PHL

54060000048198

THE
PAUL HAMLYN
LIBRARY

DONATED BY
THE PAUL HAMLYN
FOUNDATION
TO THE
BRITISH MUSEUM

WITHDRAWN

opened December 2000

CRIME AND PUNISHMENT IN ANCIENT ROME

THE
BRITISH
MUSEUM
WITHDRAWN
THE PAUL HAMLYN LIBRARY

345.009 376 BAW

CRIME AND PUNISHMENT IN ANCIENT ROME

Richard A. Bauman

London and New York

For Sheila and Nicola

First published 1996
by Routledge
11 New Fetter Lane, London EC4P 4EE

Simultaneously published in the USA and Canada
by Routledge
29 West 35th Street, New York, NY 10001

© 1996 Richard A. Bauman

Typeset in Garamond by Keystroke, Jacaranda Lodge, Wolverhampton
Printed and bound in Great Britain by Mackays of Chatham PLC,
Chatham, Kent

All rights reserved. No part of this book may be reprinted or
reproduced or utilized in any form or by an electronic,
mechanical, or other means, now known or hereafter
invented, including photocopying and recording, or in any
information storage or retrieval system, without permission in
writing from the publishers.

British Library Cataloguing in Publication Data
A catalogue record for this book is available from the British Library

Library of Congress Cataloging in Publication Data
Bauman, Richard A.
   Crime and punishment in ancient Rome / Richard A. Bauman.
      p.   cm.
   Includes bibliographical references and index.
   1. Punishment (Roman law) 2. Criminal law (Roman law)–
Philosophy. I. Title.
KJA3612.B38   1996
345′.00937′6–dc20
[342.509376]   96–21587
                                                         CIP

ISBN 0–415–11375–X

CONTENTS

vi

PREFACE

Roman Criminal Law has attracted steady attention ever since Mommsen gave it form and definition nearly a hundred years ago. Of the many scholars who have clarified and amplified Mommsen's ideas, a special place is occupied by Kunkel. Other important contributors include, in chronological order, Greenidge, Strachan-Davidson, Girard, Rogers, Siber, Vittinghoff, Brasiello, Brecht, Avonzo, Bleicken, Waldstein, Genin, Eder, Cloud, Ungern-Sternberg, Gioffredi, Wieacker, A.H.M. Jones, Pugliese, H. Jones. The writer's contributions appear in the Bibliography.

The above works can all be classified, to a greater or lesser extent, as general surveys. The present study does not aim to produce another such survey. Our focus is a more specialized one. We are concerned primarily with punishment, over the period of the Republic and the Principate; substantive law and procedure fill a subsidiary, though still important, role. Mommsen made some valuable observations on punishment, as did Kunkel, but no special lens was trained on the topic until Levy's seminal study of capital punishment which appeared in 1931 and was included in the collected edition of his works in 1963. Dupont's investigation of Constantine's criminal law is marginal to our period but instructive, and so is Biondi's work on the law of the Christian emperors as a whole. Within our period Levy was followed by the several studies of De Robertis and Cardascia, and Garnsey's full-length study in 1970 which is the only major work in English. (Drapkin focuses only in part – and inadequately – on classical antiquity.) Since 1970 there has been something of a minor proliferation. The works of Fanizza, Ducos, Rilinger and Cantarella call for special mention, as do the symposia edited by Thomas and by Diliberto. There are also the shorter studies by André, Archi, Brunt, Cornell, Crifó, Eisenhut, Ferrary, Flach, Fraschetti, Garofalo, Grelle, Grodzynski, Lassen, Liebs,

Marino, Monaco, Mouchova, Richardson, Robinson, Spruit, Thome, Volterra and Wolf.

A number of studies have an important bearing on our theme although covering private law as much as, and in some cases more than, criminal law. *Humanitas* and *utilitas publica*, which are central to our interpretation, have been discussed by Buchner, Gaudemet, Heinemann, Honig, Jossa, Lapicki, Longo, Maschi, Mignot, Riccobono, Schadewalt and Schulz; and criticism of the law by the lawyers has been (uniquely) investigated by Nörr.

While drawing massive support from the extant literature, the present study uncovers a substantial amount of unexplored terrain, both in its overall approach and in a number of specific matters. Details will be found in the last two paragraphs of our first chapter. It is hoped that some of the proposals will win acceptance, but even on those that do not, the writer welcomes debate, when documented and reasoned.

My sincere thanks are due to Richard Stoneman, Senior Editor at Routledge, in correspondence with whom the topic was clarified at the outset. I also wish to thank Nigel Eyre, Editorial Manager at Routledge; Kate Chenevix Trench, Desk Editor; and Seth Denbo, Copy Editor. I greatly appreciate the unfailing assistance and courtesy that I have received from the librarians and staffs of the Law Library, University of New South Wales; Fisher Library, University of Sydney; and Macquarie University Library.

R.A.B.
Sydney
April 1996

LIST OF ABBREVIATIONS

Except where otherwise indicated, abbreviations of the names of periodicals, classical authors and their works are as listed in *L'Année Philologique* and/or the *Oxford Latin Dictionary* and/or Liddell and Scott, *A Greek–English Lexicon*.

ANRW	H. Temporini and W. Haase (eds), *Aufstieg und Niedergang der römischen Welt*, Berlin/New York 1972–
Ascon./St.	T. Stangl (ed.), *Ciceronis Orationum Scholasticae* 1912, repr. 1964
CD	Cassius Dio
CJ	*Codex Justiniani*
Coll.	*Mosaicarum et Romanarum Legum Collatio*
CTh	*Codex Theodosianus*
D.	*Digesta Justiniani*
EJ	V. Ehrenberg and A. H. M. Jones (eds), *Documents illustrating the Reigns of Augustus and Tiberius*, 2nd edn, Oxford 1955
FIRA	S. Riccobono et al. (eds), *Fontes Iuris Romani Anteiustiniani*, 3 vols, 2nd edn, Florence 1942–3
Gai.	*Gai Institutionum Commentarii Quattuor*
ILS	H. Dessau, *Inscriptiones Latinae Selectae*
J. Inst.	*Institutiones Justiniani*
Kl.P.	K. Ziegler and W. Sontheimer (eds), *Der Kleine Pauly*, 5 vols, Stuttgart 1964–75
L.	Livy
Lenel	O. Lenel, *Palingenesia Iuris Civilis*, 2 vols, Leipzig 1899
Lex. Tac.	A. Gerber and A. Greef, *Lexicon Taciteum*, Leipzig 1903
OLD	*Oxford Latin Dictionary*
PS	*Pauli Sententiae* (= 'Sententiarum Receptarum Libri Quinque Qui Vulgo Iulio Paulo Tribuuntur')
RE	A. Pauly et al. (eds), *Real-Encyclopädie der classischen Altertumswissenschaft*, Stuttgart, 1894–1978
SA	Suetonius *Augustus*
SC	—— *Claudius*
SD	—— *Domitian*

SG	—— *Gaius (Caligula)*
SJ	—— *Julius (Caesar)*
SN	—— *Nero*
ST	—— *Tiberius*
TA	Tacitus *Annales*
TH	—— *Historiae*
TLL	*Thesaurus Linguae Latinae*
VIR	*Vocabularium Iurisprudentiae Romanae*
VM	Valerius Maximus
Warmington	*Remains of Old Latin*, Loeb edn., vol. 4, 1961

1

INTRODUCTION

Scourging, the executioner's hook, the dread of the cross – these things have long been obsolete. The credit belongs to our ancestors who expelled the kings and left no trace of their cruel ways among a free people. Many brave men followed them and protected our liberty by humane laws rather than by savage punishments.

(Cicero in 63 BC)

Those who commit capital crimes are, if from the upper classes, decapitated or exiled; those from the lower orders are crucified, burnt alive or thrown to the beasts.

(Legal manual, c. 300 AD)

CRIME AND PUNISHMENT

The expression 'Crime and Punishment' covers a number of different things. It can be used conjunctively, taking in both philosophical ideas about the suppression of crime and the practicalities of the criminal law. Or it can be used disjunctively, covering 'Crimes and Punishments' and thus simply describing positive law, enumerating the acts that are treated as criminal and the procedures and penalties by which offenders are brought to book. But the distinction between the two meanings is little more than a notional one. They are interdependent and both will be covered, though with different degrees of emphasis. Our primary focus is on punishment, with substantive law and procedure in a supporting role. But as we are also interested in what Roman thinkers felt about crime and punishment, some attention will be given to philosophical ideas.

Another question of definition arises. What do we mean by 'a crime', and what do we mean by 'punishment'? In general terms a crime is a wrongful act giving rise to a remedy, but it was only relatively late in

1

the piece that the investigation of the act and the imposition of the remedy were regulated and controlled by the state. In primitive society a wrong was a private matter to be avenged by direct retaliation by the victim or, if he had not survived, by his family. As the community became more cohesive it began to involve itself in the repression of wrongful acts, at first by restricting the private vendetta and later on by abolishing it and placing the machinery of repression and punishment under public control.

The assumption of public control sparked off a new differentiation. Wrongful acts were divided according to the nature of the remedy to which they gave rise. A crime generated a *poena*, or penalty, which inured for the benefit of the community rather than that of the victim. The penalty might be capital, which meant that it affected the status of the wrongdoer; primarily this meant death, but over time an alternative emerged in the shape of exile. Or it might be sub-capital; the most common form was the fine (*multa*), but the money went to the state treasury, not to the victim. The acts penalized under this head included both crimes against the state (treason and sedition) and common law crimes that primarily affected only the injured party, such as murder, forgery, corruption, kidnapping and adultery. But a number of wrongful acts affecting individuals retained a remedy which inured for the benefit of the individual. These included damage to property, affronts to personality, and – with less logic – theft. In these cases the *poena* (the same word was used) took the form of monetary compensation payable to the injured party. The state provided the judicial machinery for the settlement of these delicts (roughly the torts of Anglo-American law), but it had no interest in what was recovered.

This study is concerned with the first category, crimes whose punishment was pursued in the interests of the community. Those interests were designated as *utilitas rei publicae, utilitas publica*.[1] The furtherance of that concept was the fundamental *raison d'être* of Roman criminal law. The civil wrongs known as delicts will be touched on only in passing.

PUNISHMENT: THE GREEK EXPERIENCE

The first explorations of Crime and Punishment in its philosophical mode were conducted by Greek thinkers. They took their inspiration from Plato. As it is not our intention to embark on a comparative study, we content ourselves with an outline of Plato's theories in a few broad strokes. In works like *Gorgias, Protagoras* and *Nomoi* ('Laws') he explores punitive theory in depth, focusing on the purpose of punishment, its ability to achieve its perceived purpose, and the extent to which that purpose is in harmony with the *mores* of society. Why is the wrongdoer being punished? Is it in order to make him suffer? Or to make him mend his ways? Or to protect society? Or to deter others from following his example? Should there be different punishments for different classes of person? Or for different degrees of fault?

Plato's most famous contribution to penal theory is the curative purpose of punishment. The wrongdoer, plagued by his criminal propensities, derives a positive benefit from punishment. He is reformed by it. Even death is a boon to the tortured criminal soul. But if he fails to respond to curative treatment (in the non-lethal forms of whipping, imprisonment and fines) he should be exiled or put to death. Thus the idea of an increased penalty for a second conviction takes shape. The other important purpose is deterrence. The wrongdoer should be deterred from repeating his crime, and the penalties should be severe enough to discourage others. But Plato rejects retribution as a legitimate purpose; it merely inflicts suffering without reforming or deterring.

In his last work, the *Laws*, Plato comes closer to reality by anchoring his theories in the positive criminal law of the imaginary state of Magnesia on Crete. Magnesia is exposed to the stresses and strains of the real world, and its penal code includes laws currently in force in Plato's Athens. The approach is still philosophical, but it is pragmatic, almost usable, philosophy. The union between theory and practice would be taken further by Aristotle and Theophrastus.[2]

ROMAN PUNISHMENT IN THEORY AND PRACTICE

The criminal law is the poor relation on the Roman legal scene. The jurists, though not ignoring criminal interpretation nearly as much as is generally believed,[3] certainly devoted more attention to the private law. It was not until the second century AD, under the inspiration of the enlightened despotism that we know as the Antonine period, that legal literature began giving serious attention to crime. Prior to that we have to depend mainly on literary works. This is not altogether a bad thing. The accounts of actual trials in Cicero and Tacitus present contemporary thinking in real-life situations, thus supplying a window on public opinion that is not often accessible in the smooth, storyless facade of the private law. But there are disadvantages. The literary sources tend to concentrate on the upper classes. The test was whether a trial made a good story, and the best stories were provided by those who stood in the corridors of power. This leaves us in the dark as to how the ordinary citizen fared, especially when brought up for common law (non-political) crimes. Nevertheless, even with this qualification the cases give valuable insight into how the Romans thought about crime and punishment.

The philosophical approach to punishment is exemplified by Cicero and Seneca. But Cicero is an equivocal guide. His most informative work should have been *De legibus* ('On the laws'), which promised to naturalize Plato's *Nomoi* in a Roman setting. But the work is only partly successful in that regard, and has to be supplemented by, especially, *De officiis*. But even then Cicero does not provide much more than the bare bricks for a cohesive theory of punishment.[4] The truth of the matter is that in this particular area Cicero was not altogether comfortable with philosophy. His work as a barrister got in the way. His views depended on whether he was defending or prosecuting, and this might have created an imbalance that had not troubled the non-practising Greek philosophers. Cicero was also a politician, in which capacity he might have seen law reform through a different lens. Nevertheless, despite the diversity of his repertoire Cicero was able, at the end of the day, to preserve a surprising degree of consistency between what he practised and what he preached. His legal philosophy can best be described as pragmatic conceptualization.

Seneca, writing a hundred years after Cicero, was able to present his ideas more cohesively. One does not need scissors and paste to assemble a collage of Seneca's ideas; they are already there in *De clementia* and *De ira*. Also, the special relationship between Seneca and Nero gave a unique practical twist to the philosopher's work, for the pupil made strenuous efforts to put his teacher's precepts into practice. His failure was not entirely his fault; conflicting Stoic doctrines also had something to do with it.

CRIMINAL COURTS AND PUNISHMENTS

The study covers the Republic and Principate, with occasional forays into the Later Empire. Chapters 2 to 9 are built around the changes in the court systems over the period, with special reference to the changes in penalties. At any given point of time punishment depended on what courts were in operation. An outline of the systems will make this clear.

Three different systems occur in succession. None is completely isolated from its neighbour; there are overlaps right down the period.

4

But each of the three phases has a dominant system which determines what criminal acts can be charged, the procedure by which charges are tried and, most important of all, the punishments that can be imposed.

The first phase is that of the *iudicium populi*, trial by magistrate and people. A magistrate, in most cases a tribune of the plebs, conducts a preliminary examination, at the end of which he brings the accused before the popular assembly. The magistrate proposes a penalty, which may be either capital or sub-capital, in his discretion; if it is a fine he stipulates the amount. After hearing speeches the people vote on the proposal. The salient fact is that there is no fixed penalty; it depends on the magistrate's discretion and the endorsement by the people.

The first phase was at its peak until the mid-second century BC, after which it started tailing off; by about the mid-first century it was obsolete. It was supplanted by the *iudicium publicum*, trial by jury. Starting in the mid-second century, a series of permanent courts, each consisting of a magistrate sitting with a jury of about fifty, was put in place. This system dominated the trials of the first century BC and continued into the Principate, though with gradually decreasing importance; it ceased to exist in the first quarter of the third century AD. One of its most important features was its reversal of the punitive system of its predecessor. Instead of discretionary penalties, a *poena legis*, a fixed penalty, was laid down by the statute that created the court in question.

The third phase is that of the *cognitio extraordinaria*, or *cognitio extra ordinem*. Its introduction coincided with the foundation of the Principate by Augustus. At first concurrently with the jury-courts, and eventually without them, criminal justice was dispensed by a number of new jurisdictions. The senate conducted trials, thus exercising a function that it had not possessed in the Republic. The emperor did the same, and in two ways. He tried cases in his own court, and he delegated trials to his subordinates, the most important of whom were the urban and praetorian prefects and provincial governors.[5] All these 'extraordinary jurisdictions' had one feature in common: they were 'liberated' from the constrictions of the public criminal laws, that is, the laws that had created the system of jury-courts. This meant that they could exercise a free discretion, but on a much broader basis than had been possible under the old *iudicium populi*. The new courts took as their benchmark the public criminal laws pertaining to the jury-courts, but were free to depart from those laws in two ways. They could add to the categories of wrongful acts that could be charged under a given public criminal law. And they exercised a discretion on punishment; the *poena legis* for a crime could be applied as laid down by the statute or it could be mitigated or intensified in the discretion of the sentencing authority. The principal agent in the exercise of these discretionary powers was the emperor himself. He performed that function through what are generically known as 'constitutions'. The emperor could define additional categories of crimes, and new penalties, in four ways. He could issue an edict; he could reply to both official and private petitioners by rescript; he could hand down verdicts in trials over which he presided; and he could give mandates to officials, especially governors.

If anything sums up the punitive situation over the three phases, it is the position of the fixed penalty as the meat in the sandwich. It is flanked on both sides by discretionary punishments. The discretion which emerged in the Principate is, of course, vastly different in both quality and quantity from that of the *iudicium populi*, but the broad principle is the same.

HUMANITAS, SAEVITIA AND PUNISHMENT

The death sentence is a lurid beacon right across our period – and beyond. But although capital punishment was never abolished, it presents differently in different epochs. In the Late Republic there was, both in public opinion and in the minds of legislators, a desire to reduce the incidence of death sentences. That desire was inspired by *humanitas*, the civilizing instinct that is one of the hallmarks of the Roman ethos, both in the Later Republic and, at times, in the Principate. In the Republic the impulse was given practical expression in two ways. First, sentence of death continued to be pronounced, but there was a convention under which the condemned person had access to voluntary exile. By managing, with the connivance of the government, to leave Rome and Roman Italy he was safe. If he ever returned he would be put to death, but in practice the facility made all the difference to his future prospects. Then, in the first century BC, the convention was given formal expression by being written into some of the criminal laws. The unexpected architect of the reform was Sulla. The convention is discussed in chapters 2 and 3.

Even in the Republic, however, the humane impulse was hedged around with reservations drawn from the overriding doctrine of *utilitas publica*, the public interest. This is discussed in chapter 4. Then, in the Principate, ambivalence is almost institutionalized. On the one hand rulers like Augustus and the Antonines used their free discretion under *cognitio extra ordinem* to import notions of equity into punishment.

Humanitas and the cognate notions of *clementia* and *aequitas* are prominent. The theme is pursued in chapter 5 and is prominent in chapters 10 to 12. The final three chapters abandon the chronological approach, in favour of a number of themes which bring together and amplify matters touched on in the chronological section of the work.

As against the humane influences, the Principate also exhibits some of the worst features of *saevitia*, cruelty. *Saevitia* is probably the most pejorative term that the sources can apply to an emperor. Cruelty in punishment is examined in chapter 6 and, with special reference to its link with *utilitas publica*, in chapter 7. It is seen in another special context in chapter 8, in connection with the punishment of Vestal Virgins. But the very excesses of some of the first-century rulers provoked a reaction. In one sense it was a reaction by the punishers themselves. Starting with Claudius, the emperors began decreeing *liberum mortis arbitrium*, a free choice of the manner of death; one of the most important motives was the wish to spare the condemned the indignity of public execution. An even more curious phenomenon is the perception by some emperors of the damage that the capital penalty does to their own image; starting with Nero, they make strenuous efforts to deflect the odium from themselves to subordinates. There were also strong reactions against *saevitia* by public opinion. There was almost a literary sub-genre devoted to black comedy in this regard.

The supreme ambivalence is, however, displayed in another direction, one that applies to 'good' and 'bad' emperors alike. It is the emergence of grading, of different scales of punishment according to status. Those above the dividing-line, the *honestiores* (the upper classes) were punished less severely than the *humiliores* (the lower classes). Capital punishment for the *honestior* was often in the form of exile, but even when he was put to death he was spared the horror of being crucified, burnt alive or thrown to the beasts in the arena, all of which awaited his more humble counterpart. Even liberal-minded emperors failed (if they ever tried) to halt the sharp differentiation between the two echelons of society. The topic is discussed in chapter 11 and is also touched on in chapter 12.

Finally, chapter 12 examines attitudes to punishment, with special reference to the death penalty. The discussion includes the debates on punitive theory that Aulus Gellius claims to have attended. The chapter also offers some suggestions as to the purposes of punishment, especially in its nastier forms.

A word about aspects of the work for which originality can perhaps be claimed may not be out of place. The overall theme, namely looking at punishment across a time-span of some five hundred years, with successive phases based on different court systems, and correlated with both theory and practice, does not appear to have been tried before. The theme has drawn massive support from, in particular, Mommsen, Strachan-Davidson, Brasiello, De Robertis, Cardascia, Levy, Kunkel, Garnsey, Cloud, Gioffredi, Jones, Nörr, Fanizza, Pugliese, Ducos, Rilinger and Cantarella. The symposia respectively edited by Thomas and Diliberto have also been most helpful. But the particular approach, buttressed by the bifocal inspection through the twin lenses of Roman law and Roman history, may be the first of its kind.

Specific innovations, in the sense of matters which have either not been raised before, or not in the form in which they are presented here, include the following: voluntary exile; *humanitas* and capital punishment; interdiction from water and fire; the magistrate's role in a jury trial; the penalty for *parricidium*; the right to kill under the adultery law; Cicero on punishment; Augustus and *cognitio*; criticism of the criminal law; Julio-Claudian innovations with special reference to Caligula and Claudius; the free choice of the manner of death; parodies of punishment; Seneca's exposition of *clementia* and Nero's attempts to apply it; the Stoics and the *poena legis*; deflecting the odium of death sentences; *humanitas* and *utilitas publica*; Domitian and the propaganda value of punishment; aspects of the prefectorial juris-dictions; the *De poenis* genre; *honestiores* and status symbols; attitudes to punishment and to human rights; catch phrases; the *poenae metus*.

2

TRIAL BY MAGISTRATE AND PEOPLE

THE EARLY *POENA LEGIS*

The first king of Rome, Romulus, is said to have allowed the death penalty for women who committed adultery or drank wine. His successor, Numa, is more credibly reported to have provided for the perpetrator of an accidental homicide to compensate the victim's family by tendering a ram; and Tullus Hostilius carefully defined the punishment of being affixed to 'an infertile tree' and beaten to death for treason.[1] In the Early Republic the primitive code known as the XII Tables prescribed fixed penalties for some crimes. Stealthily pasturing animals on another's crops by night earned the offender death by hanging, which a later age considered harsher than the penalty for homicide. For deliberately setting fire to a barn or a heap of grain the culprit was burnt alive; and for incantations that either cast a spell on someone or charmed away his crops the perpetrator was beaten to death.[2]

There was no general formulation of penalties in early legislation. Acts considered especially dangerous were singled out for ad hoc sanctioning. There were not many; Cicero tells us that the XII Tables decreed a capital penalty for very few crimes (*Rep.* 4.12). But when it did so decree, the method of execution was clearly spelled out. This degree of precision was essential, for only if the penalty had originated in a *lex* was it insulated against the charge of cruelty, *saevitia*. According to the annalists, the Alban leader Mettius Fufetius was punished for treachery by being torn apart by two chariots going in opposite directions. The king, Tullus Hostilius, justified the penalty as 'a warning to all mankind', but Livy adds that it was the first and last Roman punishment to disregard the laws of *humanitas* (L. 1.28.6–11). In reality it was no worse than being burnt alive or thrown to the beasts in the arena, but its trouble was that it did not have a statutory credential.

9

THE IUDICIUM POPULI: PROCEDURE AND PENALTIES

The origins of the *iudicium populi* have been in contention ever since Mommsen linked the process to *provocatio ad populum*, the appeal to the people. The idea is that during the plebeian struggle against the patricians, a plebeian threatened with summary punishment by a patrician magistrate would appeal to the bystanders. A tribune of the plebs would intervene to veto the imminent flogging or execution, and over time the practice arose whereunder the tribune tested the matter by submitting it to a formal assembly of the people. And so the *iudicium populi*, trial by the people, was born. But according to Mommsen's theory of universal *provocatio* it never broke its links with *provocatio*. An appeal to the people was always the indispensable trigger to the initiation of a *iudicium populi*.[3]

Mommsen's theory has come under sustained attack over the last fifty years. The ideal enshrined in *provocatio*, that capital punishment was the prerogative of the people, and that no citizen should be punished without trial, was seen in the Late Republic as the bastion of liberty, the guardian of the rights of the individual.[4] It was no doubt notionally present in the tribunician process, but as an indispensable prerequisite the theory leaks at every seam.[5] *Provocatio* was not a device to activate the tribunician process, any more than Magna Carta activates trials at the Old Bailey. Of the many alternatives to Mommsen's theory, the most persuasive is that of Kunkel, who argues that the regular tribunician process evolved quite independently of *provocatio*. The only role of *provocatio* was to restrict a magistrate's abuse of *coercitio*, that is, when he summarily punished fractious citizens and exceeded the authorized punishments that could be inflicted in this extra-judicial way. The victim would invoke *provocatio*, and this might or might not induce the magistrate to initiate a hearing by the people. But that was quite separate from the regular (and gradually evolving over time) tribunician process.[6]

A tribunician trial began when a tribune of the plebs summoned the suspect to an enquiry known as an *anquisitio*. The enquiry was held over three sessions (*contiones*), on different days. The proceedings were held in public and attracted crowds of spectators, whose vocal interjections often influenced the tribune's decisions. In this way public opinion made itself felt. At the end of each *contio* the tribune announced a penalty, and asked the accused whether he admitted his guilt. If he did, the tribune sentenced him without any more ado, as a *confessus*. But if he denied it three times a triable issue emerged, and the tribune proceeded to the fourth hearing, the *quarta accusatio*. This took place at a formal assembly of the people convened by the tribune. If he was proposing a capital penalty the people assembled as the *comitia centuriata*, the assembly by centuries. If the proposal was for a sub-capital penalty, usually a *multa* or fine, the thirty-five tribes assembled as the *comitia tributa/concilium plebis*. There was no discussion at the meeting of the assembly; public opinion had been expressed at the *contiones*, and all that the centuries or tribes were required to do was to vote.[7]

PUNITIVE ASSESSMENTS BY TRIBUNES

As no *lex* regulated the penalty,[8] the tribune had a discretion on sentence. But it was only a relative discretion. He decided whether to proceed capitally or sub-capitally, but he did not have to make a decision until the conclusion of the third *contio*. Up to that point he could switch from a sub-capital to a capital proposal from one *contio* to the next; or public opinion might force him to do so. During the Second Punic War the tribunes charged Fulvius Flaccus with dereliction of duty in connection with his disastrous defeat by Hannibal (L. 26.1.9–3.12). At the first two hearings the tribune proposed a fine, but at the third hearing it appeared that the panic which the accused blamed for the rout had in fact been started by his cowardly desertion of his men. The spectators demanded that a capital penalty be substituted for the fine. Fulvius appealed to the college of tribunes for a ruling as to whether a change of penalty in midstream was permissible. The college ruled that it was.

> They would not prevent their colleague from conducting the *anquisitio* in the manner allowed by ancient custom, that is, by proceeding according to either the laws or custom, as he preferred, until either a capital or a pecuniary penalty emerged.
>
> (L. 26.3.8)

The 'laws' are the XII Tables rule making the *comitia centuriata* the exclusive venue in capital cases (Cic. *Leg.* 3.11, 44–5). 'Custom' is the de facto jurisdiction of the tribal assembly in sub-capital cases. There being no *lex* in that instance, there was no *poena legis*, no statutory penalty spelling out the sentence. But this did not deprive the sentence of respectability, because it received the people's imprimatur from their verdict, which was tantamount to a *lex*.

The tribune could also switch in the opposite direction, from a capital to a sub-capital proposal. When the tribunes brought a capital charge against Titus Menenius in 476–5 for losing an important military post, much was made at the *anquisitio* of the services rendered to the infant Republic by the accused's father, and a fine of 2,000 *asses* was substituted (L. 2.52.3–5).

It was also possible to use both kinds of penalty in successive prosecutions based on the same facts. In 249 P. Claudius Pulcher was charged capitally for losing a fleet at Drepana in the First Punic War. The disaster was seen as divine retribution for a remark of his before the battle. When told that the sacred chickens refused to eat, he had replied, 'Then let them drink!' and had thrown them into the sea.[9] A storm forced the capital trial to be abandoned, in terms of the rule that the assembly had to complete its business without adjourning. The tribunes ruled against double jeopardy (*Schol. Bob.* p. 90 St). But the ruling only banned a second capital charge; it said nothing about pecuniary charges. The tribunes were able to charge him again, this time before the tribes, and he was fined 120,000 *asses*, calculated on the basis of 1,000 for every ship lost (Cic. *Nat. Deor.* 2.3.7).

A similar technique was used, in reverse, in 212. A publican, Postumius Pyrgensis, was charged with claiming compensation from the state for vessels lost by shipwreck, whereas in fact he had fraudulently sunk old ships. The tribunes proposed a fine of 200,000 *asses*, but Postumius' publican friends stormed the assembly and the trial was aborted. The tribunes then indicted him on a capital charge, and ordered that if he did not furnish sureties for his appearance he was to be imprisoned. Postumius did not appear at the trial, whereupon the tribunes went to the people, meeting in a legislative capacity this time, and secured a landmark decree:

> If Marcus Postumius does not respond to a summons by the first of May he is to be deemed to be in exile, his property is to be auctioned (= confiscated) and he is to be interdicted from water and fire – *ipsi aqua et igni placere interdici.*
>
> (L. 25.3.8–4.9)

Thus was born the penalty known as *aquae et ignis interdictio*, the conditional death sentence. If the accused remained in Rome or Roman Italy he was liable to be killed; but if he went into exile he was safe.[10] (But his property was still confiscated.)

PUNITIVE ASSESSMENTS BY AEDILES

The tribunician process was largely political, being primarily concerned with persons in official positions who were accused of dereliction of duty, brutality, corruption, extortion against subject peoples, and the like. The other important *iudicium populi* is that of the aediles, the market-masters who tried market-related offences such as usury, grain speculation and prostitution. From the mid-fourth century the patrician state encouraged their jurisdiction as a counterweight to the tribunes.[11]

The aediles added a new dimension to punishment. When they imposed a fine they often used the proceeds for a *munus*, a public service to the Roman people which would both benefit the community and stand as a monument to the aedile's term of office. In 295 an aedile raised so much money from prosecuting patrician women who were trading as prostitutes that he built a temple of Venus which was still standing in Livy's day (L. 10.31.9). Thus the moral issue, the provision of a communal amenity and the glory of the aedile were all fostered by criminal punishment. The technique was unique to the aediles; the tribunes did not perpetuate their memory in this way.

The aediles sometimes made new law through their prosecutions. A case with a profound effect on the general criminal law cropped up in 246. A patrician matron, Claudia, was jostled by the crowd when leaving the theatre and loudly regretted that her brother was not there to reduce the rabble as he had done when losing a fleet at Drepana three years before. The aediles invented the new crime of *maiestas minuta*, diminishing the majesty, or 'greaterness', of the Roman people, and the assembly approved a fine of 25,000 *asses*, with which the aediles built a Temple of Liberty on the Aventine.[12] The case would ultimately lead to the adoption of *maiestas minuta* as the criterion for all acts of treason against the state.

HUMANITAS AND PUNISHMENT: VOLUNTARY EXILE

Humanitas is a persistent strand in Roman punitive thinking. It does not always means the same thing; it has been aptly described as a chameleon that changes colour according to the background.[13] But its beneficial influence on some features of punishment right across our period – and for that matter in the Later Empire – is not in doubt.

The word *humanitas* is often seen as an original Roman concept. Taking as their raw material two Greek ideas, *philanthropia* (human kindness) and *paideia* (education), the Romans are said to have moulded them into an ideology that was greater than the sum of its parts. A working definition of *humanitas* would thus cover both a civilized attitude towards all people and a cultural background appropriate to that attitude.[14] The word first appeared in the later second century BC, when Scipio Aemilianus and his circle came into contact with the Stoic philosopher Panaetius and the Greek historian Polybius. But the underlying ideas – *aequitas, iustitia, fides, venia/clementia, indulgentia, maiestas populi Romani* – were known long before that.[15]

The first significant application of *humanitas* in the penal sphere was in the institution known as voluntary exile. The earliest description is in Polybius:

> Only the people have the right to confer office or to inflict punishment, the two bonds that hold society together. The people have a notable custom. When those who are tried capitally are found guilty they are given an opportunity to depart openly, thus sentencing themselves to voluntary exile (*hekousios phugadeia*). They may do this even if only one of the tribes[16] has not yet voted. Such exiles are safe in Naples, Praeneste and Tibur, and in other cities with whom Rome has treaties.
>
> (Pol. 6.14.4–8 adapted)

Interestingly, Polybius makes punishment a partner with the magistrates in holding society together. Both were features of popular sovereignty, an idea that was attracting much attention in Polybius' Rome. The expression *hekousios phugadeia* was invented by him. There is no Latin equivalent in the sources; the usual word is *ex(s)ilium*.

Cicero gives a detailed account which stresses the technical aspects:

> Exile is not a capital punishment; it is an escape from punishment. In no *lex* of ours is exile a punishment for a crime. Those who would avoid imprisonment, death or disgrace (*ignominia*) seek refuge in exile as if at a sanctuary. If they remained in Rome they would only lose their citizenship when they lost their lives. But when they go into exile they do not lose their citizenship by law, they are stripped of it by their own act of abandonment. The fugitive loses it as soon as he becomes an exile, that is, when he acquires the citizenship of the other state.[17]

Cicero, it will be observed, allows voluntary exile before or after a verdict. This is correct; Polybius did not quite get it right. Cicero's inclusion of *ignominia* alongside death as something to be avoided by exile is important. An accused awaiting trial was technically a *reus* and was already in an invidious position. It was customary for him to go about in an unkempt and dishevelled condition in order to arouse sympathy. When Augustus investigated a congested criminal roll he struck off the names of long-standing defendants, 'whose sordid state was serving no purpose except to gratify their enemies' (SA 32.2). Even a pending sub-capital charge might prompt a departure.[18] In 171 Furius and Matienus, accused of extortion for which the penalty was monetary restitution, departed for Praeneste and Tibur (L. 43.2.11). In 476–5 Titus Menenius had drawn no comfort from the replacement of a capital penalty by a fine; he was unable to endure the *ignominia* and fell ill and died (L. 2.52.5). And in 391 Camillus, facing a penalty of 15,000 *asses*, went into exile despite an undertaking by his clients to pay the fine for him (L. 5.32.8–9).

What were the practicalities of voluntary exile? In strict law the magistrate had the power to imprison the offender pending trial or execution. But if he claimed his release there was a convention which put pressure on the magistrate to comply, and on giving sureties the offender was released and was free to depart. In effect the sureties were a down payment on his life. But if he delayed his departure beyond the period of grace the sentence could be carried out.[19] If he left before the verdict a decree of outlawry, of interdiction from water and fire, was enacted against him, as was done in Postumius Pyrgensis' case. In order to be completely safe from either sentence or interdiction he had to acquire his new citizenship, which meant that he had to go to a state with which Rome had a treaty regulating this contingency (cf. Pol. 6.14.8). The annalists attributed the institution to the infant Republic: Coriolanus was left free to go into exile and went to the Volsci, 'who received him with kindness' (L. 2.35.6). In other words they gave him citizenship, in intelligent anticipation of the position in Cicero's day.

Sometimes escape into exile was blocked by the government. In 204 Q. Pleminius was accused of barbarous acts of plunder against provincials; he had also tortured two military tribunes to death when they tried to restrain him, justifying that act by a novel principle: 'No one knew how to name the penalty for a crime except someone who had learnt its savagery by suffering.' According to some accounts he tried to go into exile at Naples but was arrested on the way and died in prison.[20] And in 141 Hostilius Tubulus was accused of taking bribes to condemn innocent persons for murder. He left Rome before the trial, but was brought back and imprisoned; he took poison before he could be put on trial. A possible explanation for this obscure episode is that, like Pleminius, he was caught before reaching safety.[21] At that time there was no legal barrier to the frustration of the right of exile in this way. The right was purely a conventional one[22] and would not receive legislative entrenchment until Sulla.

THE LIMITS OF VOLUNTARY EXILE

Was voluntary exile a resource open to every citizen, or was there an elitist barrier? Current thinking favours the latter view, holding that *humiliores* did not have access to the escape option.[23] But neither Polybius nor Cicero attests such a limitation. The evidence suggests that class differences had very little to do with it. Some criminal jurisdictions, especially the tribunician, achieved heavy concentrations of departures into exile. Others achieved few or none, and in some cases were prevented from doing so by the very way in which they were constituted.

Voluntary exile did not come into existence by legislation. It was entirely a de facto creation, a convention rather than a legal rule. The idea may have grown out of Rome's treaties with federate allies like Naples, Praeneste and Tibur. Such a treaty, the so-called *foedus aequum* or treaty on an equal footing, provided for the mutual recognition and acquisition of citizenship.[24] People began using the treaty as a means of escape. This gradually hardened into a positive feature of *libertas*, and any interference brought in the traditional champions of liberty, the tribunes. That is why we find the tribunes deciding all contentious cases in this area.

There is, to start with, no case in which a tribune conducting a *iudicium populi* was allowed to breach the convention. In the paradigm case of Quinctius Capitolinus in 461 the college of tribunes overrode an attempt by one of its members to imprison the accused pending trial; he was released on giving sureties and went into exile (L. 3.13.4–10). In Postumius Pyrgensis' case the tribunes knew that the accused was not going to appear at the trial, but their only reaction was to pass the first *aquae et ignis interdictio*. And even then they stipulated that it was only to take effect if he failed to appear by a certain date (L. 25.4.8–9), thus giving him a period of grace. And when Scipio Asiaticus was fined by a *iudicium populi*[25] for embezzling public funds, the presiding tribune threatened to imprison him unless he furnished security. The ruling was appealed to the college of tribunes, and eight members held that he was only to be imprisoned if he refused to give security. Scipio did refuse, whereupon the presiding tribune ordered his arrest. But another tribune, Tiberius Gracchus, vetoed the order of arrest anyway.

However, the tribunes did not always safeguard voluntary exile. Cicero notes, although without comment, that a man convicted of *parricidium* had no way of avoiding the penalty of the sack (*Inv.* 2.149). When Pleminius was arrested on his way to Naples, the arrest was carried out by two tribunes and an aedile (L. 38.52.7). What is of more immediate interest is the fact that there were two cases in which there was no room for voluntary exile at all. As Kunkel has argued, *iudicia populi* were used only for political crimes or for common-law crimes which touched the interests of the state. For other crimes the primary remedy was the *iudicium privatum.* Starting as the simple exaction of vengeance, the process evolved into a criminal version of the *legis actio sacramento* before a praetor sitting with a *consilium* of advisers. Instead of a stake consisting of a sum of money,[26] the criminal version put the wrongdoer's person at stake; if the verdict went against him he was adjudged to the party whom he had wronged, who could kill him, sell him into slavery or imprison him, as he saw fit.[27] There is clearly no room for voluntary exile in this process.

The other case is the jurisdiction of consuls and praetors in mass trials. The classic case is the Bacchanalian *quaestio*, or special commission which in 186 investigated a cult movement considered to be dangerous. Thousands of suspects were brought up, and if found guilty they were put to death. The offenders included men and women of rank, but there is no trace of voluntary exile. Indeed one of the features of the episode is the total absence of any reference to the tribunes in the accounts of the affair.[28] Other special commissions in which the condemned included men and women of rank followed, but again the sentences of death were carried out.[29]

There are, finally, cases where the tribunes were not precluded from intervening by any special feature of the sentencing authority, but either declined to interfere or did so conditionally. The examples are linked to the *tresviri capitales*, the three-man board for capital cases whose primary function was the supervision of prisons, executions and related matters. They also had some sort of power to adjudicate on crimes, but only to the extent of dispensing rough justice to the Roman underworld, to the lowest levels of the free, the non-Roman and the unfree.[30] Our concern is with appeals to the tribunes by persons detained in prison by the *tresviri*. For example, in 206 the poet Naevius was imprisoned for his constant abuse of leading men; a tribune freed him when he apologized. He is said to have died at Utica after being driven from Rome by a group of nobles.[31] In other words, after being released he went into exile. But before releasing him the tribune had, in effect, substituted his own sentence of an apology for that under which Naevius was being held.

That members of the elite were by no means entitled to exile as of right is shown by the case of Cornelius, a much-decorated military veteran who was imprisoned by the *tresviri* after being convicted of homosexuality. He appealed to the tribunes. But they rejected his appeal despite his offer of sureties, and he committed suicide (VM 6.1.10). As a veteran Cornelius belonged to a stratum that would later be classified as *honestiores*, but this did not secure his release. The only concession to his status was that he was allowed to choose the manner of his death.[32]

The tribunes again refused to interfere when P. Munatius was imprisoned by the *tresviri* for taking a chaplet from the statue of Marsyas and placing it on his own head (Plin. *NH* 21.8.3). The Munatii were quite a well-known family; they boasted of a consul in the triumviral period.[33]

HUMANITAS AND CAPITAL PUNISHMENT

Humanitas undoubtedly introduced a civilizing element through voluntary exile. Limited as it was, it did represent a current of thought opposed to capital punishment. The same impulses achieved a more direct breakthrough in the 80s BC, when the right of exile was, in effect, written into some of the criminal laws.[34] But a larger question remains. Was *humanitas* able, while accepting the retention of the death penalty in principle, to modify the methods of execution? Cicero delivered ringing denunciations of barbaric methods, Sallust thought along similar lines, and Livy wrote a trenchant criticism into the legend of Mettius Fufetius.[35] But was all this anything more than a ripple on an otherwise unruffled surface?

An execution was a public occasion to which the populace was summoned by trumpet, there to be regaled with the spectacle of criminals being decapitated, beaten to death, drowned in a sack, hurled from the Tarpeian Rock, burnt alive, or thrown to wild animals.[36] As most methods required the victim to be stripped, women were executed in private in the interests of modesty. Even when the Pontifex Maximus merely whipped an unclad Vestal Virgin for a minor fault, he did so from behind a curtain (Plut. *Numa* 10.4). But curtained modesty cannot hide the fact that women were put to death by being strangled, after those who were virgins had been deflowered by the executioner.[37]

18

There does not seem to be much room for humanitarianism in this catalogue of horrors. It has been suggested that *summum supplicium* ('the ultimate punishment') does not mean the death sentence in general. It means modes of execution other than 'standard' decapitation, the purpose being to inflict the maximum suffering in order to achieve maximum deterrence.[38] There may be something in it.[39] It is supported, for example, by the fact that there was something of a controversy when Livy wrote about Mettius Fufetius. The debate was not about the death sentence in principle, but about some of the methods. One school justified the most extreme cruelty; Livy puts the justification into the mouth of Tullus Hostilius. But some argued that if it had to be done, it were well that it be done decently.

There was, however, one matter on which there was a consensus, and that was if the technicalities of punishment were not observed. In 193 a proconsul decapitated a Gallic prisoner of war for the entertainment of his mistress, who complained that she had never seen a man die. This earned him severe punishment.[40] But the condemnation was on a highly selective basis. It was argued in the schools of rhetoric that there was nothing wrong with beheading if it was done under a law, and for the purpose of inspiring terror at the might of the empire; but it was unacceptable if done at the whim of a courtesan (Sen. Rhet. *Controv.* 385 M).

There is one more point that should be made. Public opinion was by no means a negligible factor. As we have seen, it was able to guide a tribune into a capital or pecuniary option, depending on the current climate. That climate fluctuated. Pyrgensis' fraud did not attract a capital penalty until it was aggravated by violence bordering on treason. But serious as Claudia's ill-timed remark was, *humanitas* ruled out a capital charge. Dislike of frightfulness also came into it. In 217, when Hannibal's irruption into Italy was in its early stages, a number of ominous prodigies evoked a new kind of response; instead of looking for an errant Vestal to bury alive, the senate decreed a supplication. But this modest improvement was abruptly reversed after the disaster of Cannae, when two Vestals were sacrificed and some Gauls and Greeks were also buried alive for good measure. But in 207, with the Carthaginian threat receding, some alarming prodigies were expiated by hymn-singing maidens.[41] *Humanitas* would never sweep away benighted superstition entirely, but it did keep chipping away at the monolith.

CONCLUSION

The punishment of Mettius Fufetius acquires new importance. The tribunes' punitive discretion, endorsed by the college but still exposed to public opinion, is an important contribution to the changing picture of punishment. The picture is further filled out by the special use to which the aediles put the proceeds of fines. But the most important item is voluntary exile, including the limits on its exercise. The seemingly irreconcilable conflict between *humanitas* and capital punishment raises an interesting issue.

3

TRIAL BY JURY

THE DECLINE OF THE *IUDICIA POPULI*

Iudicia populi survived into the first century BC, but only in a state of obsolescence, becoming more of a museum-piece than a vital cog in the machinery of criminal justice. The mid-second century saw the start of a radical reorganization of the criminal courts. Permanent jury-courts (*quaestiones perpetuae*) were created for a broad range of crimes, and by the end of the first century BC the new *iudicia publica* had completely supplanted the *iudicia populi*.

Why did the *iudicia populi* go into decline? One reason is that trials by the people were cumbersome and time-consuming, but that is only part of the story. As so often, law reform was not transferred from the drawing-board to the courthouse until society was ready for it. A specific incentive was needed, and it surfaced in the second century. Rome emerged from the wars of expansion as the undisputed mistress of the Mediterranean world, but at a price. Postwar Italy was shaken by a climate of violent protest, by great rents in the social fabric.[1] And thinking people began asking whether the institutions of a small city-state were up to the task of governing an empire. The search for a new approach was spearheaded by the criminal law. It would take another 150 years to put a suitable constitution in place, but the courts adapted more quickly.

The first response to the crisis was a series of special commissions, of mandates to magistrates to investigate and punish without needing to have the final sentence confirmed by the people. The people (or the senate) only participated to the extent of establishing the commission. The first of these special *quaestiones* was the Bacchanalian commission of 186 which investigated, and punished, thousands of people who were alleged to have committed common-law crimes, such as adultery, murder and forgery, in pursuit of social justice. The sheer magnitude of the investigation, if nothing else, ruled out the use of the regular jurisdictions.[2]

Special commissions were also used in the external sphere. The trigger was supplied by the Roman imperial idea, as encapsulated in the notion of *maiestas populi Romani* which stressed the importance of moral probity in Rome's dealings with other peoples. In 172–3 the consul Popillius Laenas persuaded a Ligurian community to surrender at discretion, but then proceeded to demolish their town and to sell the populace into slavery. The senate set up a special commission under the praetor, Licinius Crassus, 'to punish those who had enslaved the Ligurians'. Crassus held the first two sessions of Laenas' trial, but then succumbed to corruption; he adjourned the final session until 15 March 171, on which date he would vacate the praetorship, thus aborting the investigation. And so, says Livy, the commission was frustrated by a trick.[3]

The commission might have been frustrated, but it points to a new attitude to punishment. Laenas had been guilty of the most persistent kind of maltreatment, namely *repetundae* or extorting money or property from subject peoples. The focus of enlightened opinion was on redress, on restoring to the victims what had been taken from them. That is why the commission's terms of reference included 'the restoration to the Ligurians of their liberty and so much of their property as could be recovered' (L. 42.8.7–8).

Further attempts at restitution were made over the next two decades, but with mixed results. In 171 one accused was absolved and the other two avoided repayment by going into exile. There was a slight improvement in 170, when a *iudicium populi* was tried instead of a special commission. A commander was fined two million *asses* by the people, and instead of the money going into the state treasury it was used to make good the losses of the provincials. But the death-knell of ad hoc remedies for *repetundae* was sounded in 149, when a skilful blend of sentiment and chicanery enabled Ser. Sulpicius Galba to escape the consequences of selling some 8,000 Lusitanians into slavery.[4] It was time for a fundamental reform, for the introduction of the system of *quaestiones perpetuae*.

THE *QUAESTIONES PERPETUAE*

The first *quaestio perpetua* was created by the *lex Calpurnia de repetundis* of 149 BC, in the immediate wake of the scandalous absolution of Galba. The new law established a permanent jury-court to regulate claims by non-Romans,[5] both in Italy and in the provinces, for the restitution of what had been exacted from them by Roman officials. Henceforth there would be no need to face the hazards of a special commission whenever relief for exploited subjects was wanted.

The *lex Calpurnia* was followed by an obscure *lex Junia* and, in 123–2, by the *lex Acilia de repetundis* which survives in an inscription and is our major source both for the *repetundae* court and for the jury-courts as a whole. The primary purpose of all three laws was restitution, but there was also a specifically criminal penalty. Under the *lex Calpurnia* it was simply *infamia*, which carried certain civil disabilities. To this the *lex Acilia* added a penalty of double the amount exacted, and so the specific statutory penalty, the *poena legis*, was born.[6]

Proceedings in the *quaestio de repetundis* were started by the laying of an information (*nominis delatio*) with the praetor appointed to preside over the court. Originally the *nominis delatio* could only be lodged by, or on behalf of, aggrieved members of subject communities. But by 103 at the latest, by which time the extension of the new system to other crimes was well under way, it could be lodged by any adult male citizen of good repute, whether or not he had any personal interest in the case. This marked the birth of the famous right of public accusation. Trials depended on private initiative. There was no official prosecutor, and if no member of the public came forward as an accuser there was no prosecution. Public accusation remained a feature of Roman criminal justice even after the disappearance of the jury-courts in the early third century AD.[7]

A *repetundae* jury was made up of fifty to seventy-five *iudices* presided over by a praetor. The names of the *iudices* were drawn from an album kept by the praetor. The jury was charged with two functions: it first adjudicated on the wrongful conduct of the accused; and if it returned an adverse finding on that score, it went on to the *litis aestimatio*, the assessment of the amount that he was to repay.[8]

The new system was an impressive demonstration of *humanitas*; treating subjects in a civilized fashion was even more laudable than doing so with fellow-citizens. The idea had at last found a permanent home. And once in place it began expanding its punitive horizons in an almost exponential manner. The *lex Servilia de repetundis* of c. 101 created a two-tier system of penalties. The penalty of double restitution was retained for simple exactions, but if the money had been received for a purpose impinging on national security a capital penalty was imposed. Thus in 92–1 Aemilius Scaurus was charged with receiving money from Mithridates of Pontus to betray Roman interests in Asia.

He could also have been charged with treason under the *lex maiestatis*, but there was an easier burden of proof under the *repetundae* law; all that had to be shown was that the accused had received money, and for an unlawful purpose.[9] The element of forced exaction did not need to be canvassed in Scaurus' case; no one was interested in assisting Mithridates to recover his money.

The *lex Servilia* had expanded the penalty on the basis of state security. Caesar's *repetundae* law of 59 expanded it on the basis of *humanitas*. Where exactions had been carried out in circumstances of extreme cruelty (*saevitia*), a capital penalty was prescribed. Double restitution was retained; it still took care of the victims' interests. But if the act offended the conscience of the nation, the state now demanded a more severe penalty as well. Caesar's law would play an important part in controlling governors in the Principate.[10]

The new court system was rapidly extended to all major crimes, both political and common-law. The *lex maiestatis* created a permanent court for treason in 103; it may have been the first to prescribe a capital penalty, although it only just anticipated the *lex Servilia de repetundis* by a narrow margin. Other crimes were soon brought in.[11] But the real starting point is the reorganization of the system by Sulla in the 80s. Only two of Sulla's laws went down to posterity under his name, but they are of special importance. The *lex Cornelia de sicariis et veneficis* restructured the *quaestio* for homicide, and the *lex Cornelia testamentaria nummaria* (= *de falsis*) penalised forgery of wills and coining.[12] These were followed by Pompey's law on *parricidium* (murder of, primarily, a parent) and Caesar's laws on *repetundae*, treason and violence. Electoral corruption (*ambitus*) was also given a *quaestio*. At some point a *lex Fabia de plagiariis* penalized kidnapping.[13] Augustus broke new ground with the *lex Julia de adulteriis coercendis* which established a public jury-court for offences against morality that had possibly been the exclusive preserve of family courts until then.[14] Augustus also consolidated the procedure of the *iudicia publica* as a whole. He created a jury-court for thefts of public and temple property, updated the *maiestas* law, and consolidated the laws of violence and of *ambitus*. He also made manipulation of the grain supply a public crime.[15]

VERDICT AND SENTENCE IN THE *QUAESTIONES PERPETUAE*

The course of a jury trial is described in numerous works[16] and needs no addition here. Our interest is in the verdict and the sentence. The functions of the court were sharply divided. A magistrate (either a praetor or a *iudex quaestionis*) presided over the proceedings and the jury delivered the verdict. As soon as the magistrate had ascertained from the voting tablets what the jury's verdict was, he announced it with the words *fecisse/non fecisse videtur*, 'he appears to have done it/not to have done it'. This brought the *poena legis* into operation without any act of sentencing by the magistrate. The only thing that he had to do after his announcement was to record it in writing. When M. Servilius was charged with *repetundae* in 51 the jurors were equally divided between condemnation and acquittal. The magistrate correctly announced that he was not ordering restitution. But instead of recording this as an acquittal he simply recorded the verdicts of each of the three classes of *iudices*,[17] and when that was queried he merely added the facts of the case. Thus the acquittal, although announced orally, remained unrecorded, and Servilius stood neither acquitted nor condemned (Cic. *Fam.* 8.8.3).

A question arises at this point: Do we have the full picture of the magistrate's role? Did he really do no more than supervise the proceedings and announce and record the verdict? The question is prompted by an observation of Cicero's. He says that condemnation is for the jury, the penalty is for the *lex* (*Pro Sulla* 63). So firmly was the *poena legis* embedded in concrete that Cicero cites the case of the man who was charged with *parricidium*, only to find that no proof that he had murdered a parent was tendered at the trial. But there was evidence of other crimes, and that was enough to secure his conviction as charged, thus bringing the barbaric penalty for *parricidium* into operation. The only way to avoid an outrage, concludes Cicero, is to persuade the jury to acquit (*Inv.* 2.58–9). In other words, the shadow of the penalty was capable of influencing the verdict. Cicero made good use of the technique of horrifying the jury when he defended Sex. Roscius on a charge of *parricidium*.[18]

Now, the point is this: Was the magistrate able to reinforce the message that a cruel penalty transmitted to the jury? Did he deliver something like a summing-up in which he might steer the jury away from condemnation – or towards it, for that matter? Most investigators would deny the magistrate a speaking role,[19] but they may be wrong. Whenever Cassius Longinus presided over a *quaestio* on a murder charge he pressed the jurors to ask themselves, '*Cui bono?*' – 'Who benefited by it?' (Ascon. p. 39 St). He could have said this when he was summing up prior to the vote, or even by interjections during the trial. When the same Cassius Longinus presided over the trial of some Vestals for unchastity, he allowed circumstantial evidence on an unprecedented scale, inviting the jury to draw inferences against some for whose involvement there was no direct evidence.[20] Sallust criticises M. Scaurus for allowing hearsay evidence at the Mamilian commission (*Jug.* 40.4–5); there must have been argument on admissibility and a ruling by Scaurus. Also, the corruption that destroyed Hostilius Tubulus may well have consisted in misdirecting the jury. And at Verres' trial Cicero accuses the defence of prolonging the case until the new praetor, M. Metellus, takes over the court; Cicero says he would rather have Metellus voting as a juror under oath than counting the votes of others (*Verr.* 1.31–2). Cicero was well qualified to make this criticism. He admits that when he himself presided over the *repetundae* court he could have given the historian Licinius Macer a fairer hearing, but popular favour was worth more to him than Macer's gratitude (*Att.* 1.4.2).

HUMANITAS: THE ALTERNATIVE CAPITAL PENALTY

> The laws lay down that citizens shall not lose their lives but shall be allowed exile. But who, you ask, will complain of a verdict against traitors? I reply that these men may deserve their fate, but consider how it will affect others. Good cases do not make good precedents; bad rulers will use them badly. Sulla's proscriptions may have been justified at first, but they started a wave of bloodshed. Our ancestors did not hesitate to take over the honourable institutions of other people, but they also took over the death penalty of the Greeks. Later on, with increasing maturity, they passed laws which allowed the condemned the alternative of exile.
>
> (Sall. *Cat.* 51.22–40 adapted)

Sallust here makes Caesar, speaking in the senatorial debate on the Catilinarians in 63 BC, the mouthpiece for the classic statement of the humanitarian position on punishment.[21] But despite the hostile reference to Sulla, the main thrust of the humane laws to which Sallust refers was devised by Sulla.[22]

Prior to Sulla the capital penalty (*poena capitis*) simply meant death. No particular method of execution was specified; *capite puniatur*, 'let him be punished capitally', was all that was required. It was only in earlier times that specific methods of execution had been spelled out – at the trial of Horatius and under the XII Tables. The first century BC saw a radical change. In some of his laws Sulla, and after him Caesar, replaced actual and immediate execution by *aquae et ignis interdictio*, the interdiction from water and fire which denied the wrongdoer shelter and sustenance and made him an outlaw liable to be killed by anyone with impunity. In other words, Sulla gave formal expression to the procedure used against Postumius Pyrgensis in the *iudicia populi* period. In effect he placed voluntary exile on the statute-book. The penalty was not formulated as a specific right of exile; the *interdictus* still depended on being left at liberty in order to make his escape into exile. But the opportunity to avail himself of that resource was now guaranteed; instead of being a convention, it had become a right. This is a necessary inference from the words *aqua et igni interdicatur*, 'let him be interdicted from water and fire', which we know were used in the statute. There would have been no point in that expression if the culprit was still exposed to the possibility of immediate execution – by, for example, being imprisoned and not being able to persuade the tribunes to interfere. In short, interdiction presupposed freedom of movement.

The new penalty has been aptly described as a conditional death sentence; if the condemned man remained in Rome or Roman Italy he would be at risk.[23] It can also be described as compulsory exile, looked at from the point of view of a community which wanted to expel a wrongdoer from its ranks; departure was how the community hoped he would respond to the sentence of interdiction. Thus both *humanitas* and *utilitas publica*, the public interest, were served by the new dispensation. The word 'exile' was not used in the statute, but over the last half-century of the Republic the condemned responded as expected so regularly that the death penalty became a virtual dead letter, and the sources began using *exilium* as a synonym for interdiction.[24]

So far so good, but the idea that interdiction was named specifically in the statute has not gone unchallenged. It has been argued by Kunkel that it was merely an administrative measure by the magistrate. The offender had been sentenced to death, but instead of handing him over to the *tresviri capitales* for execution the magistrate took it upon himself to release him, but issued an interdiction in order to retain a hold over him.[25] This argument cannot be allowed to stand. In the first place, the jurists unanimously describe the penalty in terms which clearly make it *the* statutory punishment. The Severan jurist, Domitius Ulpianus, puts it as follows:

The *lex Cornelia* (*de sicariis et veneficis*)[26] laid down that arsonists were to be interdicted from water and fire – *incendiariis lex quidem Cornelia aqua et igni interdici iussit.* But nowadays they are punished differently. Those who deliberately light fires in urban areas are, if of the lower orders, usually thrown to the beasts; if of some standing and the crime was committed in Rome they are put to death (*capite puniuntur*) or at all events deported to an island.[27]

Ulpian draws a distinction of the utmost importance. He contrasts the penalty as laid down by the original homicide law with the current penalties under the *cognitio extra ordinem* of the Principate. In particular, interdiction is contrasted with the *capite puniuntur* which currently overtakes people of standing. When Ulpian says that Sulla's law *iussit* he is quoting from the text of the law; exact documentation is a feature of Ulpian's writing.[28]

Ulpian is corroborated by other jurists,[29] and only one text calls for a comment. Ulpian's contemporary, Iulius Paulus, says that 'Capital *iudicia publica* are those in which the penalty is death or exile, that is, interdiction from water and fire' (*D.* 48.1.2). *Exilium* is mentioned here because it is the usual word in common parlance, but the jurist adds the correct technical term.

Sulla made interdiction the specific penalty for two common-law crimes, homicide and testamentary fraud.[30] Caesar brought in political crimes. Two of his laws made interdiction the penalty for violence and treason. The language is again explicit: *iubent ei qui de vi, itemque ei qui maiestatis damnatus sit, aqua et igni interdici* (Cic. *Phil.* 1.21–23). But by increasing the number of avenues leading to exile Caesar was obliged to intensify that punishment. Suetonius says that as the rich turned to crime without any qualms because they simply went into exile with their property intact, Caesar prescribed total confiscation of property for *parricidium* and half-confiscation for other crimes (SJ 42.3).

Interdiction was also the penalty for *parricidium* under Pompey's law for that crime.[31] It continued to be the penalty under Augustus' legislation, for example in his updated restatement of Caesar's *maiestas* law (*PS* 5.29.1). At some later point in the Principate, probably in Tiberius' reign, the exile component became mandatory expulsion to a specified place, often an island. From that time the sources frequently refer to the penalty as deportation. But they also continue to use the expression *aquae et ignis interdictio*.[32] The probable form of the sentence is that the offender was both interdicted and deported. If he left the specified place of deportation he was exposed to the usual consequences of not going into exile.

There is no basis for the supposition that so many different sources were simply describing administrative action by a magistrate. Why would the jurists have recorded that instead of the actual penalty? This is not to say that the magistrate did not frame an edict giving effect to the interdiction. But that was no different from any other administrative action to give effect to a sentence, such as handing the culprit over to the *tresviri* when actual execution was decreed. In substance, then, the magistrate took the same action as he had taken prior to Sulla; he left the culprit at liberty and he issued an edict. But the difference was that he now did it because a *lex* ordered him to do it, not merely because of a convention.

SUB-CAPITAL PENALTIES

Sub-capital penalties lack the homogeneity of the capital penalty; they are not linked by descent from a common archetype. But they compensate for this by offering some special insights into punitive thinking. When the lawgiver was free to choose between civil disabilities (*infamia*), fines (*multae*) and temporary expulsions (*relegatio*), the scope for experimentation was very wide.

The potential is illustrated by the legislation on electoral corruption (*ambitus*) in the mid-first century BC. Enactments from 67–52 BC covered a whole range of penalties. Sulla created a *quaestio perpetua* for *ambitus*; the penalty was that offenders were disqualified from again standing for office for ten years (*Schol. Bob.* p. 78 St). In 67 the tribune C. Cornelius proposed an *ambitus* law with severe penalties; he was very hard on *divisores*, electoral agents whose main function was to distribute bribes. He also carried a law requiring praetors to keep to the programmes announced in their edicts.[33] This had a bearing on electoral corruption, because such a programme was the platform on which a would-be praetor sought election. The senate opposed Cornelius' legislation and gave an interesting reason: while harsh punishment was of some value as a deterrent, it was counter-productive because it discouraged juries from convicting (CD 36.38.4–5). *Humanitas* was not the only inspiration of lenient punishment; sometimes the public interest demanded it.

The senate having recommended a less drastic law than that proposed by Cornelius, the *lex Calpurnia* was passed. It expelled the culprit from the senate, fined him, and repeated Sulla's ten-year ban. Then, in 63, Cicero's *lex Tullia* prescribed banishment. It was not exile in the full sense; the offender was only expelled for ten years, and he did not forfeit either his civic rights or his property. In other words, his *caput*, or status, was not diminished.[34] A feature of the penalty was that the ten years' banishment applied not only to senators, the group most susceptible to electoral malpractice; it also applied to *divisores*, most of whom were plebeians (Cic. *Mur.* 47).

In 55 the *lex Licinia de sodaliciis* created a special charge of *ambitus* for the highly organized bribery operations of political clubs. The penalty may have been banishment for life instead of for ten years.[35] In 52 a law of Pompey's took the unusual step of banning character evidence in favour of the accused, a resource that had often saved the guilty. The law was criticized for being made retrospective (Plut. *Cat. Min.* 48.3). The penalty may have been exile for life.[36] Finally a law of Augustus imposed a five years' ban on seeking office, but that could be avoided by successfully prosecuting someone else for *ambitus*. There may also have been provision for a fine.[37]

Penalties under other *leges* included confiscation of a third of the property for private violence under a *lex Julia*, fines for profiteering in grain under another *lex Julia*, and for kidnapping under the *lex Fabia*.[38] Imprisonment was not a penalty under any of the public criminal laws; it was only a prelude to trial or execution.[39]

MIXED PENALTIES: *PARRICIDIUM*

We have already noticed one example of mixed penalties in the shape of the two-tier system for *repetundae*. We now address two other examples, one capital (*parricidium*) and the other sub-capital (*adulterium*). Both raise anomalies which emphasize the incompleteness of the Roman position on punishment.

Parricidium is the Roman crime most resistant to clear definition.[40] A working description makes it the crime of killing parents or close relatives, as defined in Pompey's law on the subject (*D.* 48.9.1). Our interest is in the penalty for this special kind of murder. Traditionally the culprit was subjected to the *poena cullei*, the penalty of the sack. He was sewn into a leather sack in company with a dog, a monkey, a snake and a rooster, and was thrown into the sea or a river. Whatever the date on which the penalty was first introduced,[41] the first specific example surfaces in 101 BC, when Publicius Malleolus was drowned in a sack for killing his mother. Then, in 80 BC, Sex. Roscius was charged with the murder of his father. The young Cicero, defending, has so much to say about the *poena cullei* that it must be taken as a real punishment – and as an important factor in persuading the jury to acquit Cicero's client.[42]

Complications arise when we turn to the *lex Pompeia de parricidiis* which was enacted by Pompey in 55 or 52. The penalty is described by the Severan jurist, Aelius Marcianus, as follows:

> The *lex Pompeia de parricidiis* provides that if anyone kills a father, a mother, a grandfather or a grandmother . . . or maliciously causes any such person to be killed, he/she incurs the penalty laid down by the Cornelian law on homicide – *ea poena teneatur quae est legis Corneliae de sicariis.*
>
> (*D.* 48.9.1)

The first point to be noticed is that this text delivers the final blow to the claim that *aquae et ignis interdictio* under Sulla's homicide law was not a specific penalty. If, as has been argued, Sulla simply established a court for homicide without specifying a penalty,[43] how did they cope with Pompey's law? In other words, how did they apply to *parricidium* a penalty that was non-existent in the homicide law? It is clear that there *was* a known *poena legis Corneliae.*

The real complications begin with a text in *Pauli Sententiae*, a compendium based largely on the writings of another Severan jurist, Iulius Paulus: 'Under the *lex Pompeia de parricidiis* those who killed a father, a mother, a grandfather or a grandmother . . . were previously sewn in a sack and thrown into the sea, but today they are burnt alive or thrown to the beasts'(*PS* 5.24). If the compiler of the compendium is to be believed – and his record on the contents of laws is generally good – Pompey, far from abolishing the *poena cullei*, incorporated it in his law.

The problems do not end there. A generation after Marcian and Paul the jurist Modestinus wrote as follows:

> By ancestral custom (*more maiorum*) the penalty for *parricidium* required anyone who killed a father, a mother, a grandfather or a grandmother to be thrashed, sewn into a sack with a dog etc. and thrown into the sea. If the sea is not adjacent a constitution of Hadrian substitutes being thrown to the beasts.
>
> (*D.* 48.9.9 pr.)

Modestinus refers the *poena cullei* to ancestral custom, not to the *lex Pompeia.* But he has the penalty still in use in Hadrian's reign, although effectively Hadrian substituted throwing to the beasts.

At the bottom of which well does the truth lie? Any solution must be tentative, but one possible approach is to suppose that all three accounts are substantially correct.[44] Pompey did not actually include mixed penalties in his law, but a mixture results from a careful examination of the evidence. We begin with a passage in Suetonius, in which he cites as an example of Augustus' leniency a case in which the emperor was trying a man for *parricidium*. Suetonius says that the punishment of being sewn up in a sack was inflicted on those who were clearly guilty or confessed their guilt, and in order to save the man from that penalty Augustus put the question thus: 'You surely did not kill your father, did you?'[45]

Pompey had done one of two things. He had either retained the *poena cullei* for the manifestly guilty and the confessed; or he had only concerned himself with the penalty of interdiction which he adopted from Sulla's homicide law. The latter is more likely. It was only if guilt was neither manifest nor confessed that a jury-court trial took place at all. In the two special cases there was no triable issue to go to a jury; the magistrate went ahead with punishment without any more ado. In fact, therefore, Pompey said nothing about the *poena cullei*; it had no place in his jury-court. *Pauli Sententiae* can perhaps be excused for thinking that the penalty had been retained by Pompey; but technically Modestinus is more correct when he refers it to ancestral custom. But whichever way it was, Pompey must be credited with a major contribution to *humanitas*. The contemporary climate influenced Pompey as much as it did Caesar.

MIXED PENALTIES: *ADULTERIUM*

In 18–17 BC Augustus established a *quaestio perpetua* for *adulterium* and *stuprum* – respectively intercourse with a respectable married woman or with a widow or unmarried free woman who was not registered as a prostitute. This court had the longest life and the heaviest workload of any jury-court in the Principate.[46] Its constituent statute, the *lex Julia de adulteriis coercendis*, laid down penalties of some severity, but they were still sub-capital. A married woman forfeited half her dowry and a third of her other property, and was relegated to an island; her lover lost half his property and was relegated to a different island (*PS* 2.26.14). Banishment was specifically in the form of *relegatio*, thus leaving civic rights largely intact.[47] But unlike *ambitus*, relegation for adultery appears to have been for life rather than for a term of years.

So much for the *poena legis* under Augustus' law. But Augustus also made provision for an alternative, in the shape of a traditional punishment. Since time immemorial the power-holder, whether a woman's father under *patria potestas* or her husband under *manus*, had had the right to kill her if he caught her in the act of adultery.[48] This *ius occidendi* was incorporated in the *lex Julia*, but in a circumscribed and carefully regulated form. The father retained the right to kill both his daughter and her lover. But he must catch them in the act in his or his son-in-law's house, and he must kill both of them; if he only killed the man he was liable for murder. The husband's traditional rights were more severely curtailed. He no longer had any legal right to kill his wife, but he might kill her lover if he was of base degree.[49]

Failing entrapment *in flagrante delicto* neither father nor husband had any right to kill. Their remedy was a prosecution in the jury-court. They had a sixty days' preferential right of accusation, but if they failed to avail themselves of it any adult male citizen could come forward as the accuser. It was a condition precedent to a prosecution that the husband divorce the wife. Failure to do so exposed him to a charge, under the same statute, of *lenocinium*, or pandering.

The right to kill was one of the thorniest problems of the new law, especially in respect of the husband's right. The curtailment of what many saw as a pillar of family life taxed the skills of the lawyers to the full. For example, although the husband might not kill the wife, he was not allowed, any more than the father was, to take revenge on only one of the guilty pair. After killing the lover he had to divorce the wife and lodge a charge against her if he wished to avoid an indictment for homicide.[50] Thus in a certain sense killing by the husband was linked to the *poena legis*. But the same did not apply to the father, for he simply killed both parties. The anomaly worried the jurists. Their uneasiness is shown by the reason that one of them gives for the father's superior right: 'The father is motivated by concern for his children's interests, the husband by passion' (Papinian *D*. 48.5.23.4). The statement, fatuous as it may seem, is not entirely misconceived, for the husband's passion was given considerable weight. It was very difficult to restrain enraged husbands from killing their wives, and in the second century AD (if not before) the *crime passionel* was accepted as a mitigating factor in charges of homicide:

> The extreme penalty can be remitted against a husband who admits that he killed his wife whom he caught in adultery, for it is very hard to restrain just grief. He must be punished because he went too far, not because he should not have avenged himself. But a lesser penalty will suffice.
>
> (Antoninus Pius in *D*. 48.5.39.8)

Similar leniency was shown where the husband killed the lover in circumstances that did not justify it:

If Gracchus, whom Numerius killed when he caught him in adultery at night, was of such a status that under the *lex Julia* he could be killed with impunity, what was done lawfully merits no punishment. But if he killed outside the limits of the *lex* he is guilty of homicide. Yet because night and just feelings mitigate his act, he can be given a lighter sentence.

(Severus Alexander in *CJ* 9.9.4)

The restrictions on the right to kill were intended to steer husbands away from vengeance towards regular adjudication. And it was not done only by restrictions; there were also positive inducements. As an alternative to killing it was laid down that anyone entitled to kill an adulterer could with a much better right (*multo magis iure*) treat him with *contumelia* (*D*. 48.5.23.3). This means that he could abuse him both physically and verbally with impunity; no action for damages in delict would lie. The choice was only open to the husband; the father's obligation to kill both his daughter and her lover cannot be reconciled with it. Another rule laid down that where the husband caught the parties in the act but was unwilling or not entitled to kill, he could imprison the man for up to twenty hours in order to obtain evidence of the crime (*D*. 48.5.26 pr.). This seems to be linked to the *contumelia* facility; the lover would be given rough treatment to persuade him to make a clean breast of it, and pending charges the husband would enjoy some immediate satisfaction.[51]

CONCLUSION

The decline of the *iudicia populi* puts the creation of permanent jury-courts in clear perspective. That the first such court gave a remedy to non-Romans rather than to citizens is not in doubt. Mixed penalties for *repetundae* are secure. The magistrate's participation by directing the jury is new. His duty to register the verdict is also important. One of the most significant items in the chapter is the detailed validation of the fact that *aquae et ignis interdictio* was the actual penalty laid down, and not merely an administrative act by the magistrate. The *ambitus* laws include the interesting reason for the senate's opposition to Cornelius' law. The solution to the intractable problem of *parricidium* is at least arguable. The analysis of the right to kill under the adultery law brings in some new factors.

4

CICERO ON PUNISHMENT

CICERO AND PRAGMATIC CONCEPTUALIZATION

In *De legibus*, a philosophical dialogue written in the late fifties,[1] Cicero declares that the science of law (*iuris disciplina*) is not to be drawn from the praetor's edict or the XII Tables, but from the depths of philosophy – *ex intima philosophia* (*Leg.* 1.17). Two or three years before he had said the direct opposite, praising the XII Tables and denigrating the Greeks (*Orat.* 1.195). But no matter. Our concern is with Cicero's pragmatic conceptualization, with the extent to which his thinking on punishment in his theoretical mode agrees with what he said and did in his practical mode, as a barrister and a politician.

On the practical side our yardstick is Cicero in 63, the turbulent year in which he held the consulship, defended Rabirius, and executed the Catilinarian conspirators. That was when Cicero dramatically confronted the two notions that have already been prominent in our discussions, namely *humanitas* and *utilitas publica*.[2] If Cicero is to be cleared of the charges of duplicity that are so often levelled at him in connection with the events of that remarkable year, an attempt to reconcile his positions on the two notions is an indispensable, though hitherto neglected, prerequisite. The first step is to investigate what he thought about *humanitas* and *utilitas publica* when wearing his theoretical hat.[3] The second step will be to investigate what he did about them.

For the first step our focus will be primarily on *De legibus* and *De officiis*; although written after 63, those works reflect ideas long held by Cicero and expressed by him on a number of earlier occasions. This analysis will provide us with a convenient basis for comparison with the events of 63. The discussion will be a selective one, being confined for the most part to items bearing on those events. Cicero will also be our principal guide for the second step. His speech in defence of

35

Rabirius and his four orations against Catiline will tell us most of what we want to know.

CICERO IN THEORETICAL MODE

The keynote is struck by a passage in *De officiis* in which Cicero compiles a minor conspectus of Platonic and Stoic ideas on punishment. He counsels total devotion to the *res publica* in order to further the interests of all (*Off.* 1.86). First and foremost, then, consideration is given to *rei publicae utilitas*, which is equivalent to *utilitas publica*.[4] Turning specifically to punishment, Cicero counsels against exposing anyone to disgrace by false charges; he sounds a special note of warning against anger, which distorts one's judgement. Those who are called on to administer punishment should copy the laws, for they are moved by equity (*aequitas*), not by anger (1.86, 88–9). *Aequitas* being one of the components of *humanitas*,[5] the latter is best served by keeping in touch with the laws – specifically with the non-discretionary penalty, the *poena legis*, which is beyond the reach of anger and is at the very core of Stoic thinking.[6]

But having introduced both of our notions, Cicero proceeds to express a preference. He says that mildness and clemency (*mansuetudo atque clementia*), commendable as they are, should give way to *severitas* when the interests of the *res publica* are involved; without that proper government is not possible. Indeed the public interest (*rei publicae utilitas*) should always be the paramount consideration when inflicting punishment. The motive should never be to expose the offender to insult – *contumelia vacare debet* – or to give satisfaction to the person inflicting the punishment (1.88).

Cicero's position on *contumelia* is in direct opposition to that which the lawyers would allow an enraged husband (*D.* 48.5.23.3). But Cicero is touching on an important principle. To many wrongdoers the most frightening part of capital punishment was the affront to their dignity. Tacitus says that under Tiberius, fear of the executioner prompted accused persons to take their own lives (TA 6.29.2). This no doubt included physical fear,[7] but in the Principate the *liberum mortis arbitrium*, the free choice of one's manner of death, was seen as a boon because it preserved one's dignity. Indeed one of the reasons for the distinction, in the Principate, between 'regular' death or exile for *honestiores* and death in the most undignified forms for *humiliores* was that it enabled the former to avoid *contumelia*. It is no accident that the *contumelia* that a husband was allowed to inflict on his wife's lover was only available against someone that he could have killed, that is, a person of base degree.[8]

Cicero develops a theme close to *contumelia* when he talks about suffering as an element in punishment. After having the guilty tormented by the Furies, not by the blazing torches of tragedy but through the anguish of remorse, he turns to suffering in the context of temporal punishment. It covers death, pain, mental anguish (*luctus animi*) and adverse court decisions (*offensio iudicii*). *Luctus animi* here means the mourning attire that an accused awaiting trial put on in order to arouse sympathy, and *offensio iudicii* is the court verdicts. Thus the offender suffers *ignominia/infamia*, which is also part of *contumelia*. T. Menenius had, we recall, died of shame; and Augustus would take practical steps to reduce that source of embarrassment.[9]

Another link in the same chain is *poenae metus*, the fear of punishment that acts as a deterrent. Cicero does, it is true, distinguish between divine and temporal punishment in this regard. On the temporal scene the deterrent effect is dissipated once the fear is removed; only on the divine scene is the effect always there, since the god's punishment cannot be evaded.[10] But the distinction is only a talking-point; Cicero knows that *poenae metus* is the secret of punishment's efficacy.

A key position on *utilitas publica* is taken up by the law that Cicero prescribes for *obnuntiatio*, the pronouncement by the augurs that the auspices were unfavourable for public business. Such pronouncements, decrees Cicero, are to be obeyed on pain of a capital penalty (*Leg.* 2.21). This may be a response to Caesar's flouting of *obnuntiatio* in 59 BC,[11] but there is more to it. Cicero describes the augurs as the most important priests and applauds their ability to keep the reins of power in the right hands by manipulating the auspices.[12] And in another law Cicero assigns the primary duty of supervising private worship to the augurs, who are the interpreters of Jupiter. This law, says Cicero, pertains not only to religion but to the state of the country (*civitatis status*), for it is the people's constant reliance on the advice and authority of the Optimates that holds the country together (*Leg.* 2.20, 30).

The augurate is thus the instrument of the conservatives on whom the stability of the state depends. Once Cicero refers to stability he is touching on one of the mainstays of empire,[13] and the message is that the preservation of stability is one of the purposes of punishment. Cicero makes this clear in his *Republic*. Discussing Ennius' line about the stability of the state depending on ancient customs and great men, he blames the contemporary decline on the neglect of custom and the lack of worthy men: 'We are accountable for this and must defend ourselves as if we were accused of a capital crime.'[14]

We return for a moment to Cicero's views on the *poena legis*. After laying down that the primary function of punishment is to serve *rei publicae utilitas*, he declares that the penalty should not be greater than the crime – *cavendum est . . . ne maior poena quam culpa sit* (*Off.* 1.89). He makes the same point elsewhere: *noxiae poena par esto* (*Leg.* 3.11). Is Cicero abandoning the immutable *poena legis*? Is he anticipating the discretionary punishments of the Principate? Or is he merely advocating different *poenae legis* according to the gravity of the crime? The last is more likely. The numerous variations in penalty that we have already inspected were introduced by *leges*, not by anyone's discretion. This is in fact confirmed by *cavendum est* in the *De officiis* passage. The meaning is 'it should be laid down by statute' rather than merely 'we should take care'.[15] We may safely conclude that Cicero retains the full *poena legis*. Which is hardly surprising, for it simply confirms that he has not abandoned his long-standing support for the statutory penalty.[16] His differential penalties may go against the Stoic belief that all faults are equal,[17] but Cicero rejected that notion,[18] and rightly so. It was quite out of touch with reality. It would not be accepted, even by the Stoics, in the Principate.

HUMANITAS AND *UTILITAS PUBLICA*

We now focus on the main thrust of our theme, the link between *utilitas publica* and *humanitas*. To some scholars humanism and the name of Cicero are almost synonymous, but this view neglects the criminal law implications.[19] *Humanitas* has a special significance in that sphere that it does not quite have even in private law contexts, let alone in non-legal situations. It comes closer here than anywhere else to the modern conception of human rights. There is a qualitative difference between Cicero's attitude to the death penalty and, for example, his concern about good faith in contracts (*Off.* 3.50–75). Four questions about *humanitas* claim our attention, namely its links with penal principles, unintentional wrongdoing, *clementia* and *rei publicae utilitas*.

Cicero considers it a cardinal principle of punishment that the sins of the fathers be not visited on the children; neither divine nor human justice can tolerate the idea of punishing the descendants of a man who escapes punishment by dying (*Nat. Deor.* 3.90). This denial of surrogate responsibility when the accused committed suicide held good not only in Cicero's day but also well into the Principate.[20] An interesting principle is enunciated in *De officiis*: it is more commendable for an orator to appear for the defence than for the prosecution. The latter role should only be adopted when it is in the public interest (*rei publicae causa*), and even then conducting too many capital prosecutions may be stigmatized as inhuman behaviour. A capital charge should never be brought against someone who may be innocent. But there is no objection to defending the guilty as long as they are not depraved or impious. Indeed custom sanctions it, and *humanitas* also accepts it (*Off.* 2.49–51).

The thorny problem of the distinction between intentional and unintentional wrongdoing never ceased to interest Cicero,[21] and in a court speech in 72–1 he linked it to *humanitas*. He is discussing the XII Tables rule which laid down that where death was caused unintentionally, a ram given to the victim's family compounded the right to kill the perpetrator (FIRA 1.62). That rule, says Cicero, 'is a tacit law of *humanitas* that demands punishment for a man's intention (*consilium*), not for the accidents of fortune' (*Pro Tullio* 51). Cicero was building on the test laid down by Sulla in his *lex Cornelia de sicariis*, which penalized 'whoever walks around with a weapon for the purpose of killing someone – *qui hominis occidendi . . . causa cum telo ambulaverit*'.[22] Even when the statute was extended to the actual act of homicide[23] Cicero maintained that intention was still the test. Defending Milo in 52, he said that the case still depended on *causa*, therefore carrying a weapon for some purpose other than killing, such as self-defence, was not culpable (*Mil.* 11).

The doctrine espoused by Cicero had a very long life; by Hadrian's day the *voluntas* criterion had become a general principle applicable to all major crimes (*D.* 48.8.14). But Cicero also drew another distinction. He postulated an intermediate type of act in which both intention and accident played a part. Again referring to the XII Tables law, he says that where a weapon is thrown but goes in a different direction from that intended, throwing is an act of will, but hitting someone unintentionally is an act of fortune (*Topica* 64). The absence of intention does not always give complete absolution; it often supports a reduced penalty, as in the XII Tables case. The doctrine went down to the Principate.[24]

Cicero extends the principle of absence of intention to temporary disturbance of mind or sudden impulse. Like accidents of fortune, this should attract a lesser penalty.[25] This is based on Plato,[26] but Cicero does not try to define the less severe penalty – very wisely, for no public criminal law tailored its *poena legis* to diminished responsibility. That would have to await the discretionary penalties of, especially, the

Antonine emperors. But sudden impulse made its mark earlier than that. Tacitus reports that in 24 AD a praetor threw his wife out of the window for an unknown reason. When brought before Tiberius the praetor was confused, claiming that he had been asleep and she had taken her own life. After inspecting the premises Tiberius rejected this explanation, and the praetor committed suicide. His first wife was then charged with having driven him mad by spells and poisons (TA 4.22). She was acquitted, but at least the accuser had read Cicero.

We have already sketched the link between *humanitas* and *clementia*, in the passage in which *clementia* and *mansuetudo* yield to *severitas* when the public interest (*rei publicae utilitas*) is at stake. Although *clementia* and *mansuetudo* are constituent elements of *humanitas*,[27] Cicero was inclined to be lukewarm about them – not from conviction, but because there was no room for clemency in jury-trials. It was the prerogative of the people, later extended to Caesar and the triumvirs, and still later to the emperor and the senate.[28] In 46 Cicero, defending Ligarius before Caesar, was able to plead *deprecatio*, the appeal for mercy, because Caesar was trying the case personally. As it was a charge of treason[29] *rei publicae utilitas* was clearly involved, but Cicero found a way around that. He trusted 'not so much to the strength of our case as to Caesar's *humanitas*'; he relied on 'Caesar's *humanitas*, *clementia* and *misericordia*'; he used 'the tone that one adopts towards a parent, not towards a jury' (Cic. *Lig.* 13, 29–30). But two years later in *De officiis*, as we have seen, he restricted *clementia* to cases where the public interest was not involved. The restriction is anomalous, for it strikes at the whole basis of clemency. The delicate part of the exercise was showing mercy to political offenders. No eyebrows were raised when common-law criminals were pardoned.

The ultimate key to Cicero's thinking is supplied by the dominant role that he assigns to *rei publicae utilitas* compared with the exercise of clemency. The public interest is the most concrete expression of Cicero's fundamental ideology, of his unswerving belief in the stability of the state as the highest virtue and the highest goal.[30] It is the value that underpins his nomination of the augurate as the most important priesthood. It is the value that limits justice by allowing people to be given their deserts only if it is consistent with *communis utilitas* (*Inv.* 2.160). And it is the value that subordinates *humanitas* to the public interest. As early as the 80s Cicero wrote about the need to interpret laws according to the public interest:

> Our ancestors wrote laws whose sole aim was the stability and interests of the state – *salus atque utilitas rei publicae*. The state is

best off when governed according to laws, but all laws should be interpreted in the light of that goal. Epaminondas of Thebes rightly passed over the letter of the law, thinking it sheer madness not to interpret in terms of the stability of the state, a law that had been enacted for that stability.[31] By assuring the stability of the state and looking to the common interest he could not possibly fail to obey the laws.

(*Inv.* 1.68–9)

Cicero was still taking much the same line in *De officiis* nearly forty years later, arguing that to deprive someone of something for one's own benefit is contrary to natural law, but to do so in order to promote *rei publicae utilitas* is fully justified (*Off.* 3.30).

It can no doubt be argued against Cicero that identifying the circumstances that constitute the public interest is a highly subjective matter, but that would apply to any legal interpretation. There are no absolute mathematical values in these matters. The most that we can ask of Cicero is that he make it clear what his interpretation is and that he keep to it with reasonable consistency. He cannot be faulted on that score. To him the public interest is synonymous with the stability of the state, and the way to ensure that is by keeping the control of affairs in the right hands. That means control by the conservatives, the Optimates. This was the fundamental and consistent core of Cicero's thinking on punishment. Whether it holds good for his practice in the matter remains to be seen.

CICERO IN 63: THE BACKGROUND

Of all Cicero's eulogies on *humanitas* in his court speeches,[32] by far the most important is that which he delivered in defence of C. Rabirius in 63, when his client was belatedly charged with having been responsible for the death of the turbulent tribune, L. Saturninus, thirty-seven years before. The speech should not be read in isolation. It has to be linked to the other major event of Cicero's consular year, his suppression of the conspiracy of Catiline later in 63, when Cicero put a number of ringleaders to death pursuant to a decree of the senate, but without making use of any of the recognized judicial processes. When so linked the two episodes form a perfectly consistent whole, both parts of which are based ultimately on *rei publicae utilitas*. At Rabirius' trial Cicero vigorously pressed humane ideas on punishment, but it was precisely because Rabirius had – so the argument went – promoted the public interest that there was room for *humanitas*. There was no similar opening in the Catilinarian affair, for the defendants posed a grave threat to the stability of the state. That was the point at which *humanitas/clementia* and *rei publicae utilitas* parted company.

The background to both episodes is broadly the same. In 100 the tribune L. Saturninus was said to be mounting a campaign of public violence that threatened the stability of the state. The senate was prompted to issue a *senatus consultum ultimum*, 'a last decree of the senate' advising the consuls to see to it that the state came to no harm. The consul in charge, C. Marius, sedated the disturbances without killing, and confined Saturninus and his followers to the senate-house pending trial. This discharged the consul's mandate, but some people failed to understand that, and a mob led by Rabirius broke into the senate-house and butchered the prisoners.[33]

A further step was taken in 88–7, when Sulla invented the *hostis* declaration which declared certain named persons to be enemies of the state. The persons concerned became outlaws and could be killed with impunity, thus creating a mirror-image of the *aquae et ignis interdictio* that Sulla would include in his criminal laws a few years later. But under the *hostis* declaration the punishment was imposed without any semblance of a trial. Sulla used the new device against Marius, but the latter managed to escape to Africa. On returning to Rome, Marius secured a *hostis* declaration against Sulla, but instead of relying on a decree of the senate, Marius got the people to vote a formal interdiction, and to include confiscation of Sulla's property.[34]

THE TRIAL OF RABIRIUS

The Populares[35] wanted to reassert the judicial sovereignty of the people against the inroads of the *s.c. ultimum*, and they chose the death of Saturninus in 100 as their vehicle. They would not attack the *s.c. ultimum* as such; its validity as a suspension of constitutional guarantees in an emergency had been confirmed by the people in 120 BC.[36] But Saturninus had been killed *after* the restoration of order by the consul, therefore his death could not be justified by the senate's decree. If the killing could be justified at all, it would be on the basis of a de facto extension of the consul's *evocatio*, his call to all citizens to assist in restoring order. In fact the *evocatio* had lapsed with the *s.c. ultimum* itself, but the defence might argue that the citizens' duty had been extended by *rei publicae utilitas*. There was a possible analogy in a doctrine approved of by Cicero, that killing a tyrant was in the public interest (*Off.* 3.19).

Rabirius was charged twice. On the first occasion he was acquitted on proving that he had not killed Saturninus.[37] A second charge by regular process being barred, the Populares cast around for an alternative. They found it in the archives, in the ancient two-man tribunal known as the *duumviri*. The *duumviri* did not acquit; their only mandate was to condemn, whereupon the culprit was put to death unless he appealed to the people. Thus the process, not being an adjudication at all, did not violate the rule against double jeopardy. It was simply a second bite at the cherry, a trigger for trial by the people on a reiterated capital charge.[38]

Two leaders of the Populares, Caesar and his cousin, were duly appointed as *duumviri* and set up their tribunal with all the traditional trappings – the unfruitful tree (*infelix arbor*) on which the condemned man would be beaten to death, the lictor standing by with his rods, and (an innovation) a portrait of Saturninus.[39] The *duumviri* duly condemned Rabirius, thus presenting him with an invidious choice – either to acknowledge the people's judicial sovereignty by speaking the words, 'I appeal to the people!' or (as he saw it at the time) to lose his life immediately; there was no room for voluntary exile in the duumviral process. Rabirius appealed and the case went to the people, meeting as the *comitia centuriata*, with the tribune T. Labienus conducting the prosecution. Cicero's extant speech for Rabirius was delivered at that trial. According to Suetonius the barbarity of the duumviral process persuaded the people to acquit (SJ 12). But Dio says that the people were on the point of convicting, when the praetor Metellus Celer struck the flag on the Janiculum; this traditional signal that the enemy was at the gate terminated the proceedings.[40] Either way this was the end of the matter; there was no third trial.

There is much skilful advocacy, much obfuscation and evasion, in Cicero's defence of Rabirius, but it is his most categorical statement of *humanitas*. The speech is geared to the fact that after the duumviral condemnation Cicero had secured a decree of the senate reducing the penalty to *aquae et ignis interdictio*.[41] The change was quite legal. The *duumviri* having discharged their mandate, the senate was at large to define the penalty to be applied in the *iudicium populi*.

With the reduced penalty as its keynote, Cicero's speech became a virtual discourse on punishment, as the following adaptation shows:

> Labienus complains that I abolished the *perduellio* (= the duumviral) process. Would that I had been the first to do so. Nothing could grace my consulship more than the removal of the executioner

from the Forum, of the cross from the Field of Mars. But the credit belongs to the founders of the Republic who aimed to protect your freedom by mild laws, not to endanger it by harsh punishments. I have refused to allow the assembly and Forum to be polluted, I have kept every citizen's person inviolate and his freedom intact. The *lex Porcia* forbade the use of the rod on citizens, it wrested their liberty from the lictor. C. Gracchus forbade capital trials without your authority, but the *duumviri* condemned a citizen to death unheard, unearthing savage procedures and punishments in archaic records. Penalties under the public criminal laws, whether fines or exile, leave some trace of freedom; even if death is proposed we may die as free men. But the executioner, the covering of the head, the cross – such things should not offend the eyes and expectations of citizens. It was by my advice, influence and instigation that this cruel punishment, more suited to a tyrant than to a tribune, was discarded.[42]

Cicero barely grazes the substantive issue, the legality of Rabirius' act as seen in the context of *rei publicae utilitas*. He has a lot to say about the *s.c. ultimum* (*Rab. perd.* 20–21), but he does not mention that the senate's mandate had been discharged prior to the killing. He regrets that at the first trial Hortensius for the defence had denied that Rabirius had killed Saturninus: 'If I had been defence counsel at that time I would gladly have admitted that Rabirius struck down that enemy of the Roman people!' (*ib.* 18). In fact there had not been a *hostis* declaration against Saturninus, but the language created the right atmosphere. It is only at the very start of his speech that Cicero touches on *rei publicae utilitas*:

I am undertaking this defence because the safety of the state and my consular duty demand it. Rabirius is not in jeopardy because of any fault on his part. They would destroy the main prop of majesty and empire by nullifying the senate's authority, the consuls' powers, the concerted action of good citizens, the guarantee of the security of the state.

(*Ib.* 1–4 adapted)

But the main thrust was on *humanitas*, a line that would appeal to an audience accustomed, by now, to more civilized penalties. If Suetonius is right the appeal succeeded, and *humanitas* presents as the complement of *rei publicae utilitas* rather than as its rival; it forestalled a verdict that would have overruled the public interest. But on Dio's version *rei publicae utilitas* survived only by default.

THE CONSPIRACY OF CATILINE

The conspiracy of Catiline dominates the closing months of Cicero's consulship. The facts continue to resist full elucidation,[43] but a working model has Catiline, already a failed candidate for the consulship, trying to do better in the elections for 62. But Cicero again puts a spoke in Catiline's wheel. Thereupon Catiline conspires with C. Manlius to raise a revolt in Etruria, to march on Rome, and to assassinate Cicero. Cicero sets in train a tortuous series of manoeuvres that culminate, in December 63, in a senatorial debate on the punishment of the ringleaders (except Catiline himself who is in Etruria). The death penalty is voted, and the ringleaders are executed by Cicero.

Catiline headed a radical populist movement, the latest in the long line of alliances between second-rank politicians and the underprivileged. Cicero was determined to stamp out this threat to stability, but he had a problem. C. Gracchus' *lex Sempronia de capite civium* was still on the statute-book, thus there was still a question-mark against punishing a citizen capitally except by process authorized by the people.[44] Cicero had to tread very carefully. The senate had passed a *s.c. ultimum*, but Cicero was not sure enough of his ground to use it (Cic. *Cat.* 1.4).

Cicero's hands were tied because Catiline had not made any overt hostile move. He was still in Rome and was even attending the senate. Cicero decided to manoeuvre him into doing something that would deprive him of the protection of the *lex Sempronia*, something that would make it possible to punish him without trying him at all. If no *adjudication* was required there would be no breach of the *lex*. Cicero outlined his plan to the senate on 8 November:

> This man is an enemy. The country might well ask why I do not put him to death. Custom does not stand in the way, for even private citizens have punished dangerous men with death. There are laws concerning the punishment of citizens, *but those who defected from the Republic have never enjoyed the rights of citizens.* Yet, by merely putting Catiline to death I would not crush the trouble, *that can only be done if he leaves Rome and gathers his forces.*
> (*Cat.* 1.28–30)

Cicero here formulates the proposition that a person guilty of treason forfeits his citizenship retrospectively to the time of his crime, and is not covered by the *lex Sempronia*. The reasoning was flawed; the offender's guilt could not be known until he had been tried.[45] But

Cicero knew that, and had a second string to his bow. It is outlined in his statement that he can only act effectively if Catiline leaves Rome for Etruria.[46] This will make him a manifest wrongdoer, thus exposing him to summary punishment without trial. Since time immemorial guilt that was either confessed, or so notorious that it did not require proof, had been punished in this way.[47]

It all worked out as Cicero had planned. The very next day, 9 November, Catiline obliged by leaving for Etruria. Cicero delivered a speech to the people – one that was conveniently ready:

> What I have been waiting for has happened. You can all see[48] that a conspiracy has been openly mounted against the Republic. There is no longer room for leniency; the case demands severity (*Cat.* 2.6). But why do I dwell on this enemy who confesses that he is an enemy,[49] and say nothing about the dissemblers who remain in Rome? I want not so much to punish them as to cure them, to reconcile them to the Republic. Most of them can benefit from the medication of my advice. If they remain inactive no action will be taken against them; they are enemies, but they were born citizens. But if they make any move the prison that our ancestors designed as the avenger of wicked and manifest crimes is ready for them. If I have to abandon leniency no loyal citizen will perish; by the punishment of a few you will all be saved.
>
> (2.17–23, 27–9 adapted)

There are several Platonic doctrines in the passage, including the curative theory of punishment.[50] But the Catilinarians in Rome were not impressed with Cicero's carrot-and-stick approach, and events moved rapidly towards a climax. On 3 December Cicero placed before the senate incriminating letters written by the men and got them to admit that the seals were theirs. They were taken into custody. Cicero addressed the people again (*Cat.* 3), and on 4 December the senate ruled that the men had acted against the Republic.[51] Next day, 5 December, Cicero convened the senate again. He said that he was referring the whole matter to them *de novo* to enable them both to judge the facts and to frame a penalty: *et de facto quid iudicetis et de poena quid censeatis* (4.6). The invitation to adjudicate on the facts was a departure from Cicero's reliance on manifest or confessed guilt, but he was still proceeding with extreme caution and wanted all possible underpinning for his position. The invitation to frame a penalty was appropriate here because the men were not being (and in view of their manifest guilt did not need to be) brought up under any public criminal law.[52]

The greater part of the debate was on sentence. After D. Silanus had proposed the death penalty and Tiberius Nero had suggested deferring a decision until Catiline was defeated, the three principal speeches were delivered. The Populares' view was put forward by Caesar. He proposed that the men be imprisoned for life in self-governing municipalities in Italy; that their properties be confiscated; that the municipal authorities be held accountable if any prisoner escaped; and that no one try to bring their cases up for review, on pain of being held to act against the Republic.[53]

An interesting feature of the debate is the charges of novelty that Caesar and Cicero hurled at each other. Caesar described Silanus' proposal of the death penalty as an innovation because, he said, exile was the regular capital penalty at that time.[54] 'Exile' is, of course, simply shorthand for *aquae et ignis interdictio*, but the point is that Caesar may have been making a genuine plea for the formal abolition of the death penalty. If the duumviral trappings at Rabirius' trial were intended to initiate that plea, so much the better. However, Cicero was not going to let this go unchallenged. In the fourth oration against Catiline, delivered after Caesar's speech, he says that imprisonment is an extraordinary punishment for capital crimes; and it is made even more peculiar by including confiscation of property (4.7–8). Cicero is criticizing the proposal as a hybrid, a mixture of purely precautionary imprisonment and fully penal confiscation. But Caesar knew what he was doing. His proposal was not for a capital penalty, and thus it did not breach the *lex Sempronia*.

Caesar's proposal appealed to senators. There was much public unrest, and Caesar warned that the senate would incur great odium if it put the men to death without trial.[55] This reminder of the *lex Sempronia* brought a prompt response from Cicero:

> I see that some Populares are absent, no doubt because they do not wish to vote on a capital charge against citizens. But I would like to remind Caesar that although the *lex Sempronia* was enacted for citizens, an enemy of the Republic cannot possibly be a citizen. (4.10)

Thus for the third time Cicero plays one of his trump cards. But he admits that Caesar's proposal is more in line with popular thinking; yet nothing will deter him from safeguarding *utilitas rei publicae* (4.9). But not everyone was convinced. Even Silanus explained that by originally proposing *eschatēn dikēn* he had not meant *summum supplicium* but imprisonment, for that was the ultimate penalty for a senator.[56]

Cato saved the day for Cicero. His speech as reported by Sallust[57] proved to be decisive. The important part is the motion at the end:

I propose that whereas the Republic has been placed in the greatest peril, and whereas these wicked citizens have been convicted by the evidence of the Allobroges,[58] and whereas they have confessed that they planned murder, arson and other crimes against citizens and country, *let those who have confessed be treated as if they were manifestly guilty of capital crimes and let them be punished in the traditional manner.*[59]

The most interesting feature is the analogy between *confessi* and *manifesti*. The latter are the measuring-rod, which suggests that originally punishment without trial had only been inflicted on manifest wrongdoers.

Cato's speech turned the scale and the senate voted the death sentence. But in deference to Caesar, who objected to the bad part of his proposal being adopted but not the good, Cicero remitted that part of the vote that called for confiscation (Plut. *Cic.* 21.5). Cicero then delivered the five men to the Tullianum, where the public executioner strangled them.

CICERO IN 63: THE AFTERMATH

The events of 63 exposed some grave weaknesses in the Roman perception of punishment. As long as they kept to the firm guidelines of the *poena legis* they were able to maintain their equilibrium; there was no room for debate on the merits or demerits of particular penalties. As Cicero himself said, the only way for a jury to relieve an accused of an unconscionable penalty was to acquit him. The trend of the *poena legis* was steadily towards *humanitas*. Sulla knew that when he substituted interdiction for actual death. Cicero was equally clear about it (in the same extraordinary year 63) when he made exile the definitive penalty for *ambitus*.

It was when politicians began moving away from the safe haven of the *poena legis* that they ran into trouble. That is what happened to Cicero. Advance notice of what was coming was given at the end of 63, when a tribune vetoed his attempt to deliver the customary valedictory oration to round off his consulship.[60] Then, in 58, his enemy P. Clodius carried a plebiscite prescribing interdiction for 'whoever shall or has put a Roman citizen to death without trial'.[61] The law did not name Cicero, but its language left no doubt that the Catilinarian affair would be brought up. The next step would be a special commission to try Cicero, but he decided not to wait for the inevitable and went into voluntary exile. Clodius secured a second plebiscite imposing interdiction on Cicero (now specifically named) for putting citizens to death without trial on the strength of a false *senatus consultum*; his property was confiscated, his house was demolished and a temple of Liberty was erected on the site.[62] Cicero was recalled from exile in 57 and delivered three speeches of thanks.[63]

Finally, what is our reply to the question that we have posed, as to the extent to which Cicero practised what he preached? The answer is that he maintained a commendable level of consistency. There were certainly numerous dodges of advocacy, but the man who stood up for *rei publicae utilitas* even though he knew he was out of touch with public opinion (*Cat.* 4.9) was undoubtedly true to his principles.

CONCLUSION

The identification of the affront to dignity as a major factor in *poenae metus* gives new meaning to the free choice of the manner of death. The link between *humanitas* and *utilitas publica* is worked out through four themes: the principles of punishment, unintentional wrongdoing, *clementia*, and the role assigned to *rei publicae utilitas* by Cicero. After a sketch of the background to the events of 63, the trial of Rabirius and the proceedings against the Catilinarians are interpreted in terms of Cicero's position on *utilitas publica*. Cicero's consistency between what he says and what he does is confirmed. The chapter ends with a note on his exile.

5

THE NEW COURTS:
AUGUSTUS AND TIBERIUS

THE *COGNITIO EXTRAORDINARIA*

When Augustus founded the Principate in 27 BC he created the conditions for as profound a change in criminal justice as in any other sphere of government and society. The *cognitio extraordinaria*[1] was designed to 'liberate' criminal trials from the shackles of the *ordo iudiciorum publicorum*, that is, from the limitations of the jury-courts. The new-found freedom was expressed in the assumption of a free discretion both in the definitions of crimes and in the scale of punishments. Acts not encompassed by the public criminal laws could be made justiciable, and the *poena legis* for any given crime could be mitigated or intensified in the discretion of the sentencing authority – or of its superior.[2] But the link with the public criminal laws was never broken completely. No matter how radical the changes, crimes continued to be classified under the established heads making up the *ordo iudiciorum publicorum*.[3] Even punishments were referred to those heads; despite far-reaching changes in the punitive system as class differentials took hold, the jurists continued to list the *poena legis* alongside the later modifications.[4] This suggests that right up to the end of the Principate the modifications had not yet acquired an invariability that would have made them, in effect, a new *poena legis*.[5]

The new approach required new tribunals. It can also be put the other way around: new tribunals prompted a new approach. In fact both are true. In the case of political crimes the first steps saw jurisdiction being exercised by Augustus' senate and by the emperor himself, and the senatorial court – but not that of the emperor himself – expanded its operations under Tiberius. In the course of such operations experiments in punishment began being conducted. Because neither senate nor emperor owed the new authority to a *lex*,[6] there was an immediate

50

parting of the ways vis-a-vis the jury-courts, all of which owed their very existence to *leges*. That opened the door to penal modifications.

On the other side of the coin common-law crimes needed a new approach because of unconscionable delays in the jury-courts. Expedients such as striking the names of long-standing defendants off the trial-lists, operating the busiest courts in multiple sessions,[7] and introducing a statute of limitations[8] were only temporary palliatives. A more far-reaching solution was found in the emperor's own court and in the courts of his delegates, the *praefectus urbi* (the urban prefect) and the *praefectus praetorio* (the praetorian prefect). The courts of the prefects would ultimately replace the jury-courts completely, although the final point would not be reached until the 220s AD.[9] But throughout the Principate the prefectorial tribunals would be subordinated to the emperor; they would have no independent power to change the definitions of crimes or the scale of penalties.[10]

Occasionally the prefects functioned as what can best be described as scapegoats for the emperor; they were saddled with responsibility for his unpopular sentences. This was a by-product of the unintended, but hardly surprising fact that all changes under the *cognitio extraordinaria* were attributed to the emperor himself, regardless of which of the new jurisdictions was actually the source. From this arose a new factor on the punitive scene, namely criticism. In the Republic free and open debate had been the norm, and even the senate's proceedings had been published on the all-important occasion of the Catilinarian debate.[11] There was no doubt some muffled criticism as well – it took five years to bring Cicero to book – but on the whole the safety-valve worked reasonably well. But with the advent of what was, at least in theory, one-man rule the institutions that had fostered the safety-valve ceased to operate, and the emperor became the focus of literary and juristic attacks.

Common-law crimes have a higher profile in the Principate, especially from the second century AD, than they had in the Republic. This was due to two factors, the new improved machinery and the changed political climate. Cicero's court speeches reflect the same liberal climate as that which shaped at least part of punishment in his day. But in the Principate the old tearaway, devil-may-care Cicero, speaking his mind with complete freedom, made way for the time-server and sycophant, ever conscious of the imperial presence at his shoulder. Pliny's letters tell us enough about his court speeches at the turn of the first century to confirm this. The difference was reflected in the spirit, even if not in the letter, of the court situation. Quintilian, appointed to a Chair of

Rhetoric by Vespasian, might think it prudent to concentrate on the purely technical aspects of court pleading in his *Institutio Oratoria*, but his younger contemporary, Tacitus, did not hesitate to pinpoint the environmental change:

> Great oratory is like a flame, needing fuel to feed it and movement to fan it. The eloquence of our fathers flourished under such conditions. Today's pleaders exert as much influence as can be expected under a stable and settled regime, but in those turbulent times they did not need a strong single ruler; political acumen was what helped a speaker to sway the unstable populace. Hence the impeachment of powerful criminals by champions of the people's rights. The high status of the defendants was an incentive to eloquence, for it is one thing to drone on about common theft, but quite another to fulminate against *ambitus, repetundae* and homicide. On such topics was built the fame of Demosthenes and Cicero.

> (Tac. *Dial.* 36–37 adapted)

But 'droning on about common theft' was a positive improvement in the eyes of the populace as a whole. It symbolized the abandonment of pyrotechnical displays in favour of criminal jurisprudence proper.

AUGUSTUS AND PUNISHMENT: THE SENATE

The effective story of the senate's criminal jurisdiction under Augustus is confined to the last decade of the reign.[12] Over 6–8 AD the regime was embarrassed by a series of anonymous pamphlets defaming eminent men and women that were being posted up at night; the principal targets were Tiberius and his mother Livia. Before anything could be done the authors had to be identified, and in order to make this possible Augustus broke with tradition. He proposed that the evidence of slaves be admitted against their masters where the gravity of the offence and the difficulty of proof warranted it. The most vitriolic of the pamphleteers, Cassius Severus, was identified and tried by the senate under the *lex maiestatis*. But he did not receive the statutory sentence of interdiction. He was sentenced to the milder form of banishment known as *relegatio*. But Cassius failed to take advantage of his good fortune. He continued his attacks from his comfortable exile on Crete, and in 24 the senate tried him again. This time he received the full *poena legis* of interdiction and confiscation, and the inhospitable island of Seriphos was specifically named as the place of his internment. This intensified penalty, known as *deportatio (in insulam)*, was partly dictated by the fact that treaty states in which the exile could acquire the immunity of non-Roman citizenship were not very thick on the ground by this time.[13] Perhaps the Platonic doctrine of a more severe penalty for a second conviction[14] was also in senators' minds.

The designation of defamatory words as treason did not fail to arouse criticism. Tacitus reflects this when he observes with some acerbity that prior to Augustus words had not been punished; only deeds like treachery, sedition and dereliction of duty had fallen under the treason laws (TA 1.72.3–4). Others were less critical; Seneca was able to say that under Augustus words had caused inconvenience but had not endangered people's lives (*Ben.* 3.27.1). Some even gave the emperor full marks for tolerance (SA 55–56). The admission of the evidence of slaves was also controversial. The Severan jurist, Domitius Ulpianus, is clearly reflecting a justification going back to the reign when he says of the grant of freedom to slaves who identified authors, 'What of it, if it serves *utilitas publica?*' (D. 47.10.5.11).

The first trial of Cassius Severus is the one clear example of the infliction of a discretionary penalty by Augustus' senate.[15] It supports that emperor's reputation for leniency. It was in the public interest that covert pamphleteering be suppressed, but the primary purpose was to uncover the authors and destroy the material, not to punish. But leniency would not last. Insults of all kinds would become culpable over time, and under some rulers the penalty would be death. And the senate would do nothing to stop the rot.

AUGUSTUS AND PUNISHMENT:
THE EMPEROR'S THREE HATS

Augustus' personal intervention in criminal justice takes three distinct forms. None of them inaugurated a full-scale emperor's court – that would take place later in the first century AD – but the three strands are important steps along the road.

In the first phase the emperor's domestic tribunal starts functioning as an analogue of a public criminal court, and matters that would have stayed in the private domain in the case of anyone else are punished under the aegis of the public criminal laws. In the second phase the emphasis is still on matters which affect the emperor personally, but the offences are essentially public; conspiracies head this list. Third, the emperor concerns himself with matters in which he has no personal interest at all; common-law crimes make up this list. The first two strands often arouse suspicions that punishment was inflicted for improper motives; but the third passes without unfavourable comment.

The leading case under the first head arose in 2 BC, when punishment was meted out to Augustus' daughter Julia and the free spirits who belonged to Julia's circle.[16] The group had operated for a long time without interference, but in 2 BC Augustus became Pater Patriae, Father of his Country, and the moral imperatives of his new status forced him to act. He brought Julia and her friends before his domestic tribunal, but the charges were framed under the public criminal laws. Most of the culprits, including Julia herself, were sentenced to *relegatio* under Augustus' adultery law. But one member of the group was less fortunate. Iullus Antonius, a son of Mark Antony and married to Augustus' niece, was seen as a potential threat to the throne. He was charged under the *lex maiestatis*, and so adultery with the emperor's daughter was elevated to treason. He was sentenced to death, but was allowed to choose the manner of it. This is the first occurrence in the Principate of the *liberum mortis arbitrium*, the free choice of death which avoided the gross *contumelia* of a public execution.

Augustus was careful not to conduct a witch-hunt. Only leading members of the group were brought up in his domestic court. Others were referred to the jury-court for adultery. And a period of five years prescription was laid down, so that early participants in the group's activities were exonerated. But this did not stifle criticism. Tacitus reflects one of the contemporary views:

> He exiled his daughter and punished her lovers with death or exile. By giving the solemn name of broken oaths and violated majesty to a common peccadillo of men and women he ignored traditional clemency and exceeded the scope of his own laws.
>
> (TA 3.24.2–3)

Not all the criticisms were unfavourable. The punishment of Julia's lovers was received with sarcastic approval. Augustus had, it was said, dealt with them no more harshly than if they had consorted with an ordinary citizen instead of Augustus' daughter. Far from putting them to death, he had banished them for their own safety and given them travel documents.[17]

Augustus again convened his domestic court in c. 8 AD, when he banished Julia's daughter, Vipsania Julia. But her lover, D. Silanus, was not punished under the adultery law at all. He merely suffered the private remedy of *renuntiatio amicitiae*, renunciation of the emperor's friendship. It was a severe handicap – a sentence of political and social death – but it did not affect his civic rights, or even his presence in Rome, in any way.[18] The experiment of dealing with private wrongs under the public criminal law was not repeated by Tiberius. In 17 AD he vetoed an attempt to bring Augustus' great-niece, Appuleia Varilla, before the senate on a charge of adultery.[19]

From the juristic point of view the adultery trials were the least of Augustus' contributions to penal theory. He did better – if that is the right word – when it came to acts that threatened him in his public, rather than his domestic capacity. In this regard he intervened not only through his own court, but also – no less effectively – by indirect means. This is graphically illustrated by the conspiracy of Caepio and Murena that was uncovered in 22 BC. Charges were lodged with the jury-court for *maiestas*, but the accused did not appear at the trial. They were found guilty *in absentia* and sentence of interdiction was duly imposed. But for some reason the men delayed making their way into voluntary exile. Augustus sent pursuers who caught them while they were still in Italy, and killed them.[20] This doctrine of 'quick pursuit' may seem to have strained the limits of legality, but there were Republican precedents in the shape of Pleminius and Tubulus. It is also possible that by not giving sureties they had failed to qualify for the right of departure; Dio does say that when they failed to appear at the trial it was supposed that they intended to depart, hence their conviction *in absentia* (CD 54.3.5). Even more important, Dio has Augustus say, in response to criticisms, that the proceedings had not been brought in anger, but because they promoted *to dēmosion* (CD 54.3.6). In other words, *utilitas publica* overrode the Stoic precept not to punish in anger.[21]

Utilitas publica was much in Augustus' mind at this time. Shortly before the Caepio–Murena affair a certain M. Primus, governor of Macedonia, was brought before the *quaestio maiestatis* on a charge of making war without authority. The accused claimed that he had acted with Augustus' authority, whereupon the emperor went to court of his own accord to deny having given authority. The future conspirator Murena, defending Primus, asked Augustus what had brought him to court unsummoned. The emperor replied, '*to dēmosion*' (CD 54.3.3). But *utilitas publica* was also used against him. In his *Res Gestae* he boasts of having driven Caesar's murderers into exile by due process of law (*RG* 2). The reference is to the *lex Pedia* of 43 BC.[22] But the use of that law against the assassins evoked criticism: 'Cassius and Brutus died because of a feud that he had inherited, but private enmities should be subordinated to *publicae utilitates*' (TA 1.10.2). The regime's response to this criticism was not convincing:

It was in keeping with his good fortune and clemency that none of those who had taken up arms against him was put to death by him or at his order. It was the cruelty and treachery of Antony that accounted for their deaths. (Vell. 2.87.2–3 adapted)

From time to time Augustus tried conspirators in his own court. Dio notes that conspirators whom he does not name were punished in 18, and again in 9–8 BC (CD 55.4.4, 5.4). Dio is more specific about one incident in 8 BC. While Augustus was sitting in judgment and was about to sentence a number of men to death, Maecenas appeared on the scene and threw a tablet with the words, 'Hangman, call a halt!' into Augustus' lap, whereupon the emperor adjourned without sentencing anyone (CD 55.7.1–2). The notice probably reflects no more than contemporary propaganda,[23] but the point is that it was the exercise of personal jurisdiction in matters affecting his personal interests that exposed the ruler to such attacks.

A detailed example of Augustus' exercise of personal *cognitio* is furnished by the conspiracy of Cn. (L.) Cornelius Cinna, a grandson of Pompey. The accounts of Seneca and Dio differ on both dates and details,[24] but the general picture is fairly clear. A plot is disclosed to Augustus. He summons his *consilium* to sit with him in trying Cinna, but at the last minute he decides to consult Livia. She advises against harsh measures. Augustus cancels the summons to the *consilium*, releases the men, addresses a homily to Cinna, and subsequently makes him consul.

The episode is suspect,[25] not only because of the conflicting dates, but also because of a difference of emphasis. Seneca wants to contrast the brutality of the man who had taken part in the triumviral proscriptions with his clemency as emperor. It is while Augustus is agonizing over what to do that Livia breaks in with a brief comment, advising him to follow the example of the physician who, when the usual remedies do not work, tries the opposite; severity having accomplished nothing in cases like Caepio and Murena, he should now try clemency (*Clem.* 1.9.3–6). Then follows the long homily to Cinna, which was the only *poena* (= a reprimand) that was being imposed (1.9.7–11).

Dio dismisses the homily in one line (CD 55.22.1). But he regales us with a long and boring dialogue between Augustus and Livia in which the empress gives a detailed exposition of the principles of punishment (55.14–21). The account includes the simile of the physician, but for the rest Dio relies on his reading of Plato to produce a compendium of all the standard criteria – the incurable recidivist, the rashness of youth, the dangers of retribution, different punishments according to gravity, and the virtues of clemency. If the account has any value it is because it may reflect the systematic attention that was being given to punishment at Dio's time of writing, in the Severan period.

Turning to our third strand, personal *cognitio* in common-law crimes, our first case is the man charged with *parricidium* to whom Augustus put a question designed to avoid the penalty of the sack.[26] Suetonius specially cites the case as an example of Augustus' leniency (SA 33.1). Suetonius also reports a trial for forgery in which all the signatories to a will were liable under a strict interpretation of the *lex Cornelia testamentaria*. When Augustus distributed the voting tablets to his *consilium* he included not only the usual tablets for condemnation or acquittal, but also a third which pardoned those who had been induced to sign by fraud or mistake (SA 34.2).

Finally, in 10 AD a quaestor was charged with murder and was defended by Livia's grandson, Germanicus. The accuser, fearing Germanicus' influence on the jury, wanted Augustus to try the case himself, but the request was refused (CD 56.24.7). It was a wise decision; an acquittal would have stirred up a hornets' nest. But the fact that the request was made testifies to Augustus' reputation for impartiality.

THE SENATORIAL COURT UNDER TIBERIUS

The Augustan Principate had seen minimal intervention by the senate, but substantial activity by the emperor himself. The roles were reversed under Tiberius. The senate rose to great prominence, with the strong support of the emperor, and personal *cognitio* was seldom used. In 20 Tiberius was asked to take personal cognizance of the case of Cn. Piso, accused of complicity in the death of Germanicus. Tiberius refused, and in remitting the case to the senate he declared that he would not use his power as emperor to avenge private wrongs.[27] The criticisms levelled at Augustus for ignoring *utilitas publica* had not been lost on Tiberius.

Tiberius had a keen appreciation of the niceties of *utilitas publica*. He regularly attended trials in the senate and also visited the jury-courts, taking his seat at the side of the praetor's tribunal.[28] These visits, although acknowledged as contributions to the truth, were criticized as an interference with judicial freedom (TA 1.75.2). But there were some who thought them conducive to *utilitas publica*, and Tiberius himself told the senate that he did not mind offending if it served the public interest.[29] The same doctrine inspired his introduction of a systematic rescript service[30] which was the vehicle for many of his pronouncements on criminal justice, including his agenda-setting *exercendas leges esse*, 'let the laws be enforced', in response to an enquiry about the *lex maiestatis*. This ruling asserted the supremacy of the public criminal laws in every respect, including the *poena legis*.[31] But although Tiberius was the major influence on punitive theory through rescripts, speeches in the senate and his tribunician power of veto, he also allowed the senate considerable latitude. It is therefore to the senatorial debates that we turn for much of the penal policy of the reign.[32]

Tiberius' first major rulings in the senate[33] were given at the trial of Cn. Piso in 20 on charges connected with Germanicus' death in Syria the year before. In his opening address the emperor gave a memorable exposition of the principles of fair trial. He reserved private questions that might generate *renuntiatio amicitiae* until after the senatorial trial[34] – so as not to prejudge any common issues. He also said that he was placing Germanicus above the laws in one respect, by entrusting the investigation of his death to the senate rather than to a jury-court (TA 3.12.10). This implied invitation to senators to use their discretion on punishment prompted a debate that went ahead despite the accused's suicide. A proposal that Piso's name be erased from the public records was rejected by Tiberius, who pointed out that the names of Mark Antony and Iullus Antonius had not been so treated. In response to another proposal, that Piso's son Marcus be stripped of his senatorial rank and banished for ten years, but with partial retention of property, Tiberius 'relieved him of the *ignominia*'. He approved of half of Piso's property being released to his other son, Gnaeus, on condition that he changed his *praenomen*.[35]

The trial of Clutorius Priscus in 21 generated a debate on the basic issue of the death sentence. Priscus had written an elegy on Tiberius' son, Drusus, during the latter's illness, but Drusus had recovered. Priscus had, however, proceeded to read the poem at the salon of a Roman matron. Word of this got out and Priscus was tried by the senate, acting of its own accord as Tiberius was out of Rome at the time. The senators were agreed on Priscus' guilt, but not on the sentence. The trouble was that the crime did not fall under any of the public criminal laws. It belonged under the *malum carmen*, the spell or curse for which the XII Tables had ordained the death penalty. The consul designate accordingly proposed that Priscus be put to death. But Marcus Lepidus opposed it:

Abominable as the crime is, a moderate response is suggested both by the emperor's policy and by precedent. Words should be distinguished from evil deeds. This is a case for a balanced sentence. I have often heard the emperor complain when some-one forestalled his mercy by taking his own life.[36] Priscus alive will not endanger the state, nor dead will he serve as an example. I propose that he leave Rome, that his property be confiscated, and that he be interdicted from water and fire. I propose this as if he were bound by the *lex maiestatis*.

Lepidus' proposal was framed in terms of *humanitas*. But he had to find a statutory basis if he wanted to displace the XII Tables penalty. His solution was to subsume this wrongful act under the *lex maiestatis* by analogy. In that way the *poena legis* would replace the death penalty. But Lepidus failed to win support, and Priscus was sentenced to death and led off to immediate execution.[37] There was, however, a sequel of some comfort to Lepidus. When Tiberius learnt of the verdict he expressed his disapproval of so hasty a punishment for words. The senate resolved that in future its sentences were not to be carried out until the tenth day after their pronouncement, so as to give the emperor time to veto them.[38] The sources can be forgiven for blaming the emperor for punishments that had in fact been imposed by the senate; by not using his veto the emperor would in future make such sentences his own.

The trial of C. Silanus, a former governor of Asia, on charges of aggravated *repetundae* and *maiestas* in 22 is of interest. The accused having abandoned his defence (= confessed), it only remained for the senate to pass sentence. The full *poena legis* was proposed, with the island of Gyarus as the place of deportation. An amendment allowed Silanus to retain the property that had come to him through his mother, who was of the family of Augustus' mother, Atia. Another amendment, proposed by Tiberius, changed the place of internment to the more pleasant island of Cythnus. These were merely ad hoc arrangements, but there was a more substantial matter. In assessing the penalty for *repetundae* aggravated by *saevitia* the accusers went back to Republican precedents, in addition to which Tiberius cited the punishment meted out to Volesus Messala by Augustus.[39] The senate was gradually building up a set of punitive guidelines.

Experimental penalties took a further step forward in 24 when C. Silius, a former legate of Upper Germany, was charged with *maiestas* arising out of his treasonable dealings with the rebel Sacrovir in Gaul. Silius committed suicide before the verdict, but the senate continued the trial and decreed confiscation of property. This, however, did not breach the rule against posthumous confiscation,[40] for the present forfeiture was of an unprecedented kind. It only touched gifts given to Silius by Augustus; those were to be handed over to the emperor's (private) treasury, not to the public *aerarium* (TA 4.20.1). In other words, Tiberius had renounced Silius' friendship and had coupled it with another private-law remedy, the revocation of gifts for gross ingratitude. Silius' suicide threatened to defeat this, since the private action for ingratitude did not lie against the heirs. Tiberius therefore 'went public'; he got the senate to decree confiscation under the public criminal laws.[41] Interchangeability between private and public remedies was a feature of *cognitio extraordinaria*.[42]

Silius' wife, Sosia, was also charged. She was sentenced to *deportatio*. In the debate on her property one proposal was that half be confiscated and that the rest go to her children. But Marcus Lepidus succeeded with a counter-proposal that a quarter go to the accusers[43] and that her children get the balance (TA 4.20.2–3). This leading protagonist of leniency was luckier this time than he had been in Clutorius Priscus' case.

The trial of Sex. Marius in 33 confirms what we have already gathered from Priscus' case, that the senate did not always need a foundation in any public criminal law. Marius was accused of incest with his daughter and was put to death by being thrown off the Tarpeian Rock.[44] The trial was conducted in Rome, by the senate.[45] The penalty was not based on any public criminal law. In the Severan period incest attracted a penalty of deportation, compared with relegation under the *lex Julia de adulteriis*. This was because incest was contrary to divine law and was punished under the *ius gentium*, that comprehensive reservoir of principles common to all mankind.[46] The Severans add that the act of incest might also amount to *stuprum* or *adulterium* under the *lex Julia*, in which case it was a double crime (*D.* 48.18.5)

Marius' precipitation from the Tarpeian Rock needs further consideration. Even if incest raised the penalty to deportation, it was still short of actual death. Why, then, did the senate decree the ultimate penalty? We might reply that the paramount idea was to purge the pollution, which in this case specifically required precipitation.[47] But in that case why do the Severans reduce it? The only answer that occurs (it is offered *faute de mieux*) is that *humanitas* prompted mitigation in the Antonine period. But the use of the extreme penalty in Tiberius' reign is secure. In 16 the senate decreed the expulsion of astrologers and L. Pituanius, who did not leave, was thrown off the Rock (TA 2.32.5). Also, according to Dio the senate ruled that Aelius Saturninus be precipitated in 23 for reciting improper verses about Tiberius (CD 57.22.5).

A report by Tacitus suggests that the shift away from Late Republican moderation had begun to poison public opinion. There was something of a black comedy in 24, when an accuser who had falsely charged two prominent citizens with conspiracy left Rome in a hurry, hotly pursued by a mob threatening him with the dungeon, the Rock and the sack (TA 4.29.1–2). But perhaps this is simply Tacitus in lighter vein.

'ALL THE LAWS IN GOOD SHAPE EXCEPT ONE'

Appointments were based on birth and military and civil excellence, always choosing the best. The magistrates retained their authority and prestige. The laws were in good shape, with the exception of the law of *maiestas*.

(TA 4.6.2–3)

To the sources the great watershed in Tiberius' reign came in 23, when the rise of Sejanus signalled the start of the decline. Tacitus takes the opportunity to review the reign up to that point, and with one exception the review is an unqualified encomium. Tacitus thus reinforces his repeated strictures on the treason law,[48] which presents as the one blot on the landscape. But what precisely was the critics' complaint? In particular, how far were they attacking the punishments meted out by the regime?

Tacitus avoids any criticism of punitive policy as such. Laws other than *maiestas* are excluded from the attack of 23 and are usually noted without comment wherever else they appear, even when they cover political charges, as long as they are not based on the *lex maiestatis*.[49] Tacitus' message is that all the vices of criminal justice – cruel punishments, unjust accusations, unfair trials – relate to the one crime.

There is not much to support the criticism over 14–23 AD. Libo Drusus would have been pardoned if he had not committed suicide; Piso's family were treated fairly, as was Silius' wife; Clutorius Priscus died because his sentence was *not* based on the *maiestas* law. Posthumous confiscation against Silius is somewhat less defensible, but the coalescence of *renuntiatio amicitiae* and the *lex maiestatis* was demanded by the logic of events. When Vibius Serenus was accused of complicity in Sacrovir's rebellion, Tiberius vetoed both the death penalty and deportation to a waterless island; the defendant was returned to Amorgus, to which he had been deported for public violence the year before.[50] Also, a Roman knight's sentence for an insulting poem was set aside by Tiberius (TA 4.31.1). And it was a common-law crime that saw Suillius Rufus exiled for judicial corruption after Tiberius had opposed a lighter sentence, which he did on the grounds of *utilitas publica*.[51]

The year 25 brought the trial of Cremutius Cordus, whose history had attacked the Principate as an institution. After a ringing vindication of freedom of speech he went on a terminal hunger strike, but there was no posthumous confiscation of property.[52] In the same year insulting remarks about Tiberius earned Votienus Montanus no more than the regular *poena legis* (TA 4.42.1–3). It is also under 25 that Tacitus makes a rare criticism of a common-law punishment: he notes with disapproval that a certain Aquilia was deported for adultery although the first proposal in the senate had merely been for her relegation under the *lex Julia* (TA 4.42.3). Then, in 26, Claudia Pulchra, great-niece of Augustus, was deported, but the charge of adultery was joined with charges of magic and trying to poison Tiberius.[53]

Up to this point there is no hard evidence for the abuse of the *maiestas* law. Some of the cases were opening shots in Sejanus' campaign against moves by the Julian party, led by the elder Agrippina, to destabilize the regime,[54] but there was no significant break with the *poena legis*. It was only when Tiberius withdrew to Capri that things changed, especially over the last five or six years of the reign. Death began replacing deportation, the activities of professional accusers reached a new peak, with evidence being extracted by force, fear or fraud,[55] and the critical assessment that Tacitus retrojects to 23 AD received some belated confirmation.

As the absent ruler's representative in Rome, Sejanus made the *lex maiestatis* a fine-tuned instrument which gave punishment a positive, almost a creative, role in government.[56] It was on his advice that Tiberius wrote to the senate in 27, lodging charges of insubordination against Agrippina and homosexuality against her son Nero. One senator proposed a capital penalty, but as Tiberius' letter was not clear, most preferred to treat the accusations as sub-capital. The two accused were sentenced to relegation, in the form of internal exile on the mainland as had eventually been decreed against the elder Julia.[57] Sejanus then subjected them to systematic destabilization, sending *agents provocateurs* who tried to persuade them to adopt treasonous counter-measures.[58]

The technique of self-incrimination was used with success against Titius Sabinus, one of Agrippina's lieutenants. Agents got him to cast aspersions on the regime and had his words recorded by hidden eavesdroppers. On 1 January 28 Sabinus was sentenced to death by the senate and was immediately led off to execution.[59] Then, shortly after

Livia's death in 29, the final steps were taken against Agrippina and Nero. Tiberius wrote to the senate clearly proposing capital charges. The senate met against a background of violent popular demonstrations. After much hesitation and browbeating by Sejanus they condemned the defendants. Agrippina was deported to Pandateria, where she was systematically ill-treated until, in October 33, she starved herself to death. Nero was exiled to Pontia, where he took his own life in 34.[60]

The fall of Sejanus in October of 31 ushered in what the sources describe as a reign of terror. Many of Sejanus' associates perished. Some were tried, but many died in the *immensa strages* of 33, the massacre of all Sejanians held in prison that Tiberius is said to have decreed with a stroke of the pen, making no distinction of sex, age or status.[61] But despite the rivers of blood, not everyone was sentenced to death. Some still received the statutory sentence of deportation. Thus although Considius Proculus, charged with *maiestas*, was summarily condemned and executed, his sister Sancia was only deported, as was Pompeia Macrina.[62] Sancia was clearly implicated in whatever her brother had done,[63] but the senate took a different view of the gravity of her case.

The lighter sentences of Sancia and Pompeia were not due to any desire to punish women less severely. Vitia was sentenced to death for mourning her son who had committed suicide when facing charges.[64] Her crime, although going back to Republican models,[65] was less of a security threat, we may think, than that of Sancia. But perhaps Tacitus has not given us full details of Vitia's offence; the sources are inclined to be selective in these matters.

The *immensa strages* not only produced lighter sentences, but also acquittals. Indeed Apronius Caesianus was not even tried for making fun of Tiberius' baldness at the festival of the Floralia. M. Terentius was tried for *Seiani amicitia*, political friendship with Sejanus, but a spirited defence, in which he admitted the association but pointed out that the emperor had also been a friend of Sejanus, secured his absolution.[66] This verdict defused the entire theme of *Seiani amicitia*, and to give added point to the message the senate sentenced the accusers to death or deportation for *calumnia*, for lodging charges without a reasonable expectation of success.[67]

The reign ended on an ominous note, however. In 37 charges were preferred against Albucilla, whose coterie of rebellious spirits was similar in broad outline to the elder Julia's circle. This time there were no dynastic implications, but the indictment still framed charges described as *impietas in principem*, thus for the first time making disloyalty to the emperor rather than *maiestas* against the state the criterion of treason.

The charges were not instigated by Tiberius; he was already moribund. The case had not been disposed of at the time of his death, and was not heard of again. But it was an ominous pointer to the future.[68]

CONCLUSION

An outline of the new system of criminal justice is followed by some features of that system under Augustus. The senate punishes treasonable defamation, while the emperor himself proceeds (tentatively) along three roads: he operates his domestic tribunal analogously to a public criminal court; he adjudicates – and also intervenes indirectly – on acts that threaten him in his public capacity, promoting *utilitas publica*, though not without being criticized; and he sits on common-law crimes, especially in the interests of *humanitas*. Under Tiberius the main focus is on the senatorial court. Principles of punishment are debated at the trials of Cn. Piso and Clutorius Priscus; strict adherence to the *poena legis* is seen to promote *humanitas*. Experimental penalties are tried out against Silanus and Silius. Precipitation from the Tarpeian Rock is discussed. Tacitus' attacks on the *lex maiestatis* are examined as an example of criticism of the regime's punitive policy. On the whole Tiberius is exonerated, but the charges against Albucilla sound an ominous note.

6

THE MATURING *COGNITIO*: CALIGULA AND CLAUDIUS

CONSOLIDATION OF THE EMPEROR'S COURT

The first concerted attempt to put the emperor's court on a regular basis was made by Caligula,[1] and the process was accelerated by Claudius. Dio says that Caligula judged both alone and with the senate, but even in the latter case the emperor had the final say.[2] Dio adds that Caligula published his verdicts as if he were afraid that they would pass unnoticed, which is Dio's way of telling us that the emperor's *decreta* were on the way to acquiring the force of precedents. Our impression is that at this time personal *cognitio* was mainly exercised in political trials, under Augustus' second hat, but we do not know enough about the nature of the charges to be sure of this. What is certain is that common-law crimes were handled by the jury-courts in greater numbers than ever before; a fifth decury of *iudices* had to be created to cope with the workload.[3] The extra help was badly needed, for Tiberius had neglected to fill vacancies in the decuries (ST 41).

Caligula's court has a particularly high profile because of his innovations in punishment. Instead of the standard modes of execution, he devised a number of macabre alternatives. Without the lost books of Tacitus to reassure us, our first reaction to Suetonius and Dio is one of disbelief, but on reflection we realize that some of Caligula's weird penalties are, in essence, forerunners of the Later Principate; some even have Republican antecedents. But the experiments were confined to Caligula's own court; there is no sign of the *poena legis* being superseded in the jury-courts, or in the senate. Nevertheless the subsequent survival of some of Caligula's ideas is not in doubt. The only important difference between his criminal justice and that of later rulers is that Caligula failed to observe the basic rules of personal *cognitio*; he failed to judge in public or to confine himself to cases in which he had no personal interest.

65

CALIGULA: PUNISHMENT AND PRECEDENT

At the start of his reign Caligula demonstrated his civic awareness by suspending the *maiestas* law; and he kept his word for two years.[4] But after the great watershed of the reign, when 'the emperor was replaced by the monster' (SG 22.1), his career as an innovator rapidly took shape. Suetonius compiled a small compendium of the penalties emanating from the new *cognitio* (SG 27); he is supported by other sources.[5]

Suetonius says that many men of status (*honesti ordinis*) were branded and sentenced to the mines or hard labour, or were thrown to the wild beasts in the arena (*ad bestias*); some were shut up in cages or sawn in half (SG 27.3). Cages and bisections are dubious,[6] but the others are genuine penalties in later sources, and their currency as early as Caligula need not be queried.[7] They are usually reserved for the lower orders, the *humiliores*, but Suetonius applies them to *honestiores*. This, however, does not discredit the evidence, for later jurists know of cases where the dividing-line is crossed.[8] But Suetonius gilds the lily by citing the case of a Roman knight who was condemned *ad bestias* but loudly protested his innocence, whereupon his tongue was cut out and he was thrown back to the beasts (SG 27.4). However, even here there was a precedent, for Cicero notes that a slave who had not given the evidence that his mistress expected had his tongue cut out prior to being crucified (*Cluent.* 187–8).

Ad bestias did not lack Republican examples. Condemned criminals were exposed to it at the Games, victims being chosen from deserters and slaves sentenced to death by their owners.[9] But even at that humble level the practice was criticized. One of Cicero's correspondents is highly critical of Caesar's lieutenant, Balbus, who threw Roman citizens to the lions in Spain (*Fam.* 10.32.3). There was a slight improvement under Tiberius, when a *lex Petronia* obliged owners to have their slaves tried officially before consigning them to the beasts.[10] But Caligula probably went too far when he supplemented a shortage of criminals by seizing some of the spectators, cutting out their tongues and throwing them into the arena (CD 59.10.3). Claudius also came in for criticism. Suetonius says that he exceeded the *poena legis* by consigning those convicted of major crimes to the beasts (SC 14). But in Suetonius' context this is more a statement of fact than a criticism; he cites it as an example of how Claudius did not always follow the strict letter of the law, often modifying severity or leniency according to his ideas of equity. That is what *cognitio* was all about. Having changed the rules, they needed time to evolve new guidelines. Meanwhile it was not always certain whether a verdict was just or unjust. The grey area was especially opaque when, as in Caligula's case, a verdict had not been debated by the senate.

Suetonius reports that a writer of Atellan farces was burnt alive in the arena because of a joke with a double meaning (SG 27.4) – that is, an ambiguous reference to Caligula. The penalty of being burnt alive, of *vivus exuri* or vivicombustion,[11] was old enough; the XII Tables had authorized it in retaliation for deliberately setting fire to a barn or a heap of corn.[12] But this was not the penalty for arson in the jury-courts; the *lex Cornelia de sicariis* merely prescribed interdiction (*Coll.* 12.5.1). Subsequently there was a harsher penalty if the crime was committed in an urban area. But no standard penalty replaced the *poena legis*. Ulpian says that *humiliores* are condemned *ad bestias*, while *honestiores* face either death or deportation (*ib.*). But according to Ulpian's contemporary, Callistratus, the penalty was vivicombustion (*D.* 48.19.28.12). Which reflects the fluctuations of discretionary penalties in the Later Principate.[13]

Like *ad bestias*, vivicombustion had a Republican background, but one that had not escaped criticism. Cicero condemns his brother Quintus for having, as governor of Asia, threatened to burn lawbreakers (*Ad Q. fr.* 1.2.6). And in Spain the innovative Balbus burnt Fadius, a Pompeian who refused to fight as a gladiator at Balbus' Games. Pollio's graphic description warns us not to be too critical of lurid scenes in Suetonius or Dio:

> He took Fadius back to the gladiators' school, buried him up to the waist, and set him alight. While Balbus was strolling about nonchalantly, Fadius shrieked that he was a citizen. 'You'd better ask the people to help you, then', replied Balbus.
>
> (*Fam.* 10.32.3)

In 64 AD, when Nero's punishment of Christians included setting some of them alight, contemporaries were horrified; the act could not be justified, it was said, even by the doctrine of *utilitas publica* (TA 15.44). But when Vespasian tortured and burnt a Jewish rebel leader for falsely claiming that prominent co-religionists supported his revolt, there was no criticism (Jos. *BJ* 7.447–50). Suppressing armed revolt was a proper case for *utilitas publica*.

BLACK COMEDY AND PUNISHMENT

My object all sublime I shall achieve in time,
To let the punishment fit the crime, the punishment fit the
  crime.
And make each prisoner pent unwillingly represent
A source of innocent merriment, of innocent merriment.
                    (W.S Gilbert & A.S Sullivan, *The Mikado*)

Roman punishments seem to have captured the imagination of writers
with a taste for black comedy. Valerius Maximus, writing as early as
Tiberius' reign, solemnly records that in 468 BC P. Mucius Scaevola,
tribune of the plebs, burnt his nine colleagues for conspiring with
Sp. Cassius, who was reputedly the author of the first agrarian law (VM
6.3.2). This is a parody of the events of 133 BC, when the tribune
M. Octavius was deposed from office by his colleague, Tiberius
Gracchus, for trying to block the latter's agrarian law; the deposition
was orchestrated by P. Mucius Scaevola, the leading lawyer of the day.[14]

Later on the author (or authors) of the *Augustan History* took a
special interest in vivicombustion. We are told that the descendants of
Avidius Cassius, who had tried to usurp Marcus Aurelius' throne, were
not punished at the time; but when Commodus succeeded Marcus he
had all the descendants burnt alive on the grounds that they had been
caught in a rebellion (*SHA Av. Cass.* 13.6–7). The author remembered
Vespasian. The *Augustan History* also reports that in the early third
century Macrinus always fastened the bodies of co-adulterers together
and burnt them alive (*SHA Macr.* 12.10). But the real subject of
this criticism was not Macrinus. The late fourth-century author was
thinking of a law of 390 AD which condemned men who played a
woman's part in intercourse 'to expiate the crime in avenging flames in
the sight of the people' (*CTh* 9.7.6).

Despite the brevity of his reign Macrinus was something of a
coathanger for unusual penalties. The *Augustan History* has a case in
which two soldiers have relations with their host's maidservant.
Although the servant is, as a woman of ill-repute, exempted from the
adultery law, Macrinus personally tries the men and orders that two
very big oxen be cut open while still alive and that the soldiers be thrust
one into each ox, with their heads protruding so that they can talk to
each other. This, adds the biographer, had never before been ordained
for any crime (*SHA Macr.* 12.4–5). The pastiche was aimed at a law of
Constantine which made the hostess of a tavern liable for adultery but
exempted her maidservant on account of her lowly status (*CTh* 9.7.1).

The joke – apparently a good one in those days – was that they had committed a non-crime and had earned a unique punishment. Sometimes a law was its own parody. A decree of 320 AD laid down that where a nurse helped her young charge to meet her lover, 'the mouths and throats of those who offer incitement to evil shall be closed by pouring in molten lead' (*CTh* 9.24.1.1).

The macabre sense of humour even extended to cases where 'regular' punishments were administered. Tacitus presents as black comedy the spectacle of Agrippina's henchman, Titius Sabinus, being led off to summary execution on 1 January 28 and shouting, as loudly as the cloak over his mouth and the noose around his neck allowed, that 'This is a fine way to celebrate New Year!' (TA 4.70.2). And as already observed, Tacitus paints a hilarious picture of an unsuccessful accuser pursued by an angry mob (TA 4.29.1–2)

CALIGULA AND ARBITRARY *COGNITIO*

Should the burlesque tradition put us on our guard with respect to the tradition for Caligula? Suetonius did use Caligula as a coathanger, but not for criminal penalties. It was simply a matter of Hadrian's reform of the legal profession being retrojected – in a distorted form – to Caligula.[15] In principle the same could have been done with penalties, but there are two reasons against that. In the first place, the tradition for Caligula's punishments is a consistent one. It is consistent not only because it is attested by several writers in somewhat different ways, but also because it is spread across their narratives instead of being confined to a single passing mention that might arouse suspicion.[16] Second, Suetonius only ventures on a retrojection when he needs a surrogate for something that a contemporary ruler has done. In other words, he is careful not to offend the current occupant of the throne. But Hadrian's punitive policy was, by the standards of the day, a progressive one. There was no need for veiled criticism.

Suetonius has covered the main capital punishments that evolved in the Principate, and he has correctly located them in Caligula's own court. But there is a question. If Caligula's sentences are 'respectable' after all, why did he have such a bad press? Part of the answer is that he used *humiliores* punishments against *honestiores*. But there is a more fundamental reason. Caligula brushed aside the indispensable safeguards. The emperor was expected to judge in public, sitting with a *consilium* of friends who took part not only in the deliberations but also in the decision-making.[17] The accused should be heard in his defence;

and the emperor should not judge in his own cause. Only if these criteria were met was the emperor seen to consult the public interest, to foster *utilitas publica*. Otherwise there was criticism. The annalists made the last Tarquin their role model for secret trials, and they cited as a further proof of tyranny the trials of the 'wicked' Decemvirs who clung to office after completing the XII Tables. The trials held by Caesar in his house were attacked by Cicero on the grounds of secrecy and personal interest, and part of the hostile tradition about Tiberius on Capri was prompted by the fact that people simply did not know what was going on.[18] Augustus judged in secret in 2 BC, but his parricide and forgery trials were held in public; they belonged under the most acceptable of his three hats.

Caligula broke all the rules. He sat in private, without a *consilium* and in the absence of the accused; and he judged in his own cause.[19] He even outraged public opinion by his procedures for confiscating property. He used the *maiestas* law against testators who had announced their intention to make the emperor an heir[20] but had neglected to do so. The insult – treated as treasonable defamation – prompted Caligula to decree posthumous confiscations against offending testators. He would nominate in advance how much he intended to raise at each sitting, and once boasted of having condemned more than forty defendants in a single judgment.[21]

CLAUDIUS, *PARRICIDIUM* AND *HUMANITAS*

> By concentrating all the functions of the laws and the magistrates in his own hands he had opened the door to the excesses of the professional accuser.
>
> (TA 11.5.1)

With these words Tacitus sums up the strong centralism that is a feature of Claudius' reign. Though exaggerated, the passage implies what all the sources agree on, that the main centralizing feature was Claudius' passion for courts and adjudication. It also confirms the importance of an accuser. No charges could be brought without one, as Nero was to discover when he set out to destroy Vestinus Atticus; as no accuser had come forward Nero was unable to frame charges and had to rely on arbitrary power (TA 15.69.1).

There is no doubt about Claudius' interest in the courts and the law. He is seen establishing a special bureau for trials, sitting on the *consilium* of magistrates, and reforming court procedure. Above all, he exercises personal *cognitio*. But unlike Caligula he keeps to the rules; he sits in public and with a *consilium*.[22]

Claudius' first act on his accession was to suspend the *lex maiestatis*; it remained in abeyance for the whole of his reign. But in order to safeguard his security he devised a number of ingenious substitutes.[23] The death penalty was much in evidence, especially in cases of manifest or confessed guilt. That doctrine dispensed with the need for charges of any sort, and therefore those public criminal laws that prescribed interdiction did not stand in the way of death sentences. The use of these surrogates was partly responsible for the charges of abusing capital punishment that his critics hurled at him.[24] He also took the first steps towards establishing the jurisdiction of the praetorian prefect. Claudius would obtain verdicts from the praetorian cohorts by acclamation. The cohorts would demand 'the names of the wrongdoers and the punishment of their crimes', and Claudius, who had his praetorian prefect sitting with him on the tribunal, would comply.[25]

So much for the technicalities behind Claudius' extensive use of the death penalty. But he also had a reputation for cruelty, for a sadistic interest in executions, especially the more esoteric varieties. There is a provocative notice in Suetonius:

> He always had interrogations under torture and the punishment of parricides carried out immediately, and in his presence. At Tibur he wished to see punishment administered in the ancient fashion, but after the guilty persons had been bound to the stake it was found that no executioner was available. He sent to Rome for an executioner and waited until the evening. At gladiatorial combats he signalled death even for those who fell by accident, especially the unhelmeted net-fighters whose faces he could watch as they died.
>
> (SC 34.1)

Leaving aside the naive suggestion that this merely confirms Claudius' antiquarian interests,[26] we ask ourselves whether the passage is true. It is, after all, a more forthright portrayal of cruelty than anything that Suetonius says about Caligula. But the circumstantial nature of the passage counsels against rejection. Moreover, it is corroborated by Dio, at least to the extent of the bloodthirsty enjoyment of gladiatorial combats (CD 60.13). The passage should therefore be approached on the assumption that it is probably true.

Our first task is to correlate the passage with a statement by Seneca. He is discussing the theory that crimes which are frequently punished must have been frequently committed, and he cites the case of Claudius, who, he says, sewed up more people in the sack within five years than had previously suffered that punishment throughout recorded time (Sen. *Clem.* 23.1). This is not a mere rhetorical flourish. Seneca is specifically arguing that harsh punishment does not reduce the incidence of crime, it encourages it by giving prominence to particular offences.[27] We therefore have two passages, both of which must be taken seriously.

The first point to be made is that Suetonius and Seneca are not talking about quite the same thing. Both are referring to *parricidium*, but the penalties are different. Seneca has the penalty of the sack, but in Suetonius it is Claudius' wish to witness *antiqui moris supplicium*, punishment in the ancient fashion. This means death by scourging, which had been the penalty for *parricidium* until it was superseded by the sack in, probably, the late third century BC.[28] That is why there was a delay at Tibur after the man had been tied to the stake; the lethal thrashing had to be administered by the executioner.

But what was Claudius' purpose in waiting around all day for an archaic demonstration? Was it just curiosity? Or did he have something more specific in mind? If there is an answer, it is that Claudius was motivated by *humanitas*. Savage as being beaten to death was, it was less so than the sack. It was less of an outrage to human dignity.[29]

The trouble with our solution is, of course, that it leaves Claudius' record-breaking use of the sack up in the air. Only one possible answer comes to mind.[30] *Parricidium* is a very flexible word. Besides meaning the murder of a parent, which is one sort of impiety, it also applies to the betrayal of the fatherland, which is another sort. But the two were interchangeable. In the regal period Horatius kills his sister for mourning an enemy, but when it comes to framing a charge against him the legend fluctuates between *perduellio* and *parricidium*, between treason and homicide.[31] The link between the two is especially strong with respect to conspiracies against the emperor's life. As Father of his Country (*pater patriae*) he is *in loco parentis*; thus the conspirators are plotting to kill both a parent and a Head of State. The interface is at its strongest in Claudius' case. He had a pathological fear of conspiracies, real or imagined, and much of the tally of sackings that Seneca ascribes to him could have come from using *parricidium* as a surrogate for charges of *maiestas*.[32]

There is a final piece of evidence that make it almost certain that Claudius did indeed reintroduce scourging as one of the penalties[33] for *parricidium*. When the senate decrees punishment *more maiorum* against Nero he asks what that punishment is, and is given a description that exactly fits scourging.[34] Scourging was not ordered by the senate as a mere preliminary to the sack; it was the definitive sentence.[35] But for what crime did Nero incur this penalty? To that there can only be one answer. It was for *parricidium* in its homicidal sense, that is, Nero's murder of his mother. His enemies never stopped harping on that tenebrous episode, and finally they charged him with it.[36]

CLAUDIUS: OTHER USES OF *HUMANITAS/AEQUITAS*

Criticism of Claudius' use of equity as a guideline for law reform was not confined to *parricidium*. Whether justified or not, his enemies do not seem to have lacked ammunition. Suetonius lists it in a long chapter devoted to Claudius' personal *cognitio* (SC 15). Some of the items belong to black comedy,[37] but others make quite good sense.[38] One is a deliberate distortion. Suetonius says that he decided against absent parties without considering whether their failure to appear was contumacious or unavoidable (SC 15.2). In fact epigraphic evidence discloses that Claudius formalized default judgments in a perfectly proper way.[39] He applied the same principle of *utilitas publica* that had led Augustus to authorize criminal trials *in absentia*.

In a chapter drawn from a less hostile source Suetonius speaks of his administration of justice in glowing terms (SC 14). He says that Claudius did not always follow the letter of the law; he modified its severity or leniency in many cases according to his notions of equity: *duritiam lenitatemve multarum ex bono et aequo, perinde ut adficeretur, moderatus est*. Suetonius cites one civil example and one criminal: He allowed a new trial where less was proved than had been claimed in the *formula*; and he exceeded the *poena legis* by inflicting *ad bestias* for major crimes (*in maiore fraude*). The rulings were proper examples of equity in Roman law; the idea that *bonum et aequum/aequitas/humanitas* always meant mildness is misconceived. They were extremely flexible notions,[40] as Seneca demonstrates in a compelling argument.[41]

Claudius abandoned Augustan leniency in a decree on testamentary forgery. He ruled that anyone who, when writing out a will for somebody, included a legacy to himself would be liable under the *lex Cornelia testamentaria*; ignorance of this decree would be no excuse (*D.* 48.10.15 pr.). Augustus, we recall, had allowed a pardon where a witness was induced to sign by fraud or mistake (SA 33.2). Claudius preferred to give equity a meaning consistent with *utilitas publica*. He may have been influenced by a personal experience, for Caligula had sent a charge to trial in respect of a forged will which Claudius had signed as a witness (SG 9.2).

Suetonius notes that Claudius devised a new type of *relegatio* which confined the wrongdoer to Rome and an area extending for three miles outside the city (SC 23.2). But this inclusion of a custodial element in *relegatio* was not entirely new. Caesar had proposed something like it in 63 BC, and Tiberius had interned Agrippina and Nero in Italy.

It was persistently claimed that Claudius condemned *indicta causa*, without hearing the accused.[42] This is nothing more than a malicious distortion of the procedure, recognized since time immemorial, where-under the manifest and confessed were sentenced without trial. Even Augustus had realized that a confession of *parricidium* would bring the immediate infliction of the sack. And Marcus Aurelius would, despite his general reputation for leniency, punish manifest wrongdoers with relentless severity (*SHA Marc.* 24.1). Where Claudius did go wrong was in his acceptance of unreal 'proofs' like dreams as evidence of manifest guilt.[43] This was the sort of thing that earned him a reputation for inconsistency.

There is one Claudian innovation whose importance is seldom recognized. In 47 Valerius Asiaticus, charged with planning to usurp the throne, was tried by Claudius personally. The trial was held in the emperor's quarters in the palace (*intra cubiculum*), in the presence of Messalina.[44] Messalina and her lackey, the consul Vitellius, were worried by the favourable impression that Asiaticus was making on Claudius, and resorted to a trick. Vitellius, pretending to speak as defence counsel, asked that Asiaticus be allowed to choose the manner of his death. Claudius, always ready to accept any stray statement as fact, took the request as a confession and sentenced Asiaticus to death, but in such manner as he might choose: *liberum mortis arbitrium ei permisit* (TA 11.3.1). The order to commit suicide – that in effect is what it was – conferred three benefits on the accused. It spared him the horror of public execution and he died with his dignity intact. It saved his property; and it gave him the right of burial.[45]

The *liberum mortis arbitrium* was thus installed as a new, *humanitas*-driven form of capital punishment. It was only humane in the context of the reintroduced death sentence of the Principate, but on those terms it was an improvement. It became a fairly regular penalty. It was frequently imposed by Nero, was confirmed as a regular sentence by Marcus, and was recognized by the jurists.[46] Formal confirmation by Marcus became necessary because of a decree of Hadrian's regarding pre-verdict suicide. Hadrian exempted the suicide's property from confiscation if the suicide was prompted by weariness of life, but not if it was prompted by a guilty conscience.[47] Henceforth a man facing criminal charges could no longer save his property by suicide; only the special sentence of *liberum mortis arbitrium* could assure him of that. That is why Ulpian does not allow this sentence to be pronounced by a provincial governor (*D.* 48.19.8.1). It was an act of clemency exclusively within the emperor's prerogative. But it was institutionalized clemency, for the rescript of Marcus and Verus (*ib.*) allowed any offender to hope for its extension to him.

'THE PUMPKINIFICATION OF CLAUDIUS'

The tradition for Claudius' forensic peculiarities was a strong one. It inspired a squib known as *Apocolocyntosis,* or 'The Pumpkinification of Claudius'. The piece is attributed to Seneca,[48] but our main interest is in what it tells us about contemporary attitudes to punishment. Claudius, having been poisoned by Agrippina, is tried by the gods on a motion to deify him. Augustus condemns him for putting people to death without a hearing. He proposes that Claudius be punished capitally, that he be allowed no delay of process, that he be banished, and that he leave heaven within thirty days and Olympus within three (10.2–11.6). This suggests that since the Republic[49] a fixed period, of three days for Rome and thirty for Italy, had been laid down, perhaps by the *lex Julia iudiciorum publicorum.*[50]

Augustus' proposal is carried unanimously and Mercury drags Claudius down to Hades. There he is tried by Aeacus, presiding over a jury-court convened under the *lex Cornelia de sicariis,* for killing 35 senators, 221 knights and many others. The reference to the *lex Cornelia* (14.1) is an encouraging sign of technical accuracy. The proceedings before the gods had been held in the senate[51] with comparable accuracy. In Suetonius, we note, Claudius is criticized for condemning 35 senators and some 300 knights.[52]

Aeacus refuses Claudius an adjournment and even denies his counsel a hearing. He condemns Claudius, and after a long debate on sentence (not consistent with a jury-trial) he devises a new penalty: Claudius is to spend his time shaking dice in a box with holes in the bottom. At this point Caligula arrives and claims Claudius as his slave. Caligula gives him to Aeacus, who hands him over to his freedman as his trial registrar, *a cognitionibus* (14–15).

The penalty imposed by Aeacus anticipates some of the pastiches that we have already inspected. The piece could have been written by a senator (which Seneca happens to have been) who wanted to contrast the considered punishments of the senatorial court with the (supposed) triviality of jury-court penalties. But the principal message is dislike of executions without proper trial. It is not the death penalty as such that is attacked. The focus is on the irregular procedure.

CONCLUSION

Caligula's penalties, outrageous as they seem, had Republican precedents and foreshadowed the punitive system of the Later Principate. But he offended against accepted standards: he sat in private, without a *consilium* and often without the accused, and he judged in his own cause. Claudius initiated the praetorian prefect's jurisdiction. His reputation for sadistic cruelty is found on an analysis of his position on *parricidium* to be exaggerated; his replacement of the sack by scourging was in fact motivated by *humanitas*. His other punishments, including *liberum mortis arbitrium*, confirm his promotion of both *humanitas* and *utilitas publica*. Dislike of cruel punishments is seen to have inspired a genre of black comedy, including *Apocolocyntosis*.

7

NERO AND THE STOICS

THE TWO FACES OF STOICISM

Nero's reign is one of the most important in the entire Principate. Theories of punishment, touched on only sporadically since Cicero, were exposed to sustained debate, and attempts were made to translate ideas into practice. But true to its dichotomous character, the dominant philosophy, Stoicism,[1] exerted two opposing influences on penology. On the one hand, Seneca sought to indoctrinate Nero with the ideology of *clementia*, which he saw as something more than a mere moral principle. It was, or ideally should be, part of positive law. The ruler should give clemency the form of a verdict, effectively one of 'Not Guilty', but arrived at through a more complex assessment of responsibility than the simple black-and-white of *fecisse/non fecisse videtur*. It would not be the equivalent of a pardon, for that implied forgiving a proven wrong.

A different scenario was written by hardline Stoics. They believed that punishment should be measured solely by the *poena legis*. There was no room for discretion, whether beneficial or otherwise, and there was no place for notions like the ruler's *clementia*. The message was reinforced by giving *utilitas publica* more prominence than it had ever had before, and by fostering the notion of *publica clementia* in opposition to that of the ruler.

Because of Seneca's unique position as Nero's tutor, he was able to inspire his pupil with a keen desire to regulate his criminal justice by what he had been taught. The results were mixed, but Nero's sincerity is not in doubt; he applied his lessons in some unexpected ways which shed new light on his character. But as Seneca's influence declined, Nero found himself in conflict with the hardline Stoics, and some of the great trials of the reign were the result. The confrontation was based on existing penalties. Nero did not contribute much by way of new

77

varieties, though he did make modifications. We must lend credence, for example, to Suetonius' claim that people sentenced to *liberum mortis arbitrium* were allowed only an hour in which to open their veins, failing which a surgeon did it for them (SN 37.2). Tacitus confirms it, and so does Nero's wife, Octavia. Her veins were opened by soldiers when she failed to do it herself, and even then the blood would not flow and she was killed by suffocation.[2] Suetonius does however spoil his case by reporting that Nero wanted to have people eaten alive by crocodiles (SN 37.2). The invention lacks the guarantee of subsequent institutionalization that saves Caligula's punishments from oblivion.

SENECA ON CLEMENCY

Seneca's thoughts on crime and punishment are mainly expounded in two works. In Claudius' reign he wrote *De ira* in which he urged the ruler to show measured restraint in his sentences.[3] Then, on Nero's accession, he composed his pupil's inaugural address to the senate in which he pledged himself to cut down on personal *cognitio* and to sit in public when he did exercise it (TA 13.4.2). This was followed, in 55 or 56, by Seneca's most important work, *De clementia*.

The fundamental notion in *De clementia* is the clear distinction between *clementia* and *venia* (pardon):

> The wise man (= the Stoic) should not grant pardon, for it is the remission of a deserved punishment. The wise man does not remit a punishment that he ought to impose. But he may give the same advantages as pardon in a more honourable way: he may spare, show consideration, rectify. One he will merely reprimand, not inflicting punishment if the wrongdoer's age holds out hopes of reform. Another whose guilt is manifest will be absolved if he was misled or influenced by wine. All this is the work of clemency, not of pardon. Clemency means a free discretion which does not judge according to a *formula* but according to what is right and fair: *non sub formula, sed ex aequo et bono iudicat.* Clemency may absolve, or it may fix an amount at whatever figure it deems fit. But it does not fall below the level of what is just, for it assumes that it is doing the most just thing possible.
>
> (*Clem.* 2.7.1–3 adapted)

In this, the ultimate statement of his position on punishment, Seneca puts two propositions. First, that *clementia* depends on the accused not being guilty. To reach that conclusion the judge must take into account not only the formal evidence of the crime, but also surrounding circumstances such as youth, error, intoxication and curative potential. Second, the formal evidence must be assigned a minor role, leaving it to equity to shape the free discretion, the *liberum arbitrium*. Private-law principles are Seneca's yardstick, and quite properly; Claudius had applied *bonum et aequum* to both civil and criminal cases (SC 14). Under the influence of the praetor the private law had relieved contracting parties of liability on the grounds of minority, mistake and so on. In strict law the contract was enforceable, but *bonum et aequum* introduced exonerating factors. Similarly in a criminal case, on a strict interpretation of the '*formula*', that is, of the *lex*, the accused may be guilty; but *bonum et aequum* lets in a verdict – not, we repeat, an act of pardon – based on *clementia*.

The principle also applies to the assessment of punishment, where the exonerating circumstances do not warrant a complete acquittal. In a civil action for damages for *iniuria* (an assault on person or reputation) the XII Tables had laid down a fixed tariff; the praetor's *formula* gave the judge a discretion to assess the amount according to gravity, status, and so on. In the same way the criminal judge ceased to be bound by the *poena legis* and exercised a discretion. This more than anything else is what separated Seneca from the hardliners. But whether it did so in practice as well as in theory remains to be seen.[4]

Although Seneca sees *clementia* as the special prerogative of the ruler, he defines it in more general terms; it is the leniency of a superior towards an inferior (2.3.1–2). This is because he wants to institution-alize *clementia*, to provide it with guidelines that will in a certain sense fetter the sentencing authority's discretion. Factors like youth, error, intoxication and curative potential will tend to arouse an expectation of absolution or leniency whenever they are present. It is not for nothing that *clementia* as an instrument of law reform is seen as a feature of *humanitas*.

Seneca even extended his theory to the private sector, that is, to the family court. He cites with approval a proposal of Augustus, sitting on the *consilium* of Tarius Rufus whose son had tried to kill him. Augustus proposed that the son be sentenced to exile instead of the sack, on the grounds that his youth had caused him to act timidly, which was tantamount to innocence (1.15). Augustus was proposing quite a drastic innovation. He was incorporating a penalty of a public criminal law, the *lex Pompeia de parricidiis*, in a *paterfamilias'* domestic jurisdiction.

Some of Seneca's elaborations of *clementia* are worth a brief glance. He draws a distinction between *severitas* and *crudelitas*, between severity and cruelty. The former is in harmony with *clementia* but the latter is not; it is displayed by those who, although they have a valid reason for punishing, act without moderation, such as when they torture guilty men (2.3–4). In justifying *severitas* Seneca makes common cause with all Stoics. He rejects the criticism levelled at the Stoics, to the effect that they allow neither pity nor pardon. They are in fact the true exponents of *humanitas*, but they blend it with service to the community (2.5.2–3). Thus *humanitas* and *utilitas publica* are made opposite sides of the same coin.

The judge's duty to avoid anger and haste is an important theme. They lead to wrong decisions. Nero, having recently become Father of his Country, should model himself on the good parent who is slow to inflict severe punishment on his children. He should only do so after long cogitation, for to condemn swiftly is to condemn gladly.[5] Anger has the same capacity to lead to a wrong decision. Seneca cites the case of a governor who, finding that a solider had returned from leave without his comrade, ordered his immediate execution on the grounds that he must have killed the comrade. When the comrade suddenly appeared the governor flew into a rage and ordered that both soldiers, as well as the centurion who had delayed the first soldier's execution, be put to death. Thus anger drummed up three charges although it had grounds for none (*De ira* 1.18.3–6).

The measured response, the impersonal character of proper punishment, is emphasized in an extraordinary way. The judge, says Seneca, should follow the example of the magistrate who adjusts his toga[6] when he is about to sentence someone to death: he acts not in anger but sternly, showing no more emotion than if he were killing a poisonous snake (*De ira* 1.16.3–6). This is pure Stoicism.

Seneca makes much of the Platonic idea that curative procedures should be tried before resorting to severe punishment. He lays down the following sequence of remedial measures: first, private criticism; second, public disgrace, *ignominia*; third, exile; fourth, imprisonment; and fifth, death which is justified because it puts an end to the criminal's suffering.[7] This raises the question of Seneca's position on capital punishment as a whole. He is very vehement about it, even more so than Cicero. He abhors modes of execution which are dictated by anger, and he makes the arena a special target of criticism:

> The trappings of anger are the rack, the cord, the dungeon, the
> cross, the bodies planted in the ground and set on fire, the corpses
> dragged by the hook, the stake driven through a man, the limbs

torn apart by chariots driven in opposite directions. Nothing is so morally degrading as the spectators at the Games. As if armed combats are not bad enough, the midday intermission when criminals have to fight without helmet or armour, are pure murder.[8] Many spectators prefer this to the regular programme. In the morning they throw men to the lions and bears, at midday they throw them to the spectators.[9]

A scathing indictment, but are the strictures directed at the death penalty as such, or only at particularly nasty forms of it?

It has recently been argued by André that Seneca did not object to the death penalty, which he saw as quite consistent with *humanitas* if inflicted for a proper reason. His only objection was to excessively cruel or derisive modes of execution.[10] This is undoubtedly correct, but it needs amplification. The specific motive justifying the death penalty was *utilitas publica* which, as we have seen, did not necessarily conflict with *humanitas*. But it depended on how one defined *utilitas publica*. And here Seneca is quite specific. A distinction must be drawn between crimes against other people (common-law crimes) and crimes against the emperor (treason). The public interest requires the suppression of common-law crimes, but wrongs to the emperor do not put the public interest at risk. Therefore he should remit the punishment if that can be done with safety; but if not, he should only inflict moderate punishment (*Clem.* 1.21–22). It seems, then, that Seneca is advocating a return to the *maiestas* penalty of interdiction/deportation which had been increasingly overtaken by death in the Principate. Nero would take the recommendation to heart, albeit in a somewhat unusual fashion.[11]

NERO AND CLEMENCY: THE PEDANIUS CASE

Nero ought to have started putting Seneca's ideas into practice during his 'good' period, that is, the first five years of the reign prior to his murder of his mother. But we have no specifics. He promised much in his accession speech, and propaganda lauded his clemency and his return of jurisdiction to the jury-courts.[12] But his only brush with *clementia* came in 57, when he personally tried P. Celer, a former procurator of Asia, for *repetundae*. Nero did not want to punish him, but on the evidence he could not acquit him. He therefore delayed his verdict until Celer died of old age (TA 13.33.1–2).

It is only over 61–62 that hard evidence appears. In 61 the urban prefect, Pedanius Secundus, was murdered by a domestic slave.[13] Under the law every slave who was under the same roof at the time of the murder had to be questioned under torture and later put to death. There was thus a presumption that every slave was an accomplice; it could only be rebutted by showing that one had done everything possible to help the victim. The death penalty was imposed under the *lex Cornelia de sicariis* – not because the regular *poena legis* under that law had been increased from interdiction to death, but because a special decree of the senate, the *senatus consultum Silanianum* of 10 AD, had prescribed punishment *vetere ex more*, by ancient custom, for slaves guilty of murder in this form.[14]

Pedanius' household, numbering some 400 men, women and children, were tried by the senate.[15] The question was whether the special *poena legis* should be enforced, reduced or remitted. The eminent lawyer C. Cassius Longinus, a hardline Stoic, spoke vehemently in favour of strict enforcement. He argued that although family slaves had shown loyalty in the past, the present hordes drawn from diverse backgrounds could only be kept down by fear. His concluding words open a new window on punitive thinking:

> No doubt innocent people will die. But when a defeated army flogs every tenth man to death, the brave must take their chances with the rest. There is an element of injustice in every major precedent, but the public interest outweighs that of individuals: *habet aliquid ex iniquo omne magnum exemplum quod contra singulos utilitate publica rependitur.*
>
> (TA 14.44.6–7).

Cassius believed that *utilitas publica* overrode *bonum et aequum*. There was no room for discretion; the *poena legis* must be enforced. This view continued to guide him. In 69, as a member of a governor's *consilium*, he said that 'It accords with *utilitas publica* for previous decisions to stand'.[16]

Cassius spoke for a majority of senators, and the mass execution of the 400 slaves was duly voted. But outside the senate-house the populace staged violent protests, though not on moral grounds; economic interests were at stake.[17] At all events Nero published an edict rebuking the demonstrators and stationed troops along the route leading to the place of execution. Nero made one alteration to the senate's verdict. It had been proposed that freedmen under the same roof be also punished, although less severely than the slaves; they were to be deported. Nero vetoed this on the grounds that 'although ancestral custom had not been tempered by mercy (*misericordia*) it should not be intensified by brutality (*saevitia*)' (TA 14.45.3–4). This limited response – he could have vetoed the entire decree – raises the whole question of the part played by Nero and Seneca in the affair.

Nero had shown *clementia* to free persons, but not to slaves. He may have wanted to try; there is a note of bitterness in his 'even though mercy had not reduced the ancient penalty'. But he was probably advised not to cross swords with the majority of senators on an issue of such importance. This was not the first time that Nero bowed to the thinking of a slave-owning society. In 57 the senate had extended liability under the *s.c. Silanianum* to some marginal categories of slaves,[18] but again there is no trace of intervention by Nero.

The advice to proceed with caution will have come from Seneca. Tacitus does not mention him in the debate. He says only that some senators protested against the number of victims, the inclusion of women and children and the clear innocence of some of them, 'but no one in particular (*nemo unus*) ventured to make a counter-proposal' (TA 14.42.2, 45.1). Seneca's general position on the treatment of slaves[19] does not oblige us to contradict Tacitus. If anything, the man who said that 'Every slave is an enemy'[20] would not have found much to quarrel with in Cassius' speech.

Ambiguity continued after Nero. Pliny describes a case in 105 when a consul was killed. After the slaves and freedmen had been tortured, Pliny moved that the freedmen be acquitted; another senator proposed their deportation; and a third proposed their death. After a long debate – on voting procedures, not on the justice of the case – the two punitive proposers joined forces and deportation was voted (Plin. *Ep.* 8.14). Trajan did not intervene. A few years later Hadrian condemned an *ancilla* who had not assisted her mistress although she was in the room at the time of the murder. Her excuse was that the murderer had threatened to kill her if she interfered, but Hadrian ruled that she could have cried out but had preferred her own safety to that of her mistress. He sentenced her to the supreme penalty which would remind other slaves not to think of themselves first (*D*. 29.5.1.28).

The *s.c. Silanianum* aroused as much debate in antiquity as it does today.[21] Relaxations were allowed from time to time,[22] but no attempt was made to repeal the law. Seneca and Nero are in good company.

NERO AND CLEMENCY: INSULTS TO THE EMPEROR

Claudius' suspension of the *lex maiestatis* remained in operation for the first eight years of Nero's reign. He did not even lift it in 55, despite the rising tensions with his mother, Agrippina, whom he suspected of plotting to make the wealthy Stoic, Rubellius Plautus, emperor in his place. Nero tried to indict her for *parricidium*, using that flexible crime as a substitute for treason, as Claudius had done. But with Burrus' connivance Seneca was able to defeat the move.[23]

Personal insults, the most awkward *maiestas* category under Tiberius and Caligula, were now treated with the moderation that Seneca had recommended to Nero. Even after Agrippina's death in 59 he reacted without anger. An actor who mimed drinking and swimming while singing a song beginning 'Farewell father, farewell mother!', thus alluding to Claudius' drinking habits and Nero's attempt to drown Agrippina, was only relegated.[24] And when pamphlets were circulated bearing such messages as 'Nero Orestes Alcmeon matricides', Nero took no steps to uncover the authors, and when they were identified he vetoed attempts to punish them capitally.[25]

It was not until 62 that the suspension of the *lex maiestatis* was lifted, and even then it was done against Nero's wishes. The praetor Antistius Sosianus having recited defamatory verses about Nero at a dinner party, an accuser came forward and the matter was debated by the senate. The consul designate proposed execution by ancestral custom, *more maiorum*.[26] According to Tacitus – and there is no reason to doubt his word[27] – this was done by arrangement with Nero, who wanted to gain credit by vetoing a death sentence (TA 14.48.3). But the proposal was opposed by that intractable Stoic, Thrasea Paetus. Following a similar line to that pursued by M. Lepidus at Clutorius Priscus' trial, Thrasea spoke to the following effect:

> This House is not obliged, under such an excellent ruler, to impose the maximum sentence that the act deserves. The executioner and the noose were abolished long ago; the laws lay down penalties (*poenas legibus constitutas*) which inflict punishment without brutalizing the judges or disgracing the times. Let him forfeit his property and be sent to an island, where the longer he drags out his guilty life, the better example will he be of private misery and public clemency (*publica clementia*).
>
> (TA 14.48.5–7 adapted)

We particularly note the description of the statutory penalty of deportation as an example of *publica clementia*. This was not the emperor's clemency which he exercised in his discretion. It was clemency built into the statute. The *poena legis* provided all the clemency that was required. We have here an unequivocal stand against the death penalty. Thrasea has given us what Seneca with all his effort and erudition has not. But there is still a qualification. Thrasea opposed the death penalty because the *lex* opposed it, not because of a crisis of conscience. If the *lex* had prescribed death Thrasea would have had no complaint. There is no sign of his having attacked the *s.c. Silanianum*.

In proclaiming *publica clementia* Thrasea was partly motivated by the general Stoic opposition to pardon; it was considered alien to a strict interpretation of the *poena legis*.[28] It was also a reaction against the idea that clemency was the special prerogative of the hereditary monarchy that the Julio-Claudian dynasty had become. To those Stoics who disliked that sort of ruler in principle, the *leges* were the one sure shield against tyranny.[29]

Thrasea's speech persuaded a majority of senators to switch their support from the consul designate's proposal to Thrasea's (TA 14.49.1). Thus the scheme to gain credit for Nero, an idea that bears Seneca's imprint, was blocked. However, the consuls did not carry out the deportation immediately. They deferred registering the senate's decree, for only on such registration would the long dormant *lex maiestatis* revive.[30] Being well aware of Nero's views, they decided to refer the matter to him. Nero wrote back as follows:

Without any provocation Antistius has uttered the gravest insults against me. The senate could justifiably have imposed a penalty commensurate with the gravity of the crime. But I would have blocked severity in any case, therefore I do not veto your *moderatio*. Decide as you please; you are free to acquit him if you so wish.

(TA 14.49.3–4)

Nero was clearly offended, but Thrasea did not alter his proposal and the consuls did not change the decree (14.49.5). The *lex maiestatis* therefore stood revived. As Tacitus says (although some modern critics do not believe that it was ever suspended), this was its first revival: *tum primum revocata ea lex* (TA 14.48.3). However, the idea of creating artificial conditions for the exercise of clemency was not dead. It would be used to good effect by Domitian.[31]

NERO AND CLEMENCY: THE DEFLECTION OF ODIUM

Prior to the appearance of *De clementia* Nero said something that gave Seneca the idea of writing on the subject. Burrus, who held office as praetorian prefect, was about to execute two bandits. He pressed Nero to record their names and the reasons why he wanted them put to death. Such a step had been mooted before without result, but now Burrus insisted on it. With great reluctance Nero complied, but when he handed the warrant (*charta*) to the prefect he exclaimed, 'Would that I had not learnt to write!'[32]

Nero regretting his literacy is a striking proof of his espousal of *clementia*, but there is also another message embedded in Seneca's account. It seems that until then Burrus had carried out death sentences under his own steam, acting under a general mandate from Nero which did not identify individual cases. Consequently, in the public perception the prefect was the author of the executions. But Burrus wanted to change this because he was as anxious as his superior to avoid the odium of putting people to death. He also wanted the reasons for imposing the supreme penalty to go on record in every case. Thus we already have an example of an elaborate game of cat-and-mouse, designed to deflect the odium between the emperor and his subordinate.[33]

The game continued under Nero's successors. In 69, during the ephemeral reign of Vitellius, Dolabella was accused of trying to revive the party of Otho. Charges were lodged with the urban prefect, Flavius Sabinus, but he was reluctant to accept them because capital punishment was repugnant to his gentle nature (TH 2.63). But when the emperor's sister-in-law, Triaria, warned Sabinus not to seek a reputation for clemency at the emperor's expense, the prefect put Dolabella on trial and sentenced him to death. Triaria had done her work well. Vitellius needed a judicial verdict for the execution, but he did not want to be seen to sentence the man whose wife had previously been his own wife (TH 2.64). He therefore delegated the task to the prefect. But Vitellius still had to authorize the execution. The urban prefect did not have the power to sentence capitally, and the emperor's *charta* was required. But Vitellius tried to conceal his ultimate responsibility. He wrote to Dolabella to avoid the crowded Flaminian Way and to come to him via Interamnium. He had given orders for the execution to be carried out there, but the executioner cut Dolabella's throat at a tavern on the way. The incident redounded to the great discredit of the regime (*ib.*). Domitian would do his best not to fall into the same error.[34]

UTILITAS PUBLICA AND ENTERTAINMENT

Nero began moving away from Seneca's indoctrination in 64, when he blamed the Christians for the Great Fire. Tacitus reports as follows:

In order to dispel the belief that he was responsible for the fire, Nero drummed up defendants and inflicted the most exquisite punishments on the Christians. Many were convicted not so much for arson as because they were hated by the human race. He made a sport of it, dressing them in animal skins and having them torn to pieces by dogs, or crucifying them and setting them on fire for use as lamps after dark. He staged the spectacle in his Gardens and also put on displays in the Circus, mingling with the populace dressed as a charioteer. It was felt that they were not being sacrificed to *utilitas publica* but to one man's *saevitia*.

(TA 15.44.3–8 adapted)

Nero justified the performance on the grounds of *utilitas publica*. He probably used the expression in an edict celebrating the entertainment. The edict will have emphasized that although the technical charge was arson, for which the XII Tables penalty was vivicombustion (*D.* 47.9.9), a more drastic penalty was needed because of the hostility towards (or of) the Christians.[35] That was the factor that brought in *utilitas publica*. Nero had moved sharply away from Seneca, to whom the idea of making capital punishment a public entertainment was anathema. In fact, at the end of the day the gap between teacher and pupil was even greater than that. Seneca did not subscribe with any enthusiasm to the notion of *utilitas publica*; its occurrences in his works are few and desultory.[36] Cicero is much closer to this mainstream Stoic line; he even anticipates Cassius' comment about the public interest justifying injustice.[37]

Nero's apparent conversion to an orthodox Stoic line raises a question. Why did he arouse such strong criticism? The answer is actually quite simple. In itself *utilitas publica* was neither 'good' nor 'bad'. It depended on the motive behind it, as Cicero knew (*Off.* 3.30–31). This was always the criterion. Tiberius did not mind giving offence as long as he was acting in the public interest; but he knew the limits.[38] Augustus had exceeded those limits when he took action against Caesar's assassins.[39] Oddly enough, the criticism of Nero can be based on Seneca's own words: 'Kings should only put people to death when they are satisfied that it is in the public interest, for brutality is for tyrants' (*Clem.* 1.12.3). Nero's problem, then, was that he did not have the right motive.[40]

NERO AFTER SENECA

The abuse of *utilitas publica* in 64 was the watershed in Nero's criminal justice. After that he moved rapidly away from Seneca's measured precepts. The immediate trigger was the conspiracy of Piso in 65. Whether or not Seneca was actually implicated in that opaque episode,[41] Nero treated him very roughly. An accuser denounced Seneca, alleging that he had said that his own safety depended on Piso's impunity. Seneca denied this, but Nero convened the special *consilium*, consisting of Poppaea and Tigellinus, that sat with him when he bypassed his regular advisers in order to cut loose. Seneca was sentenced to death *in absentia*; he was allowed *liberum mortis arbitrium* and with some difficulty killed himself (TA 15.60–64). Nero gave the verdict some credibility by blocking the attempt by Seneca's wife, Paulina, to die with him; Nero said he had no quarrel with her (15.64.1). The consul designate, Plautius Lateranus, was not even allowed a short time in which to carry out a *liberum mortis arbitrium*; he was dragged away unceremoniously and executed like a slave (15.60.1). Vestinus Atticus fared even worse. Where Seneca had at least been formally charged, no one came forward to accuse Vestinus. He could therefore not be indicted under the public criminal laws, and Nero sent soldiers to force him to a suicide not backed by a verdict (15.68–69).

The ultimate absurdity was perpetrated against Antistius Vetus, father-in-law of the Stoic, Rubellius Plautus. Learning that he was about to be tried by the senate, Vetus decided to anticipate the verdict. He, his mother-in-law and his daughter opened their veins. But after the funeral an indictment was lodged against them and the senate sentenced them to death *more maiorum*. Nero vetoed this and allowed them *liberum mortis arbitrium* (16.10–11). Tacitus comments acidly on the farce, but in terms of Nero's Gilbertian logic it made some sort of sense. As no one had frustrated his plan by proposing the *poena legis*, he at last had a cruel sentence to veto. There was even one beneficial feature: the defendants' property was preserved.

The confrontation with the Stoics came to a head in 66, when Thrasea Paetus and others were tried by the senate. Nero was now attacking the sect itself, not merely individuals whose crimes may have been linked to Stoicism. As Tacitus says, 'After butchering so many eminent men, Nero finally planned to extinguish Virtue itself.'[42] The main thrust of the charges against Thrasea was his persistent boycotts – of the senate, of Nero's 'divine voice', of the deification ceremonies for Poppaea. Nero had twice renounced Thrasea's friendship, but the philosopher's only response had been to ask for details of the charges so that he might refute them. Thrasea did not consider *renuntiatio amicitiae* a proper response to unlawful conduct; the determinant must, as always, be the *lex* and the *poena legis*. That message was his sole reason for asking for details; for he boycotted the trial, was condemned in his absence and was sentenced to *liberum mortis arbitrium*.[43]

PUBLIC OPINION AND THE DEATH OF OCTAVIA

In 62, the year that saw the death of Burrus and Seneca's withdrawal from public life, Nero staged one of his most bizarre performances. Faustus Sulla and Rubellius Plautus, both suspected of designs on the throne, were murdered at the instigation of the Grey Eminence, Tigellinus. But Nero wrote to the senate denouncing them as if they were still alive and alleging that they threatened the security of the state. The senate solemnly found them guilty and expelled them from its ranks (TA 14.59.5–6). Tacitus thinks Nero welcomed the verdict because it gave the senate's imprimatur to his next atrocity, the destruction of his wife Octavia.[44]

Nero divorced Octavia in 62 in order to marry Poppaea. Although 'no fault' divorce was the rule, Nero wanted to prove adultery in order to have her dowry forfeited under the *lex Julia de adulteriis*. But despite the best efforts of Tigellinus a case could not be concocted against her, and she retained her dowry. But Octavia remained a problem. She was the focal point of a Claudian lobby that did not fully accept the idea of a united Julio-Claudian dynasty. Nero had her removed to Campania under armed guard, but this sparked off a wave of popular demonstrations. Nero now redoubled his efforts to convict Octavia of adultery. Anicetus, commander of the fleet at Misenum, was suborned to make a perjured claim of adultery with Octavia, adding that she had done it in order to win over his fleet for the Claudian cause. Armed with 'proof' of adultery compounded by a threat to *utilitas publica*, Nero banished Octavia to Pandateria. After a few days she received an order to die, which points to a penal innovation – deportation for the purpose of being put to death, no doubt because secrecy was essential.[45] Octavia protested that she was no longer Nero's wife, only his sister, but the soldiers bound her and opened her veins. But the blood flowed too slowly, and they put her in a hot bath and suffocated her. Her head was cut off and taken to Poppaea.[46]

Tacitus observes in disgust that thanksgivings were voted. He asks his readers to take it for granted in future that whenever an emperor ordered a banishment or a murder thanks were given to the gods (TA 14.64.5). But this is only the tip of the iceberg, for the treatment of Octavia inspired the most detailed criticism of punitive policy that we possess. It is in the tragic mode rather than the comic, being expounded in *Octavia*, the only extant example of Roman historical drama. The play is attributed to Seneca,[47] but again the cardinal fact is that it reveals public opinion, whoever the author was.

There are some reminiscences of Seneca. The philosopher is one of the *dramatis personae* and advises Nero to cure his fear of usurpers by clemency: *magnum timoris remedium clementia est*. Nero replies that destroying an enemy is a greater virtue, to which Seneca responds that for the *pater patriae* to save citizens is greater still (442–4). In reply to Seneca's injunction to give just commands acceptable to public opinion, Nero replies that respect for the sword will make them acceptable (459–61). He shows his familiarity with Seneca's sequence of remedies (*De ira* 1.15–16) by declaring that exile has not broken Faustus and Rubellius, and it is now time for the sword.

The climax is Nero's decision to treat Octavia as a *hostis*. When Burrus baulks at the idea of putting Octavia to death and Nero takes him to task for sparing a *hostis*, Burrus asks, with perfect logic, how a woman can be called a *hostis*.[48] Nero replies that her crimes authorize it. Burrus asks who charges her and is told that the accuser is the people's rage. The idea of red rage justifying the immediate punishment of the *manifestus* was not new,[49] but here it deliberately contradicts Seneca's stand against haste and anger. Another tilt at Seneca is implied in Nero's claim that fear of punishment will break her (870–2); there is no thought of curing her. Nero therefore decrees that she be taken to a remote island and killed (873–6).

What were Seneca's views on how a *hostis* should be treated? We cannot be sure, because we do not have his full coverage of the question. He says he will deal with Sulla's proscriptions later on when he considers what sort of anger should be felt towards citizens who have broken away and become enemies (*Clem.* 1.12.2–3). But we do not have the section of *De clementia* in which he returned to the subject. We do, however, have the passage in which he says that *hostes* who go to war for reasons of loyalty, treaties or liberty are entitled to clemency-driven acquittals (*Clem.* 2.7.2). But this refers to external enemies. The only mention of internal enemies is when Augustus extends leniency to Cornelius Cinna. But when Seneca tells Nero, in *Octavia*, that the *pater patriae* should cure his fear by clemency (442–4), he is referring to fear of internal *hostes*. This may reflect what the real Seneca had said in the missing part of *De clementia*.[50]

CONCLUSION

Two opposing Stoic views on punishment colour Nero's punitive policy. Seneca moulded *clementia* into something more than mercy/leniency; it became, at least in part, an interpretative canon of total exoneration. Seneca did not object to capital punishment as such, but only to cruel and derisive uses of it. Nero tried to apply Seneca's precepts by instigating savage sentences in order to veto them. But the hardline Stoics frustrated the attempts, preferring their notions of the *poena legis*, *utilitas publica* and *publica clementia*. Nero devised the technique of deflecting the odium of death sentences authorized by him. He moved away from Seneca when he claimed that his savage punishment of the Christians was, although put on as an entertainment, in fact consonant with *utilitas publica*. After that he continued to abuse the notion of *utilitas publica*; the ultimate absurdity was perpetrated against Antistius Vetus. The Stoics were attacked as a sect. Another absurdity was perpetrated against Faustus Sulla and Rubellius Plautus. An analysis of the punitive parts of *Octavia* throws up suggestions as to the possible content of *De clementia* on the subject of the *hostis*.

8

DOMITIAN AND MORALITY

INTRODUCTION

By 68 AD, when the fall of Nero signalled the end of the Julio-Claudian dynasty, the main heads of punishment were in place, even though only in embryonic form in some respects. In a certain sense, therefore, emperors from Vespasian to Severus Alexander presided over the consolidation of penal categories rather than over further innovations. It is therefore quite logical for us to turn to a thematic presentation, focusing on some key features of the consolidation rather than on developments under individual rulers. But before addressing that it is proposed to say something about Domitian's punitive policy, some features of which need closer attention than they have hitherto received.[1] This will be followed by four chapters on themes.

DOMITIAN AND THE VESTALS

Domitian has had an extremely bad press, one that cannot easily be queried because so much of it comes from contemporary sources. Both Tacitus and Pliny were members of Domitian's senate and sat in judgment on Stoics whom he wanted to destroy, though only Tacitus is honest enough to say so.[2] Suetonius was not a senator, but he was a judge and was well placed to know what was going on.

From the punitive point of view Domitian's principal innovations were in the area of morality. Most of the picture has been canvassed often enough,[3] but what has not been noticed is his deliberate use of punishment as a means of propagating the message of moral reform. He did this, in eccentric but effective fashion, through the *lex Julia de adulteriis*. And he did it even more dramatically through his attacks on the Vestal Virgins. Those attacks claim our immediate attention.

In the Republic, Vestals accused of unchastity (*incestum*)[4] had been tried by the pontifical college presided over by the Pontifex Maximus; the penalty for those found guilty was to be buried alive. But early society had persuaded itself that this was not execution at the hands of the secular authorities. The condemned woman was sealed in an underground chamber in which a small quantity of food and water had been placed, and it was then for the goddess, Vesta, to say whether the victim should live or die. This forerunner of the medieval ordeal was designed to expiate the pollution that the *incestum* had brought on the city.[5] In the Late Republic the procedure was changed. Jurisdiction began being exercised by secular tribunals, starting with the scandal of 114–13 BC, when the Pontiffs had tried three Vestals but had condemned (and buried alive) only one of them. The other two were tried again by a secular commission appointed by a *lex* of the people, and were condemned. But the traditional penalty could not be imposed by secular officials, and death by secular means was decreed. It was because of the necessary difference in the penalty that the two Vestals could not plead double jeopardy. After this there were one or two (secular) trials in the first century BC, but no convictions resulted.[6] Consequently the pontifical process and its attendant penalty were dormant from 114–13 BC until revived by Domitian some two hundred years later.

There were two series of trials for Vestal unchastity in Domitian's reign. Our principal informants are Pliny and Suetonius, both of whom were there. On the first occasion, probably in 83 AD, the Senior Vestal, Cornelia, was acquitted,[7] but convictions were recorded against three other Vestals and their lovers. The women were sentenced to death but were allowed to choose the manner of their death (SD 8.3–4). For their lovers the traditional penalty was to be beaten to death, but Domitian also treated them leniently, merely sentencing them to exile.[8] He specially drew attention, in an edict, to the fact that he had not inflicted live burial on the women (CD 67.3.4[1]).

Some six to eight years later[9] the Senior Vestal, Cornelia, was charged again. Domitian summoned the pontifical college over which he presided as Pontifex Maximus; they met out of Rome, at his Alban villa, instead of at the pontifical headquarters at the Regia (Plin. *Ep.* 4.11). Cornelia was condemned in her absence and unheard and was sentenced to be buried alive. The people then witnessed the dreadful spectacle of the distraught woman being paraded through the streets on her way to the Polluted Fields near the Colline gate, where the interment was to take place.[10] Desperately appealing to Vesta and all the gods, she now made the defence whose formal pronouncement had been denied to her. But she still displayed something of her patrician dignity. When her robe caught on a snag as she was descending the steps to the underground chamber, the executioner offered her his hand; but she drew away in disgust, rearranged her clothing and made a dignified descent. Her lovers were also charged. They were not as lucky as those condemned in 83; they were publicly beaten to death, although one man's confession dispensed with the need of proof and earned him a comfortable exile.[11] If Dio is to be believed one of the Pontiffs, Helvius Agrippa, was so horrified at the spectacle that he dropped dead in the senate-house (CD 67.3.3[2]).

What caused Domitian to switch from the leniency of 83 to the savagery of 89/91? The tired stereotype of the tyrant who throws off the mask is not the answer. A new interpretation of the trials is needed. It must proceed from the fact that Domitian was obsessed with the idea of restoring traditional morality; such a restoration had possibly been mooted by Vespasian,[12] but convention had been openly flouted by Titus. As early as the second year of his reign Domitian legislated, probably by edict, against the practice of castration that had been encouraged by Titus for his own reasons.[13] That the edict was enforced by subsuming castration under the *lex Cornelia de sicariis* is likely enough.[14] Domitian also encouraged prosecutions for homosexuality and strictly enforced the *lex Julia de adulteriis* – including, it is said, the indictment of women with whom he himself had consorted.[15] These and other measures[16] make up the *correctio morum*, the reform of morals, which is not so much a synonym for his censorship[17] as a convenient label for his programme as a whole.[18]

So much for the general moral background. But our concern is with something more specific. Domitian used shock therapy as a weapon in his campaign. The public display of punishment in order to transmit a message gave Cicero's *poenae metus*[19] a new dimension; fear was inspired in stages, rising from relative leniency to frightfulness as more traumatic demonstrations became necessary. The idea of making the propagation of a message one of the purposes of punishment was not entirely unknown to the Greeks,[20] but its full exploitation had to wait for the Romans. It was, if one likes, the dramatic promotion of a redefined *utilitas publica*. One example of it is the report that Domitian killed his wife's lover, the actor Paris, 'in the middle of the street' (CD 67.3.1). Dio's report should not be dismissed. The killing was perfectly legal under Augustus' adultery law, given the lowly status of the actor (*D.* 48.5.25 pr., 1). Domitian even obeyed the rule requiring the husband to divorce the wife without delay after killing the lover; he divorced Domitilla after killing Paris, although he subsequently took her back because the people demanded it (CD 67.3.2). The only slight irregularity is the place chosen for the revenge killing, if the rule requiring the husband to catch the guilty pair in his house means that he had to kill the lover on the spot.[21] But even if Domitian acted irregularly on this detail it was a small price to pay for the publicity that he wanted for his message.

The Vestal trials represent the most important move in the campaign to pitchfork society into morality. Pliny says as much: 'He had set his heart on burying the Senior Vestal, Cornelia, alive under the belief that exemplary punishment of this sort would lend lustre to his reign' (*Ep.* 4.11.6). And Suetonius cites the trials as an important aspect of *correctio morum*, adding that Vestal immorality had been left unchecked by Vespasian and Titus (SD 8.3.)

The involvement of no less than four Vestals, out of a total order of six, together with a number of men, invites comparison with the trials of 114–13 BC. On that occasion immorality had been institutionalized; the Vestals had virtually been running a brothel.[22] Something similar may well have been happening now. It was simply a variant of a secular form of group activity that was illustrated most graphically by Julia's circle in 2 BC; even before that it had manifested itself in the Bacchanalian movement of 186 BC, and it was again prominent at the end of Tiberius' reign.[23] That the Domitianic Vestals were simply expressing dissatisfaction with their lot, as the Vestals of 114–13 BC had done,[24] cannot be positively asserted, although it is likely enough. But whatever their motive, two-thirds of the Vestal order faced Domitian with what was not only a challenge to *correctio morum* but a deadly threat to the very existence of Rome.[25] Domitian thus had good reason, according to his lights, to respond vigorously to the threat. But the live burial of the Senior Vestal was a late item on the agenda; it only surfaced in 89/91. A careful analysis of the sequence of events will make this clear.

The key to the whole matter is the punitive differential between the cases of 83 and those of 89/91. The differential is clearly adumbrated by Suetonius:

> Having undertaken the correction of morals, . . . he punished the unchastity of Vestal Virgins in various severe ways, first by capital punishment and later on in the traditional fashion (*priora capitali supplicio, posteriora more veteri*). For while he allowed the Oculata

sisters and Varronilla *liberum mortis arbitrium* and banished their seducers, he later ordered that the Senior Vestal, Cornelia, who had been acquitted but rearraigned after a long interval and found guilty, be buried alive and that her lovers be beaten to death in the Comitium.

(SD 8.3–4)

Suetonius tells us, then, that the two series of trials employed different procedures and were bound by different rules of punishment. Trial by the Pontiffs resulted, and could only result, in live burial for the women and fatal flogging for the men. Those penalties were unalterable. They had originated as measures to purge the pollution, to placate the gods, and if the gods required purgation in a particular way it was not for mortals to say otherwise. In other words, there was no room for leniency in this process. But Domitian *was* lenient on the first occasion, thus Suetonius' *capitale supplicium* does not denote a pontifical trial. It implies a secular process going back ultimately to the special *quaestio* of 114–13 BC. The offence was analogous to Vestal *incestum*, but it was not specifically that crime.[26] It fell under one of the public criminal laws, namely the *lex Julia de adulteriis*.[27] Domitian, sitting not as Pontifex Maximus but either with a *consilium* in a secular capacity or at a trial by the senate – the former is more likely[28] – was not subject to any restrictions on his punitive discretion. He may even have applied the strict *poena legis* to the men, for Suetonius describes it as *relegatio* (SD 8.4); but the distinction between that and *deportatio* is not always clear.[29] The punishment of the women certainly exceeded the statutory limits, but in the aftermath of the Julio-Claudian developments there was ample room for that.

The second series of trials dates to Domitian's 'bad' period. If this series can be dated to 89 rather than to 91 it will furnish a concrete reason for the use of the traditional penalty. In the past live burials had been prompted by crisis situations, or at the very least by omens that presaged disaster.[30] There was arguably such an event in 89, when the revolt of Antonius Saturninus faced Domitian with the supreme crisis of his reign.[31] The trials of 83 having failed to stamp out Vestal unchastity because of the (fortuitous) acquittal of Cornelia,[32] the events of 89 may well have been seen as a pollution-generated crisis demanding purgation. Domitian would have needed a new propaganda campaign to transmit the message of *correctio morum* more forcefully, and he would have needed it in a hurry. It so happens that there is evidence of haste. While one of the condemned, the Roman knight Celer, was being beaten to death, he kept on asking, 'What have I done?' (Plin. *Ep.* 4.11.10). Like Cornelia, he seems to have been hastily condemned without being heard, and on insufficient evidence. Another of the men, Licinianus, was given a lighter sentence because he confessed; he was interdicted from water and fire and was given time to remove some of his property before confiscation took effect (*Ib.* 4.11.11). This reward (that is what Pliny calls it) was granted because his confession had dispensed with the need for proof.[33] Again there are indications of haste and insufficient evidence.

Cornelia herself furnishes support for the idea that her punishment was a response to a particular omen. While being paraded through the streets she repeatedly asked how she could be stigmatized as a source of pollution when Domitian had celebrated two triumphs during her priesthood (Plin. *Ep.* 4.11.9). Pliny is not sure whether this was meant seriously or ironically, and it is true that Domitian's triumphs were something of a joke (Tac. *Agr.* 39). But either way her remark indicates that there was something that was being interpreted as a bad omen. Pliny also concedes that her innocence may have been more of a semblance than a reality, but he still criticizes the fact that she was condemned unheard and at a secret trial outside Rome.

The Vestal penalty did not surface again for a hundred and twenty-five years, but when it did it was again invoked against two-thirds of the order. Dio, an eye-witness this time, reports that Caracalla condemned four Vestals to be buried alive. Three of them suffered that fate, although one protested that she was a virgin, but the fourth killed herself (CD 78.16.1, 2[2]–3). It has been suggested that this is connected with the Severan revival of the cult of Vesta.[34] At some time between then and the late fourth century the pontifical and secular processes coalesced; a Vestal at Alba[35] was condemned by the Pontiffs but the execution was entrusted to the urban prefect. But he begged off on the grounds that his office did not allow him to leave Rome (for Alba), and the matter was handed over to the local governor (Symmach. *Ep.* 9.147–8). Symmachus adds that the entrustment of the execution to the secular authority was in accordance with recent precedent. It is clear that live burial was not employed; the Vestal was to be executed at Alba, not at the Polluted Fields in Rome where live burials took place (L. 8.15.8).

CLEMENCY AND THE DEFLECTION OF ODIUM

Domitian had an acute fear of odium, and in order to counteract it he constructed elaborate charades. Suetonius says that he never pronounced an especially dreadful sentence without a preliminary promise of clemency, so that a lenient preamble came to be regarded as a guarantee of a cruel death. Suetonius cites a case in which he brought some men charged with *maiestas* into the senate and declared that he would find out that day how dear he was to senators. The senate took the hint and sentenced them to death in the traditional fashion. Thereupon Domitian, appalled at the brutality of the penalty, vetoed it in order to lessen the odium – *ad leniendam invidiam*. He went on to outline an appropriate replacement for the vetoed sentence. Suetonius quotes his exact words:

> Allow me, Conscript Fathers, to seek from your loyalty some-thing which I know I shall obtain with difficulty, namely that you grant them *liberum mortis arbitrium*. In this way you will spare your own eyes and everyone will know that I was present in the senate.

(SD 11.2–3)

Domitian had avoided the trap into which Nero had fallen. The charges against the men almost certainly covered insults to the emperor rather than attempts on his life. The case was thus on all fours with that of Antistius Sosianus in 62. But where Nero had failed to get from the senate a traditional punishment that he could veto, Domitian invited such a punishment as a proof of the senate's loyalty. Armed with that proof, he was able to demonstrate his clemency. And in case anyone thought of crediting the milder sentence to *publica clementia* rather than to *clementia principis*, the record would show that Domitian was the author. This time the Stoics would not be able to steal the emperor's thunder.

The episode has another important message. It suggests that the trauma of public executions was becoming a problem. Domitian thus enlisted *humanitas* in support of his strategy on this occasion. But it was a qualified *humanitas*. Death in the form of immolation in the arena was an even more important spectator attraction in the eyes of the builders of the Colosseum than it had been before.[36]

Domitian played a variation on the odium theme at Cornelia's trial. As Pliny tells it, he was disturbed by the reputation for cruelty that his treatment of the Vestal had earned him. He devised a devious response. Licinianus was arrested for having concealed a material witness, and on the advice of Domitian's agents he confessed in order to avoid being beaten to death. Thereupon Domitian exclaimed in great relief that 'Licinianus has absolved us!' (Plin. *Ep.* 4.11.5, 3). He expressed similar

98

relief when he was instituted as heir in the will of Tacitus' father-in-law, Agricola. He was, says Tacitus, as elated as if he had been tried and honourably acquitted (Tac. *Agr.* 43). Doing odious political things and then straining every nerve to avoid odium is not a modern invention.

CONCLUSION

The message of Domitian's punishment of the Vestals is that he was using a most terrifying punishment, live burial, as a means of propagating *correctio morum*, his policy of moral reform. It was an extreme use of the *poenae metus*. Two series of Vestal trials are uncovered. The first was conducted by the emperor in a secular capacity and under the public criminal laws. It resulted in the discretionary secular penalty of *liberum mortis arbitrium*. He held the second trial as Pontifex Maximus and inflicted the mandatory sentence of live burial. Domitian also used the technique of deflecting the odium of capital punishment; his approach was more effective than that of Nero.

9

PREFECTS AND CRIMINAL TRIALS

INTRODUCTION

Our first thematic presentation focuses on the two major prefects, the urban prefect (*praefectus urbi*) and the praetorian prefect (*p. praetorio*). The theme sheds important light on punishment theory. As both prefects were mandated by the emperor, changes in the scope of their authority reflect the changing perceptions of the government on the question of increasing the efficacy of criminal justice, especially in the area of common-law crime. The changes largely coincide with the formal establishment of punitive differentials between *honestiores* and *humiliores* which will be discussed in our next chapter.

THE URBAN PREFECT IN NERO'S REIGN

In 61 AD a certain Valerius Ponticus was exiled by the senate for having lodged charges concerning the forged will of Domitius Balbus with the jury-court under the *lex Cornelia testamentaria* instead of with the urban prefect. The two courts had concurrent jurisdiction at that time, but it was claimed that Ponticus was in league with the defendants, who included his relative Valerius Fabianus. Ponticus had deliberately bypassed the new court with its streamlined procedure and had chosen the court whose chronic congestion[1] promised indefinite deferment of the case.[2]

Originally an ex-consul with essentially police powers of coercion, the urban prefect became a regular official under Tiberius.[3] At some point of time he began adjudicating at trials. The date of his first exercise of jurisdiction proper is not known, but Nero's reign looks likely, and testamentary fraud looks like the first crime to which it was applied. Nero had a special interest in the *lex Cornelia testamentaria*. He wrote a number of safeguards against fraud into that law.[4] He also framed what may have been a comprehensive wills ordinance that may have given the urban prefect power to try cases.[5]

The forgers whom Ponticus had wanted to save were tried by the senate after all; the praetor in charge of the jury-court had probably remitted the case.[6] All but one were condemned. Ponticus received a similar sentence to that of an accomplice who was interdicted from Italy and Spain.[7] So far so good, but there is a question that has not been asked before. If Ponticus *had* taken the case to the urban prefect, what power of punishment would the latter have had? Would he have been bound by the *poena legis*, which means that he would have exercised capital jurisdiction,[8] or would his mandate from the emperor have restricted him to sub-capital penalties – relegation, for example, but not interdiction/deportation? If Tacitus' *interdictum est* (TA 14.41.1) means that the Spanish accomplice was sentenced capitally by the senate, we might think that he could not have got less from the prefect. But this needs further consideration. There is no more evidence from Nero's reign, but a great deal after that. It will show that the prefect was probably restricted to sub-capital penalties at first, and that it was only by degrees that his reach was extended.

THE URBAN PREFECT FROM VITELLIUS TO DOMITIAN

As we have seen,[9] the question of a capital mandate first cropped up in 69, when C. Dolabella was tried by Flavius Sabinus. This looks like the urban prefect's first exercise of capital jurisdiction. Although Tacitus implies that Sabinus refused the mandate at first because he abhorred bloodshed (TH 2.63), he also knew that he did not have capital jurisdiction. Vitellius' sister-in-law, Triaria, saw to it that he got it.

The next stage is reached with two of Domitian's prefects. The incumbent in 83, the jurist Pegasus, attended a meeting of the emperor's *consilium* at which a reorganization of the prefect's functions was discussed. Domitian wanted to vest him with the *ius gladii*, to give him capital jurisdiction, and so to formalize the tentative step taken by Vitellius.[10] Domitian wanted this for two reasons. First, he was about to leave for the war against the Chatti, and if the prefect was to protect his back while he was away he would need capital powers. Second, the first (secular) series of Vestal trials was being organized at this time, and it is possible that Domitian wanted the prefect to conduct the trials. In principle there was nothing against this, since Domitian would not be sitting as Pontifex Maximus on that occasion.[11] But Pegasus rejected the idea, declaring that 'Even in such critical times everything should be done *inermi iustitia*, by justice not armed with a sword'.[12] Pegasus shared his profession's dislike of bloodshed,[13] so that again an aversion to the death penalty is evident.

A similar stance was taken up by our other Domitianic prefect, Rutilius Gallicus, who held office in 89.[14] Statius says the following in a poem celebrating Rutilius' recovery from an illness:

> Favouring neither imprisonment nor scourging, reluctant to follow the road marked out by your high office (*alta potestas*), you renounced much of your armed force, heard the petitions of the humble (*humiles*), and rendered justice in court without driving away the curule magistrates (*nec proturbare curules*), and tempered the sword by the gown (*et ferrum mulcere toga*).[15]

The passage covers both summary punishment by *coercitio* and judicial punishment by *iudicatio*. Rutilius believes that even *humiliores* should be heard before being punished. The crucial words are 'without driving away the curule magistrates', that is, without supplanting the jury-courts. Concurrence exists, as it did in Nero's day, but Rutilius favours milder punishments than those prescribed by the *poenae legum*, 'he tempers the sword by the gown'. But the exact meaning needs careful attention.[16] Does it imply that he does not possess capital jurisdiction, having rejected it as Pegasus had done? Or does he possess it but use it only sparingly?

Elsewhere in the poem Statius has Rutilius relieving the pressure on the congested jury-courts, even hearing cases remitted from outlying areas. The poet blames the prefect's illness on the workload (1.40.10–12, 52–7). Statius seems to confirm Rutilius' preference for sub-capital penalties when he speaks of 'the one in whose merciful hand is placed the custody of war-free Rome' (1.4.16). But a complication is introduced by Juvenal, who has Rutilius slaving away from dawn to dusk, trying cases of poisoning and *parricidium*, as well as other crimes that Juvenal finds too numerous too mention (Juv. 13.154–8). Juvenal's choice of crimes is unfortunate; they are the least likely to have prompted sub-capital sentences. But there is a way out.

The solution lies in determining, if possible, what types of case took up Rutilius' time. Statius gives a useful pointer when he praises Rutilius for the judgment and understanding that he made available to the Hundred Men (1.4.24–5). The reference is to the Centumviral Court, the most prestigious Roman court, which tried cases of wills and related matters. This meant a whole network of issues fanning out from the court's principal function. If any hint of a fraudulent will came to light it might generate charges under the *lex Cornelia testamentaria*; disentitlement under the *lex Papia Poppaea* also stirred up criminal, or quasi-criminal, process.[17] Thus Rutilius' special expertise, which made him as much an adviser to the Centumviral Court as a pleader,[18] was the springboard for a heavy case-load in the testamentary area when he became urban prefect. The *lex Cornelia*, the second busiest criminal law, is the probable source of most of the workload that undermined his health. Juvenal has made a feature of isolated poisoning and *parricidium* cases, or he has even blown up a single *cause célèbre* of *parricidium* by poisoning. The murder of a parent has obvious testamentary connotations.

Two conclusions can be drawn at this point. First, the bulk of the prefect's work was in the testamentary area, especially on the criminal side. Second, the prefect may have been given a general capital authority, but it is more likely that the emperor only gave it ad hoc when the gravity of the crime required it. Even then Rutilius seldom used it. But the status of the offender was not a factor in Rutilius' mind; he gave the same consideration to *humiliores*. And that policy left a permanent imprint on the *lex Cornelia testamentaria*. As late as the Severan period punitive distinctions between *honestiores* and *humiliores* did not apply to this law. There was a standard penalty of deportation and confiscation, and only slaves were sentenced to death (*D.* 48.10.1.13).

THE URBAN PREFECT IN THE SECOND CENTURY

The period sees the gradual consolidation of the prefect's powers, culminating in their formal entrenchment by the Severans. Our first piece of hard evidence appears in a rescript of Antoninus Pius addressed to his urban prefect, Erucius Clarus. The rescript laid down that the prefect of the watch (*praefectus vigilum*) was to try cases of arson and of breaking and entering, unless the gravity of the crime or the notoriety of the offender (= a previous conviction) warranted a remittal to the urban prefect (*D.* 1.15.3.1–2). As the prefect of the watch was limited to giving a reprimand or a (non-lethal) beating (*ibid.*), the greater penalty open to the urban prefect was not necessarily capital: even *relegatio* might have met the case. It was also in Pius' reign that Apuleius of Madura was tried under the *lex Cornelia testamentaria* (Apul. *Apol.* 2.3.23–4). But as he was acquitted we do not know what penalty would have been imposed.

The position under Marcus calls for a close look. According to the *Augustan History* Marcus personally tried capital charges against *homines honesti* and punished all crimes with lighter penalties than the *poenae legum*, except the serious felonies of manifest offenders (*SHA Marc.* 24.1–2). Mommsen took this to mean the end of capital jury-trials in Rome,[19] but that is not right. In the same passage Marcus reprimands a praetor for conducting trials in a summary fashion. The convictions are set aside and the praetor is told to try the cases again: 'It is of importance to their status (*dignitas*) that they be tried by some-one who judges on behalf of the people, *pro populo*' (*ib.* 24.2). Judging *pro populo* is a plebeian catch phrase, and the passage must mean that *humiliores* – but only they – continued to be tried by jury-courts on capital charges. Let us look again at the context in which the reprimand is noticed: 'He tried capital charges . . . and always with great fairness (*summa aequitate*), so much so that he reprimanded a praetor etc.' The praetor had failed to live up to *bonum et aequum*, he had failed to avoid haste as recommended by Seneca and endorsed by the Stoic emperor.[20] That haste was linked to capital penalties, not to sub-capital.

This brings us to the urban prefect, and the *Augustan History* again assists. Marcus took it amiss (*non libenter accepit*) whenever the prefect sentenced anyone to interdiction.[21] The prefect was now imposing capital sentences regularly.[22] But was he, in common with the emperor himself, restricted to *honestiores*, or did he also share the *humiliores* with the jury-courts, thus perpetuating the rivalry between the prefect and the curule magistrates? It can safely be concluded that he was trying persons of all classes, as Rutilius Gallicus had done;[23] and he was sentencing capitally.

But what was it about the prefect's sentences of interdiction that caused Marcus 'to take it amiss'? The answer must be that the emperor was annoyed with the prefect for a similar reason to that which he raised against the praetor. The prefect had also disregarded *bonum et aequum*; he had failed to observe *clementia* (in the Senecan sense). (Seneca had, we recall, defined *clementia* as an attribute of any superior, not only the emperor, vis-a-vis an inferior; *Clem.* 2.3.1–2.) *Humanitas/clementia* in that sense was very much in the air at this time. Marcus and Verus ruled that a man who had killed his mother in a fit of madness need not be punished; he suffered sufficiently from his madness, and need only be kept under restraint (*D.* 48.9.9.2). The same emperors modified a ruling of Antoninus Pius, who had told his urban prefect that where documents that could not be proved were produced in court, sentence should be passed according to the gravity of the offence. Marcus and

Verus modified this 'out of their *humanitas*' by stipulating that where the document was handed in by mistake the act should be pardoned (*D.* 48.10.31) – that is, absolution should be granted. The emperors also commended a governor for his prudence and *humanitas* in absolving a slave who had falsely confessed to homicide through fear of being returned to his master. The governor had found on investigation that the slave had had nothing to do with the murder, and had set aside the conviction and ordered the slave to be sold (*D.* 48.18.1.27). And Marcus and Commodus exonerated a father who killed the lover but only wounded his daughter, on the ground that he intended to kill her but she was saved by fate (*D.* 48.5.33 pr.).

The message was being vigorously propagated, and all mandated jurisdictions were expected to familiarize themselves with it. But one prefect[24] failed to give due weight to the guidelines and earned a reprimand. There is no sure way of identifying the culprit, but there may be a case for Q. Iunius Rusticus, consul in 133 and 162, and urban prefect over 162–168. A Stoic whose lectures were attended by Marcus, he may have belonged to the *poena legis* school; his father was Q. Iunius Arulenus Rusticus, one of Domitian's Stoic martyrs who had earlier, as tribune of the plebs, offered to veto the *senatus consultum* against Thrasea Paetus.[25]

The urban prefect's jurisdiction was formally defined in c. 199, when Septimius Severus addressed an *epistula* to his prefect, Fabius Cilo, empowering him to try all crimes committed in Rome or within a hundred miles of the city. He was authorized to sentence to *relegatio* and *deportatio in insulam*, subject to the particular island being designated by the emperor; he could also inflict other punishments, including the condemnation of *humiliores* to the mines.[26] He does not appear to have had the power to sentence *honestiores* to death, as distinct from exile. Even in the Later Empire the prefect had to forward the record to the emperor for that (*CTh* 9.16.10, 40.10). Not much had changed since Flavius Sabinus. There are no cases on the prefect's infliction of the death penalty on *honestiores*, but one suspects that Antoninus Pius' senator who confessed to *parricidium* but was merely marooned on a desert island (*SHA Pius* 8.10) had been tried by the prefect, who referred to the emperor in view of the mandatory *poena cullei* for confessed parricides. There is also no specific mention of death sentences on *humiliores*, but it is a fair guess that the prefect did not have to refer to the emperor. The *dignitas* of *humiliores* did not trouble the Severans as much as it had Marcus.

To some extent Severus merely formalized current practices, but the extension of the prefect's authority to all crimes of whatsoever nature

– *omnia omnino crimina* (*D.* 1.12.1 pr.) – looks like an innovation. The jury-courts were in a chronic state of congestion; Dio found 3,000 cases on the trial-list when he investigated it during his first consulship (CD 76.16.4). The congestion was particularly bad in the adultery court, but the Cornelian laws on forgery and homicide also posed problems, and the alarming increase in kidnapping was putting pressure on the *lex Fabia*.[27] Also, the increasing use of *crimina extraordinaria*, charges that did not even pretend to be based on the public criminal laws, could no longer be maintained on a casual basis.[28]

The formalization of the prefect's powers was not quite the end of the jury-court system, for one court, the *quaestio de adulteriis*, ran concurrently with the prefect's tribunal. A last attempt to streamline the jury-courts was made by Elagabalus, who created a sixth decury of *iudices* drawn from the lower income levels of the *humiliores*, but Severus Alexander put an end to that.[29] He entrusted the reorganization of the criminal courts to the jurist Ulpian, praetorian prefect from 222 until his murder in 228.[30] Under Ulpian's guidance the *quaestio de adulteriis* was abolished, thus finally dismantling the jury-court system. And the urban prefect, now the sole regular jurisdiction in Rome and its environs, was given a panel of fourteen urban curators of consular rank, to assist him.[31]

THE PRAETORIAN PREFECT: CONDEMNATIONS BY ACCLAMATION

The jurist Arcadius Charisius, who flourished under Diocletian, writes about the origins of the praetorian prefect's jurisdiction as follows:

> Some say that praetorian prefects were instituted on the analogy of the master of the horse who deputized for the dictator in olden times. When governance was transferred to emperors they made analogous appointments of praetorian prefects, giving them fuller authority to correct public discipline. From this simple beginning their authority grew to such an extent that no appeal lay from the prefect's judgments. Previously the point was controversial, but finally appeals were forbidden by imperial edict. The emperor believed that their industry, loyalty and authority qualified them to give judgments of equal efficacy to his own.
>
> (*D.* 1.11)

As so often, the sources manage to tell us everything except what we want to know. At all events, the praetorian prefects were late starters. We have only one example in the first century AD, that of Burrus and the robbers in Nero's reign. The period is in fact taken up with a somewhat different process, condemnations by acclamation by the praetorian cohorts, orchestrated by the prefect.

The paradigm case emerges in 48 AD, when Claudius and the freedman Narcissus, appointed prefect just for the day, sat with the cohorts judging Messalina's lovers. The cohorts set up an insistent demand for 'the names of the culprits and the punishment of their crimes – *continuus dehinc cohortium clamor nomina reorum et poenas flagitantium*'. Claudius allowed the defendants to plead in mitigation, but as their guilt was either manifest or confessed he did not put formal charges.[32]

The Claudian precedent was put to good use by Vespasian's son, Titus. It was his custom, as prefect, to obtain verdicts against his enemies at the praetorian camp; he would then have the verdicts confirmed by the emperor and would put the victims to death.[33] This precedent was followed by Nerva's prefect, Aelianus. He persuaded the cohorts to demand the surrender of Domitian's murderers 'in order to put them to death', and Nerva was forced to surrender two of his close friends.[34] This was a critical moment, for the prefect had got the cohorts to adjudicate in defiance of the emperor's wishes. Nerva was so alarmed that he promptly adopted Trajan (CD 68.3.4). This was not the end of condemnations by acclamation, however. In 212 the praetorians condemned their prefect, the jurist Papinian, and took him before Caracalla, who confirmed their verdict with the words, 'I rule for you, not for myself, and I yield to you both as accusers and as judges.' The soldiers then killed Papinian in the emperor's presence.[35]

Caracalla's ruling deflected the odium of being seen to punish the lawyer who had refused to justify the murder of the emperor's brother, Geta.[36] It also established a precedent for the murder of Ulpian in 228. A reluctant Alexander was forced to confirm the cohorts' verdict and Ulpian was killed in his presence.[37]

THE PRAETORIAN PREFECT: CONDITIONAL ADJUDICATION

Early prefects like Sejanus and Macro had not adjudicated; they had merely gathered evidence which they passed on to the regular jurisdictions.[38] Burrus signals something of an advance, but the first trial to be held in public occurs in Trajan's reign.[39] A mother, suspecting that her son's freedmen had poisoned him and forged his will, laid charges with the emperor. Trajan appointed Servianus as *iudex*. Pliny appeared for the defence and secured what he (predictably) describes as a brilliant victory. The mother, not satisfied, went back to Trajan with fresh evidence. Suburanus was delegated to determine whether a new trial should be ordered. He found that there was no case for reopening (Plin. *Ep.* 7.6.8–9).

In what capacities did Servianus and Suburanus act? Servianus was not praetorian prefect,[40] but he may have been urban prefect, given the testamentary implications of the case. But he could not have been commissioned to consider the fresh evidence; he had already found for the defendants. Trajan therefore turned to Suburanus, who happens to have been his first praetorian prefect.[41] But what function did Suburanus discharge? Did he merely gather evidence, or did he actually adjudicate? The answer lies somewhere between the two. He heard argument from counsel, and he appears to have given a ruling.[42]

Regular, but still emperor-controlled, adjudication is seen under Hadrian. Dio reports that the praetorian prefect, Marcius Turbo, spent the entire day at the palace, often starting his day before midnight. One night the celebrated pleader, Fronto, was returning home when a client told him that Turbo was already holding court. Fronto went into court and greeted Turbo with the word 'Goodnight' instead of 'Good morning'. Turbo, adds Dio, heard cases even when he was ill, and in reply to Hadrian's advice to take things more easily he declared that 'A prefect ought to die on his feet' (CD 69.18).

Turbo appears to have been as hard-pressed as his urban predecessor, Rutilius Gallicus. And like the latter, his trial-roll included the lower end of the social spectrum. *The Augustan History* says that although Hadrian summoned both senators and *equites* to his *consilium*, he did not allow *equites* to try cases against senators, *whether he was present or not* (*SHA Hadr.* 8.8–9). This does not mean that the prefect presided over the *consilium* as the emperor's deputy.[43] There would not have been much point in having a deputy who, as a member of the equestrian order,[44] had to withdraw whenever a senator was charged. The prefect's trials in the emperor's absence were held *outside* the *consilium*, and defendants of every sub-senatorial degree were brought before him.

We are told of a case in which someone complained to Hadrian about usurious interest. The emperor directed his prefect to adjudicate on the complaint (*iudicabit*) and to report back by *libellus*.[45] Although a civil matter, this case adds the final point to the picture of the prefect's authority at this time. He did adjudicate, but his decisions had to be confirmed by the emperor. Not much had changed since Burrus.

Substantially the same position obtained under Marcus. We learn that he kept prefects by him and always laid down the law on their authority and responsibility – *habuit secum praefectos quorum et auctoritate et periculo semper iura dictavit* (*SHA Marc.* 11.10). Marcus thus relied on his prefects[46] for guidance through two avenues: their *auctoritas*, that is, their opinions as tendered at meetings of the *consilium*; and their *pericula*, the written judgments delivered at their trials and submitted to the emperor for confirmation. The word *periculum* is carefully chosen. It is here equivalent to *libellus*,[47] but it also retains the meaning of 'risk, responsibility'. Thus semantic flexibility enabled Marcus to use the proven dodge of shifting the odium on to the prefects.[48]

Marcus continued Hadrian's policy of excluding *equites* from the trials of senators,[49] but there is a problem, one in which a praetorian prefect is involved. The orator Herodes Atticus was accused by the Athenians and the matter was referred to Marcus. The praetorian prefect, Bassaeus Rufus, was present at the trial. Herodes began ranting against the emperors, whereupon 'Bassaeus who was entrusted with the sword threatened him with death' (Philostr. *Vit. Soph.* 2.1, 559–63). Herodes was a senator, the charges were capital,[50] and the question is, what was the prefect doing there? If he was simply performing his primary duty of protecting the emperor there is no difficulty. But if he was sitting as co-adjudicator with Marcus,[51] he was present at the trial in the prohibited sense. The solution depends on a case under Commodus.

The future emperor Septimius Severus, then governing Sicily (189–90), was accused of consulting astrologers about the succession to the throne. Commodus remitted the case to the praetorian prefects,[52] who acquitted Severus. The unsuccessful accuser was crucified. That is not a problem. Unsuccessful accusers had been punished for *calumnia* in the Republic, although the penalty of *infamia*[53] was much milder than the imperial counterparts. Trajan had staged a mass trial of informers in the arena, and had confiscated their properties and deported them *en masse*; Pliny found it 'a beautiful sight'.[54] Pertinax had laid down differential penalties according to the culprit's status; crucifixion was one of the penalties for *humiliores*.[55] Severus' accuser was of that status; astrologers were not well placed socially, nor were their associates who knew what they were doing.

The awkward part of the case is that it has the prefects adjudicating on a senator. This strengthens the possibility that Bassaeus did the same in Herodes Atticus' case. We must therefore conclude that when Marcus retained Hadrian's exclusion of *equites* he made an exception in the case of the praetorian prefects. Or to be more precise, he anticipated a decree of Severus Alexander. That ruler is on record as having conferred senatorial status on all praetorian prefects, 'so that no one who was not a senator himself might adjudicate on a Roman senator' (*SHA Alex.* 21.3–5). Marcus, and after him Commodus, may have got in first.[56]

THE PRIMACY OF THE *LEX FABIA*

The first comments by jurists on the praetorian prefect's jurisdiction appear in the Severan period. The focus is on the *lex Fabia de plagiariis* which had earlier established a jury-court for kidnapping:

> It is laid down by imperial constitutions that cases under the *lex Fabia* are to be judged by the urban prefect where the offence was committed in Rome or within the hundredth milestone; beyond that point praetorian prefects have jurisdiction. The *lex Fabia* applies to whoever conceals, imprisons, sells or buys a Roman citizen or a freedman who was given his freedom in Italy, and to any accomplice. The *poena legis* is attached to this in the same first chapter of the law. The second chapter applies to anyone who persuades another's slave to desert, or without the master's consent wrongfully and unlawfully conceals, buys or sells another's slave, or is an accomplice. The law lays down a fine of 50,000 sesterces. But recent constitutions impose a capital sentence in aggravated cases, such as crucifixion and the mines for *humiliores*, half-confiscation and exile for *honestiores*.
>
> (*Coll.* 14.3.4–6, 14.2 adapted)

The *lex Fabia* is the only criminal law in respect of which the division of function between the urban and praetorian prefects is spelled out. A similar division under the other *leges* is generally assumed,[57] but what has not been considered before is the possibility that kidnapping was the very first crime to be formally allocated to the two jurisdictions and that this was the role model for other crimes.

As so often in Roman law, the change was made casuistically, in response to a particular problem. By the turn of the second century AD the shortage of agricultural slaves, a legacy of the Augustan Peace, was assuming worrying proportions.[58] The slave-dealer, always one of the most ruthless elements in Roman society, began ranging far and wide in search of slaves to buy or abduct. His favourite stamping-ground was the great estates (*latifundia*) with their enormous slave populations. But the main concentrations of *latifundia* were beyond the hundredth mile-stone, in ranching country. As experience had shown, resistance to law and order in those areas often obliged the government to use force.[59] Thus both geography and the level of unrest necessitated a jurisdiction properly equipped to handle the situation. The praetorian prefect was the answer. Where, as quite often, the office was shared by two incumbents, if one of them happened to be a civilian he could provide the legal expertise, while his colleague provided the muscles.

It is precisely in the Severan period that a specific reason for the change surfaces. A bandit named Bulla had terrorized the Italian countryside for two years (206–7). He was not only defying the imperial dignity, but was also seizing imperial freedmen (who had been manumitted in Italy)[60] as well as skilled workmen.[61] He was eventually captured in c. 207 and put on trial. The trial was conducted by the jurist Papinian, prefect since 205. His contemporary, Dio, records an exchange between prefect and accused: 'Why are you a bandit?', to which Bulla replied, 'Why are you a prefect?' Papinian sentenced Bulla to be thrown to the beasts.[62]

Bulla's trial was based on the *lex Fabia*: he had seized duly manumitted freedmen, and at least some of the workmen were slaves. But other questions also came into it. An idea of what they were is supplied by a text taken from Ulpian. He lists as the wrongdoers causing the most trouble in the provinces temple-robbers, bandits, kidnappers and thieves; he advises governors to punish them according to the gravity of the crime, and also to punish their accomplices, 'without whom a bandit (*latro*) could not remain in hiding' (*D*. 1.18.13 pr.). The main emphasis is on the *latro*, which is how Bulla was classified by Papinian. The word does not only mean robbers in the narrow sense; it is also a pejorative term for social dissidents, for those who attack the whole edifice of privilege. Bulla had pointed out to the imperial freedman that they were being exploited; and he had sent a message to the government: 'Feed your slaves so that they do not become bandits' (CD 76.10.5).

All four of the crimes listed by Ulpian were committed by Bulla.[63] Thus the investigation under the *lex Fabia* was able to fan out beyond the strict confines of kidnapping. Even the *lex maiestatis* came into it.[64] With this diversity available under the broad umbrella of the *lex Fabia*, the prefects did not really need special decrees for other *leges*. All the issues raised at the trial under the *lex Fabia* would be recorded in the prefect's *periculum*,[65] and if that document happened to be backed by the signature of Papinian, the most prestigious of all the jurists,[66] the adoption of similar sets of rules under other laws would be almost a routine matter.

THE PRAETORIAN PREFECT:
UNCONDITIONAL ADJUDICATION

Does the *lex Fabia* establish not only a territorial division, but also a general mandate giving the praetorian prefect a similar independent power of sentencing to that possessed by the urban prefect? An affirmative answer is almost mandatory, for otherwise we would have the urban prefect sentencing independently of the emperor, while his opposite number was still in swaddling clothes. This is supported by a line of cases,[67] but the strongest proof is supplied by a passage in Ulpian:

> Those who are deported by the praetorian prefects, or by a vice-prefect who judges under imperial mandate, or by the urban prefect (for he *too* was given power to deport by an *epistula* of Severus and Caracalla), lose their citizenship immediately.[68]

Here the praetorian prefects judge under a general authority; only their subordinates, the vice-prefects, require special mandates from case to case. Moreover, the position of the urban prefect is almost secondary to that of the praetorian prefect; he is almost an afterthought. This is not merely because Ulpian himself held the praetorian office; that would not have coloured his interpretation of the law.

The praetorian prefect's importance is also shown by the practice of remitting cases to him from other jurisdictions. An example is a rescript which Alexander addressed to the owner of a warehouse that had been broken into, 'You should take your complaint to the governor of the province. But if he thinks that the caretakers of the warehouse deserve heavier punishment, he is to remit them to Domitius Ulpianus, praetorian prefect and my parent.'[69] However, this principle was not unique to the praetorian prefect. Antoninus Pius had authorized remittals to the urban prefect:

> The prefect of the watch (*praefectus vigilum*) judges arson and breaking and entering . . . unless the gravity of the crime or the notoriety of the offender warrants a remittal to the urban prefect. Occupiers whose negligence causes fires should either be whipped or given a severe reprimand. The caretakers of warehouses are usually held responsible for breaking and entering, as Pius wrote to (the urban prefect) Erucius Clarus.
>
> (D. 1.15.3.1–2 adapted)

In cases of arson the Severan emperors cut down the jurisdiction of the *praefectus vigilum*, 'You may sentence those who cause fires negligently to be beaten. But those who do it deliberately are to be remitted to Fabius Cilo, urban prefect and our friend' (*D.* 1.15.4).

The warehouse case was not the first remittal to the praetorian prefect. That had happened under Caracalla, when a knight who had been relegated to an island and committed murder while there was sent to Rome for trial by the prefects (Philostr. *Vit. Soph.* 2.32). But the warehouse case does represent an important advance, in two respects. The prefect was now taking cognisance of crimes committed in the provinces, outside Italy. And he was starting to transform the legal basis of his trials. Bulla had been charged under the *lex Fabia,* and the knight had been charged under the *lex Cornelia de sicariis.* But breaking and entering was not a crime under any public criminal law. It was a delict, *rapina* or theft with violence, which normally gave a civil claim sounding in money. But now it was being tried as a crime, as one of the *crimina extraordinaria.* This was an intelligent recognition of the fact that a monetary penalty was cold comfort against men of straw like warehouse caretakers. The cognitionary process was being enlarged, and indeed transformed. The new categories, based largely on private-law delicts,[70] lacked even a nominal link with the public criminal laws. There was no *poena legis* which could even serve as an asking bid, and punishments had to be cut from the whole cloth. This in turn caused people to rethink statutory punishments, thus accelerating the movement away from the *poena legis.* It has even been argued that the incursion of non-statutory crimes brought about a change in terminology. Instead of *crimen* signifying 'a charge' under the relevant *lex,* it will have come to denote 'the crime' itself.[71] But whether this was anything more than a popular turn of phrase, even in the Later Empire, is debatable.[72]

A further step towards the prefect's ultimate emergence as the High Court of the empire was taken by Alexander's successor, Maximinus Thrax, 'A *forma* issued by the praetorian prefect which is of general application and not contrary to laws or constitutions is of permanent force unless subsequently changed on my authority.'[73] The prefect was promulgating Rules of Court, which points to a firmly entrenched jurisdiction. It is not surprising that by the end of the same century he was seen to judge in the emperor's stead (*vice sacra*) and his judgments were (uniquely) not subject to appeal.[74]

CONCLUSION

The urban prefect started exercising jurisdiction proper in Nero's reign. He began with the *lex Cornelia testamentaria,* and forged wills remained one of his main targets. At first he only imposed sub-capital penalties, but a death sentence emerged under Vitellius. However, one of Domitian's prefects refused capital jurisdiction, and another used it sparingly. Under the Antonines the prefect tried persons of all classes and sentenced capitally. But Marcus reprimanded one prefect for failing to exercise *clementia*. Septimius Severus formally defined the prefect's jurisdiction, empowering him to try all crimes committed in, or within 100 miles of, Rome. He could sentence up to deportation but not, it seems, to death. As for the praetorian prefect, his first contact with adjudication was through condemnations by acclamation by the cohorts. Starting with Claudius, this was still happening under Alexander. Under Trajan he exercised a function somewhere between gathering evidence and adjudicating. His participation in trials of senators created problems under both Hadrian and Marcus, but it is likely that the exclusion of *equites* from such trials did not apply to the praetorian prefect. In the Severan period the *lex Fabia* placed the prefect's jurisdiction on a firm basis, parallel in every essential respect to that of the urban prefect. By the same period the portfolios of both prefects included crimes not falling under any of the public criminal laws.

10

THE GROWTH OF CRIMINAL JURISPRUDENCE: *DE IUDICIIS PUBLICIS*

THE FOOTHILLS OF PUNITIVE THEORY

As already observed, the criminal law was the poor relation of Roman jurisprudence. It did not inspire the quintessence of Roman interpretation, *responsa prudentium*, until well into the Principate.[1] But even in the Republic interpretation was practised in other ways, notably in laws which focused on the intention with which an act was done. This made interpretation a necessary adjunct. For example, when the *lex Cornelia de sicariis* penalized the cut-throat 'who walked around with a weapon (*telum*) for the purpose of killing someone or committing theft', interpretation was needed to establish the particular intent, and also to define a *telum*.[2]

But the penalty under the *lex Cornelia* did not call for much interpretation. When that law formalized *aquae et ignis interdictio* there was no doubt some uncertainty before it became clear that it was now obligatory on the magistrate to allow the offender time to escape into exile. But once that was settled the *poena legis* was a stable frame of reference – so much so that it was incorporated in Pompey's law of *parricidium* in its own (Cornelian) name.

There were however one or two Republican statutes that did call for ongoing assessment. The classic cases are Caesar's *repetundae* law and the right to kill under Augustus' adultery law. Thus when C. Silanus was charged with aggravated *repetundae* in 22 AD, the accuser cited three Republican cases that had involved cruelty (TA 3.66.1–3). The senate was reminded, too, of what it had decreed against Volesus Messala in Augustus' reign (*ib.* 3.68.1). There was a degree of continuity, of the gradual accumulation of a set of principles. But there is no trace of any systematic commentary.[3] The most that we can point to is antiquarian works, and rhetorical works like *Ad Herennium* by an unknown author and Cicero's *De inventione*, which are to a large extent collections of cases that Late Republican orators consulted for use in court. Interpretation, including quasi-philosophical ideas of punishment, is prominent.[4]

THE '*DE IUDICIIS PUBLICIS*' GENRE

Prior to the second century AD we know of only one work in this genre, the *De iudiciis publicis* of Ateius Capito who founded the Sabinian law school.[5] Although the two extant fragments deal with *iudicia populi* rather than with *iudicia publica*, they were of some relevance to Augustus' criminal justice.[6] But the genre proper does not emerge until the second century, when it was given shape and substance by two Antonine jurists, L. Volusius Maecianus and Venuleius Saturninus.[7] Maecian compiled a *De iudiciis publicis* in fourteen books, a quantitative highwater mark for the genre. Venuleius wrote three books under the same title; that he also wrote on penalties under the title *De poenis paganorum* is unlikely.[8]

Of the four extant fragments of Maecian's work, the most important is that in which he discusses the *senatus consultum* exempting slaves under age from the penalties of the *s.c. Silanianum*. Maecian notes with approval the judgment of the legate Trebius Germanus, who overrode the exemption and sentenced an *impubes servus* to the supreme penalty.[9] The jurist gives the rationale for that decision. The boy was not far off puberty, he was sleeping at the foot of his master's bed, and he did not raise the alarm. He could not have prevented the crime, but he could have raised the alarm afterwards. The senate had intended to spare *impuberes* who had merely been under the same roof. But no special consideration should be shown to one who had assisted the murderer and was of an age which, although below puberty, gave him the capacity to understand what was happening (*D.* 29.5.14).

Maecian was building on Hadrian's ruling regarding an *ancilla* who had failed to raise the alarm (*D.* 29.5.1.28). The jurist interprets the exemption of *impuberes* restrictively, putting them in the same position as the (adult) *ancilla* if they are old enough to understand. The reasoning is a corollary to the thinking which led Marcus to absolve on the grounds of defective mental capacity resulting from minority or insanity.[10] But although the Antonines took as progressive a view of the criminal responsibility of *impuberes* as Seneca had done, it should not be supposed that Maecian's interpretation went against the trend. The dangers to be feared from slaves modified Antonine *humanitas*. The ultimate arbiter was *utilitas publica*, as it had been ever since the Pedanius Secundus case.

Maecian's other important ruling is to the effect that the *poena parricidii* should be inflicted on accomplices (*D.* 48.9.6). But this does not offend against the humanitarian climate of the day, for Maecian is referring to interdiction under Pompey's law, not to the sack. Antoninus Pius did not even use the *poena cullei* against the confessed parricide. A senator who confessed was merely marooned on a desert island, and the emperor added that he was only going as far as that because it was against the law of nature to let such a person live in comfort (*SHA Pius* 8.10). As one of the most influential lawyers of the day,[11] Maecian could have been the author of the carefully formulated sentence. Indeed he may also be behind Marcus' exoneration of a parricide on the grounds of insanity.[12]

Maecian's contemporary, Venuleius Saturninus, only needed three books for his treatise, compared with Maecian's fourteen. This may have been due to a difference in readership, for it has been suggested by Fanizza that Maecian wrote for the specialist, Venuleius for practitioners and students.[13] Two of the Venuleius fragments[14] are of special interest. In one he says that although charges of opening a murdered person's will prior to the interrogation of the slaves[15] are prescribed after five years, that time-limit is waived by the *senatus consultum* of 11 AD in respect of those who are liable to the *parricidii poena* (*D.* 29.5.13). Again the penalty can only be interdiction; Augustus' senate of 11 AD is an unlikely vehicle for the entrenchment of the sack.

In another fragment Venuleius discusses the right of accusation (*D.* 48.2.12). He says that as a general rule slaves can be charged under the public criminal laws in the same way as free persons, except under the *lex Julia de vi privata* whose penalty of one-third confiscation cannot apply to a slave. He infers a similar exception for other *leges* which lay down pecuniary penalties, or even capital penalties that are not appropriate for slaves, such as exile.

Another line of reasoning is used for the *lex Pompeia parricidii*. Venuleius says that its first chapter, covering those who kill parents, blood relatives or patrons, does not apply to slaves. But, he adds, a similar punishment can be inflicted on them by analogy (*D.* 48.2.12.4). At first sight this is awkward. As the *lex Pompeia* is expressly cited, the penalty for non-confessed parricides is interdiction. But in effect that means exile, and he has already told us that exile is not appropriate for slaves. We might suspect an interpolation by Justinian's compilers in the light of Constantine's reintroduction of the *poena cullei* (*CTh* 9.15.1). But it is more likely that since the slave is, in any event, brought in under cognitionary discretion, he can be punished more harshly. First you draw an analogy and then you embellish it. Indeed that is precisely what Venuleius does in another case. He says, apropos of the *lex Cornelia iniuriarum*, that Sulla himself laid down that a slave could not be a defendant under that law; but, adds the jurist, he faces a harsher penalty *extra ordinem* (*D*. 48.2.12.4).

Whatever the arrangement of their material by Maecian and Venuleius,[16] they initiated a genre of commentaries on the public criminal laws. The main thrust came in the Severan period. Three works entitled *De iudiciis publicis* are known, namely two books each by Aemilius Macer and Aelius Marcianus, and a single book by Iulius Paulus.[17] The theme was also covered in sections of more general works,[18] the most important of which was the last four books of Ulpian's *De officio proconsulis*.[19] Ulpian also wrote a monograph on the *lex Julia de adulteriis* in five books. It covered the one public criminal law that had not been dealt with in the guide to governors. There was a reason for its appearance four years after the latter.[20] The jury-court for adultery was the only *quaestio perpetua* still operating, but it was very near the end of the road. It would cease to function in the early years of Alexander's reign. Ulpian, knowing that the change was imminent, compiled a manual to fuel the anticipated flood of rescripts to officials that would be needed when adultery was subsumed under *cognitio*.[21]

The adultery law was the only criminal *lex* to which special monographs were devoted. Papinian is credited with one work in two books and another in one. The third major Severan jurist, Paul, is credited with one work in three books and another in one.[22] Commentaries on the criminal law were continued in the early post-classical period, when they formed an important part of the compendium known as *Pauli Sententiae*.[23] But the genre was neglected by one jurist who might have been expected to deal with it, namely Gaius. There is nothing on the criminal law in the works that he compiled in the high noon of the Antonine period. The omission is most striking in the case of his *Institutes*; Justinian's *Institutes*, which was largely based on Gaius, ends with a title *De Publicis Iudiciis* (4.18). Both are students' manuals, and if Justinian's students needed instruction in the criminal law it is not clear why their Antonine predecessors did not. But Gaius was consistent, for he avoided the criminal law almost completely in his other writings.[24] One might have expected his *Commentary on the Provincial Edict* to have foreshadowed the guidance on criminal jurisdiction that the *De officio proconsulis* genre would soon be offering governors,[25] but the fragments include only one (oblique) criminal notice.[26]

MOTIVATION AND IDEOLOGY

What prompted the sudden upsurge of interest in the criminal law in the Antonine period? The question can no doubt be approached through general evaluations of how the jurists thought in the second century,[27] but something more specific is needed. The best attempt so far made to provide it is that recently undertaken by Fanizza.[28] The thrust of her argument is that Maecian and Venuleius set out to mould Augustus' criminal legislation[29] into a harmonious system capable of regulating criminal repression right across the board. Although still anchored in the jury-courts, they also took account of the fragmentary, and still fluid, *cognitio extra ordinem*. But the *leges* remained the frame of reference for the latter as much as for the *quaestiones*. In the wake of Hadrian's reforms the problem for the jurists was to reconcile the statutory rules with the regulations evolved by *cognitio*. The jurists were motivated by the ideology of Antoninus Pius' reign. That ideology included familiarity with the advanced cultural levels of the day; specialized expertise; and recognition of the distinctions between *honestiores* and *humiliores* that were starting to be entrenched in the system.

One part of Fanizza's thesis can be accepted right away. The *leges* continued to supply the frame of reference, and the link was more than nominal. At the turn of the third century, for example, *Pauli Sententiae* quoted numerous definitions of crimes taken verbatim from *leges*.[30] The same work shows, perhaps more coherently than any other source, just how interpretation had produced changes in scope and emphasis.[31] Sometimes it does more. It tells us, for example, that if someone is killed by a branch that was thrown down without a warning, the culprit is sent to the mines *etsi in legem non incurrit*, 'even though it does not fall under the *lex (de sicariis)*'.[32] The basis of liability is thus negligence. But it is not a *crimen extraordinarium* as such; *Sententiae* locates it under the rubric *Ad legem Corneliam de sicariis et veneficis*. On the other hand, it is not an extension of anything in the *lex de sicariis*. The basis of that statute was doing something with a specific intent – walking around with a weapon etc. – and if, as here, it was done negligently it cannot be interpreted into the *lex*. But it is close enough to the end result of the *lex*, causing death, to be loosely associated with it.

Now, the example that we have just cited comes from an early post-classical work, when the task of harmonizing the old and the new had (presumably) been completed. It does not follow that the same degree of harmonization had been achieved by the Antonines. Fanizza

119

is, I think, aware of this, for in her final chapter she narrows down her hypothesis: it was the Severan jurists rather than the Antonines who moulded *cognitio* into an harmonious juristic whole.[33] The modification is a wise one. The extant fragments do not have Maecian or Venuleius saying anything about the cognitionary process; even their citations of legislation lean heavily towards *leges* and *senatus consulta* rather than constitutions, and deal with matters that are equally applicable to jury-courts.[34] It is not until the Severans that the balance tilts at all significantly towards *cognitio*, with numerous citations of constitutions.[35] But having said that, we must immediately qualify it by noting a curious feature. It is shown, for example, by Marcian, who wrote on the criminal law both in his *De iudiciis publicis* and in his *Institutiones*. When Marcian is discussing the public criminal laws he says nothing at all about *cognitio*, although the urban prefect, to mention only one cognitionary jurisdiction, was judging extensively under all the *leges*. It is only when he comes to *crimina extraordinaria*, which have no roots in the *leges*, that he talks about cognitionary jurisdictions, naming prefects, governors and others.[36]

Another surprising fact is that in the whole of the *De iudiciis publicis* genre there is only one reference to the emperor's personal *cognitio*. It occurs in Paul's monograph, where notice is taken of the trial of one of the Cassian conspirators, in the course of which Marcus ruled that suicide did not protect the property where the charge was *maiestas*.[37] Paul is known to have compiled embryonic law reports in which he recorded decisions of the emperor and his *consilium*,[38] but whether that accounts for his unique *De iudiciis publicis* citation is a moot point.[39]

Perhaps the most striking example of this sort of thing is supplied by Ulpian. Discussing the homicide law in his *De officio proconsulis*, he remarks as follows:

> The ... *lex Cornelia de sicariis* lays down that the praetor ... to whom the lot has assigned the *quaestio de sicariis* for acts committed in Rome or within a mile of the city shall, with the jurors allocated to him under the *lex*, conduct a capital investigation into anyone who has walked around with a weapon etc.
>
> (*Coll.* 1.3.1)

Provincial governors, for whose guidance this information was supplied, would certainly have been interested in the 'walking around' part. They were also interested in the statutory penalty of interdiction which Ulpian noted in the same discussion of the *lex Cornelia*.[40] But were they interested in the praetor and the jury? It is possible that provincial governors sat with juries; Augustus' Cyrene Edicts are said to reflect a general practice.[41] But this creates an anomaly. It partly removes the governor from the list of those who judge *extra ordinem*. Insofar as that expression denotes a different procedure, the governor does not use the new, streamlined procedure when he sits with a jury.[42] As for discretionary punishment, his mandate may authorize that for cases where he sits alone, but not where he merely announces and registers the verdict of a jury.[43] The only time that the governor can truly be said to be operating *extra ordinem* is when he judges extraordinary crimes – that is, when he enters the area for which Marcian does discuss cognitionary jurisdictions. But how his change of hats was carried out in practice remains a mystery.[44]

It seems, then, that harmonization by the Severans was not nearly as all-embracing as Fanizza thinks. Yet *Pauli Sententiae* may measure up to what is required. In particular, a large part of Book V is almost a mini-*De iudiciis publicis*.[45] This raises an even more difficult question, namely the ultimate source of that work. If the work as we have it is substantially something that was written by the Severan jurist, Iulius Paulus, then fully-fledged harmonization was in place in the Severan period after all, despite the contrary indications in Marcian and Ulpian. But the authorship and provenance of *Sententiae* are uncertain. The current view is that Paul may or may not have written a work for the instruction of his son under the title of *Pauli Sententiae Ad Filium*, but in any event the work as we have it is not that original. It is thought to have been put together in *c.* 300, some sixty or seventy years after Paul's death, and to have drawn heavily, though not exclusively, from Paul's writings. The extant material is believed to represent only a small part, something like one-sixth, of the original compilation.[46]

That *Sententiae* was important in late antiquity cannot be doubted. But its credentials as a genuine work of the Severan jurist were called in question very shortly after the (presumptive) date of its publication. In 327–8 Constantine confirmed all Paul's writings and specially laid down that there was not the least doubt about *Sententiae*, which was to be valid when cited in court (*CTh* 1.4.2). The validation was repeated in the well-known *Law of Citations* in 426 (*CTh* 1.4.3.5).

We may wonder why controversy should have blown up so quickly. Would Constantine's decree not be more meaningful if it related to a work written something like a hundred years earlier? We may also wonder why the author borrowed Paul's name, although that is less of a problem. Sailing under false colours had been a recognized practice ever since the Late Republic.[47] Plagiarism was only penalized when it took the form of kidnapping. But it is not our purpose to enter the fray in respect of such questions. There is, however, one point that must be made. If, as we have suggested, *Sententiae* displays in full measure the harmonizing facility that Fanizza wants, is it reasonable to suppose that this was achieved for the first time at the turn of the third century? At the very least the author must have found substantial indications of a similar facility in the writings of the Severan jurists. In particular, the criminal sections of Book 5 must have been organized on a Severan pattern.

The aforementioned observations support Fanizza's thesis, but before reaching a final conclusion we should look at one of the passages that Fanizza considers of special importance. After stating the proposition that 'a system that links *crimina* of statutory and non-statutory derivation is able, while preserving diverse terminology, to iron out the tension between legislative regulation and coercive practice',[48] Fanizza cites a passage from Macer's *De officio praesidis* (= *proconsulis*):

> In regard to the status of the condemned, it makes no difference whether it was a *iudicium publicum* or not; for it is only the sentence (*sententia*), not the kind of charge (*genus criminis*), that is looked at. Therefore those sentenced to execution (*animadverti*) or to the beasts (*ad bestias*) become slaves of the penalty (*servi poenae*) immediately.
>
> (*D*. 48.19.12)

The passage tells us even more than Fanizza realizes. It hints at a perspective of a very distinctive kind: execution (*animadverti*) is the penalty resulting from condemnation under a *lex*, whereas *ad bestias* is extra-legal. In other words, the various alternatives to interdiction and 'straight' execution were not seen as *extensions* of the *poena legis*. They were extraneous to it. The point is illustrated by a passage in Gaius:

> Those who are sentenced to the supreme penalty immediately lose both their citizenship and their freedom. This fate therefore precedes their death, and sometimes by a long interval, as happens in the case of those who are condemned to the beasts.
>
> (*D*. 48.19.29)

Gaius' point is that the condemned would not face the beasts immediately. It depended on the Games producer's schedule.[49] But from the private-law point of view it was important to know exactly when the condemned suffered testamentary and proprietary incapacity. When, in other words, did they become *servi poenae*?[50] Macer (above) takes it a stage further. While still recognizing the theoretical distinction between statutory and cognitionary process, he finds a common yardstick in the sentence. This is the ironing-out technique. In earlier times the penalty might have determined the procedure,[51] and later on the *lex* determined the penalty. But now there is a simple formula: *ubi iniuria ibi poena*, there is a wrongful act, therefore there is a penalty.

One might object that elsewhere, in his *De iudiciis publicis*, Macer stresses the continued importance of the kind of charge, the *genus criminis*, 'Not all processes in which charges are canvassed are *iudicia publica*, but only those which arise from the public criminal laws, such as *Julia maiestatis*, etc.' (*D.* 48.1.1). But this simply underlines what we already know. The ironing-out process was still not complete, and probably never would be. That is why we can give only qualified assent to Fanizza's thesis. Whatever purposes the *De iudiciis publicis* genre was intended to serve, a systematic synthesis was not one of them. Nor would it ever be on the Roman scene. The masters of casuistry would remain true to their origins to the end.

CONCLUSION

Systematic commentaries on the public criminal laws originated in the Principate. After a dubious model by Ateius Capito, the genre proper was initiated by two Antonine jurists, Maecian and Venuleius. Despite appearances, neither of them went against the *humanitas*-motivated climate of the day. The main thrust of the genre came in the Severan period. The genre was prompted by the perception of a need to iron out conflicts between the jury system and the *cognitio extra ordinem*. But on the evidence the jurists achieved that purpose more successfully with extraordinary crimes than with those falling under the public criminal laws. The place of *Pauli Sententiae* in the rationalizing process is also considered.

11

THE GROWTH OF CRIMINAL JURISPRUDENCE: *DE POENIS*

THE *'DE POENIS'* GENRE

Although not as clearly defined as *De iudiciis publicis*, a genre devoted specifically to punishment did exist. But its nomenclature was not stable. The only straightforward title is the *De poenis* in four books of Ulpian's pupil, Herennius Modestinus, who flourished over the first half of the third century.[1] The Severan jurist, Iulius Paulus, also worked in the genre. He is credited with four monographs.[2] Finally, the word *poena* appears in the title of Claudius Saturninus' monograph on civilian penalties, *De poenis paganorum*. The Florentine Index to the *Digest* credits the work to Venuleius Saturninus. The accreditation is suspect, and perhaps with good reason; Venuleius may be too early an arrival on the criminal scene to have produced a specialized work.[3] But the play's the thing; the long fragment in the *Digest* (48.10.16) is a miniature essay on the categories of punishment.

The genre is rounded off by material in works not specifically devoted to punishment. Ulpian *De officio proconsulis* and Callistratus *De cognitionibus* are prominent. In the early post-classical period *Pauli Sententiae* is our principal source for punitive differentials based on class. Finally, the compilers put together a substantial *Digest* title *De poenis*, as well as a rubric in the *Institutes*.

DIFFERENTIAL PUNISHMENTS: TERMINOLOGY

Different capital punishments according to status were securely in place by the Severan period, and are visible enough over the preceding decades of the second century. It was not just a question of savage penalties. *Saevitia* was as old as Rome, and in the Early Principate it began attracting official support. But at that time it was socially indiscriminate; it was

124

not always aimed at a particular class. Caligula threw a Roman knight to the beasts and sentenced many of honourable status (*honesti ordinis*) to be branded, sent to the mines, thrown to the beasts or otherwise cruelly handled (SG 27.3). But the same thing happened to the lower orders; the plebeian writer of an Atellan farce was burnt alive in the arena (*ib.* 27.4). Domitian may have been more selective. The spectator who accused the emperor of bias and was either thrown to the beasts or burnt alive[4] was a plebeian. It is possible that those whom Claudius sentenced *ad bestias* for serious crimes (SC 14) were restricted to the lower orders, but we cannot be sure. To some extent it depends on whether 'those convicted *in maiore fraude*' means only common-law criminals or includes political offenders. Be that as it may, the overall picture is of a developing phenomenon that had not yet crystallized out as social differentiation.

The second and early third centuries are our principal target. The treatment will not be exhaustive; it would be otiose to repeat what has already been better said by others.[5] It is proposed to concentrate on some features which illustrate salient aspects of penal differentiation, starting with the question of terminology. The pattern is supplied by *Pauli Sententiae*:

> Anyone who knowingly and with wrongful intent forges . . . a will is liable under the *lex Cornelia testamentaria*. *Honestiores* are deported to an island, *humiliores* are either sent to the mines or crucified.
>
> (*PS* 5.25.1)

> The *lex Cornelia* (*de sicariis*) imposes a penalty of deportation on anyone who kills someone or walks about with a weapon etc. It is laid down (*placuit*) that in the case of *honestiores* such acts are punished by a capital penalty (*poena capitis*), but *humiliores* are either crucified or thrown to the beasts.
>
> (5.23.1)

> Under the *lex Julia maiestatis* anyone at whose instigation arms were taken up against the emperor or the state . . . used to be interdicted from water and fire. But now *humiliores* are thrown to the beasts or burnt alive, *honestiores* are punished capitally.
>
> (5.29.1)

These passages immediately raise the question of terminology. Do the consistent '*honestiores*' and '*humiliores*' of *Sententiae* reflect the usage of the Severan jurists? The passages also raise another question. Does the clear distinction between the penalties respectively prescribed for *honestiores* and *humiliores* reflect the reality of the second and early third centuries?

The short answer is that there is only a partial fit at best. The following passages from the works of Severan writers illustrate this:

The penalty (under the *lex Cornelia testamentaria*) for forgery of a will . . . is deportation and total confiscation. If the offender is a slave he suffers the supreme penalty, *ultimum supplicium*.
(Marcian *Institutes* 14 = *D.* 48.10.1.13)

Anyone who steals . . . a will or . . . writes a false will is condemned to the penalty of the *lex Cornelia*.
(Paul *Ad Sabinum* 3 = *D.* 48.10.1.2. Cf. Paul *Responsa* 3 = *D.* 48.10.16.1; Ulpian *De officio proconsulis* 8 = *D.* 48.10.9.3)

If anyone uses forged constitutions without authority he is interdicted from water and fire under the *lex Cornelia* (*testamentaria*).
(Modestinus *De poenis* 3 = *D.* 48.10.33)

There is no differential based on class here, except for slaves. And even for the latter the penalty is simply death without any lurid details. All these texts could have been written by Cicero, for it seems that for this particular crime the Severans – including Paul himself and Modestinus, who was closest in time to *Sententiae* – kept unequivocally to the *poena legis* for all free persons. Thus the offence with the longest history of adjudication *extra ordinem*[6] retained its punitive integrity until displaced by *Sententiae*. But for other crimes the Severans knew of differential penalties and adapted their terminology accordingly. For example:

The penalty under the *lex Cornelia de sicariis* is deportation to an island and total confiscation. But capital punishment (*capite puniri*) is usual these days, except for those whose status is too high to sustain the statutory penalty (*nisi honestiore loco positi fuerint, ut poenam legis sustineant*). *Humiliores* are usually (either crucified) or thrown to the beasts, *altiores* are deported to an island.
(Marcian *Institutiones* 14 = *D.* 48.8.3.5)

Although not entirely lucid,[7] the passage displays awareness of both a class differential and (almost) of *Sententiae*'s terminology. The *humiliores* are there and so, with some modification, are the *honestiores*.

But sometimes both social groups are given different labels from those of *Sententiae*:

> The *lex Cornelia* (*de sicariis*) lays down that arsonists be inter-
> dicted from water and fire, but currently they are punished
> differently. Those who raise fires in urban areas are, if of the
> lowest/a lower status (*humillimo/humiliore loco*), usually thrown
> to the beasts. If they are of some standing (*in aliquo gradu*) and do
> it at Rome, they are punished capitally, or are at least sentenced to
> deportation.[8]

Differences in terminology are even more pronounced in imperial
constitutions. Our first example – it may in fact be the first formal
enforcement of differentiation – is a rescript of Hadrian. Significantly,[9]
the regime did not at first interfere with the public criminal laws. It
directed its attention to a *crimen extraordinarium*, namely moving
boundary-stones.[10]

> This is a serious crime, but the penalty should be determined
> according to the status of the offender and his intention. If those
> convicted are of high status (*splendidiores*) they have undoubtedly
> done it in order to encroach on another's land and can be
> relegated for a time according to their age. . . . But if others (*alii*)
> have done it as a service (*ministerium*) they are to be beaten and
> sentenced to two or three years' hard labour (*ad opus*). But if they
> appropriated the stones in ignorance or by accident it suffices to
> beat them.
>
> (Ulpian *De off. proc.* 8 = *Coll.* 13.3.1–2 =
> Callistratus *De cog.* 3 = *D.* 47.21.2)

Hadrian thus defines the upper echelons specifically, as *splendidiores*,
and saddles them with a presumption of wrongful intent. But he simply
lumps everyone else together under the amorphous *alii*.[11] The latter are
not defined as a social class at all. They are simply non-*splendidiores*
who have acted on behalf of a *splendidior*.[12] But by the time of *Sententiae*
the threads had been gathered together; for moving boundary stones
slaves were condemned to the mines, *humiliores* to hard labour (*in opus
publicum*), *honestiores* to relegation with one-third confiscation or to full
deportation.[13]

Although Hadrian only used a specific word for upper-class offenders,
specific words for both classes soon appeared. In the earliest known case
under a public criminal law Antoninus Pius ruled that a man who killed
his wife whom he caught in adultery was, if *honestior*, to be relegated to

an island, and if of low rank (*humilis loci*) to be given hard labour for life (*D.* 48.5.39.8). But the terminology is not stable. Ulpian speaks, apropos of a rescript of Marcus, of those of plebeian status and those of superior status – *in plebeio, in honestiore* (*D.* 47.18.1.2). There is, however, some reason to believe that the greater precision reserved for the upper classes by Hadrian continued to influence the terminology. Callistratus says that not every free person is beaten with rods, but only those of the lower orders (*tenuiores homines*); imperial rescripts lay down that *honestiores* should not be beaten (*D.* 48.19.28.2). One wonders whether the emperors (and the jurists) were mainly interested in finding a consistent label for the upper bracket. Having got that, *alii* or an equivalent sufficed for the rest.

Sententiae has a substantial lead over the classical jurists in the use of consistent labels for both *honestiores* and *humiliores*.[14] But even *Sententiae* does not always adopt a one-word label. In its discussion of the delict of *iniuria* it says, apropos of aggravated injury (*iniuria atrox*), that when it is assessed[15] according to status (*persona*) two questions arise: Was the injured party a senator, Roman knight, decurion or otherwise of established prestige (*alias spectatae auctoritatis*)? And was the injury done by a plebeian or person of humble birth (*plebeius vel humili loco natus*)? *Sententiae* was here influenced by Gaius, who has *atrox iniuria* assessed 'according to . . . *persona*, for example if a magistrate suffers injury, or injury is done to a senator by a lowly person (*ab humili persona*)' (Gai. 3.225). But despite the similarity, *Sententiae* goes into greater detail than Gaius. Ultimately that is a reflection of Paul. His monograph on *iniuria* was much more detailed than Gaius' treatment of the topic.[16] This may suggest that when *Sententiae* does not use labels it is because Paul did not do so – and conversely. But the possibility cannot be pressed.

Sententiae does not attest punishment according to status for all the public criminal laws. It does so for temple theft, homicide, public violence, forgery, treason and kidnapping,[17] but not for *parricidium*,[18] theft of state funds, *repetundae* or electoral corruption.[19] At the sub-capital level there is no differential for adultery.[20] All this is something of a guarantee of veracity. The author was not looking for a differential at all costs. It may perhaps be suggested that the numerical discrepancy between *Sententiae* and the classical jurists[21] was not as great as might appear. Perhaps only a small fraction of the jurists' uses has come down to us. With the exception of Paul, they were denied the advantage of special validation by Constantine.[22] Justinian's compilers often saved themselves trouble by consulting *Sententiae* instead of combing through the classical works.[23]

DIFFERENTIAL PUNISHMENTS:
CUT-OFF POINTS AND STATUS SYMBOLS

How far down the social (and punitive) ladder did the *honestiores* go? They are usually taken to comprise senators, knights, the municipal aristocracy known as decurions, and military veterans.[24] But what has not been suggested before is that the status of the last two was determined by their position vis-a-vis punishment. Exemption from the harsher penalties virtually acted as a certificate of status. Even if you were never brought up on a criminal charge, it was nice to know that you would be amongst the privileged if you were.

The decurions need special attention. Their upward mobility was fostered by imperial intervention, not by jurists' interpretations. The earliest known decree emanated from Hadrian:

> The deified Hadrian forbade the capital punishment of those who were classed as decurions, except where a parent had been killed. Indeed it is very fully laid down in mandates (to prefects, governors) that they are to suffer the penalty of the *lex Cornelia* (*de sicariis*).
>
> (Venuleius *De off. proc.* 1 = *D.* 48.19.15)

Although confined to the homicide law, this marks the start of a broad extension of *honestior* status to decurions.[25] It was taken further by Marcus and Verus, who ruled that a decurion by the name of Priscus who had confessed to homicide and arson be deported to an island. The rescript went on to lay down, as a general rule, that decurions of *civitates* should be deported or relegated for capital crimes.[26] But they still faced execution for *parricidium*. Hadrian's exclusion of that crime from the privilege does not appear to have been repealed. When Pius merely marooned a confessed parricide on a desert island he did so pursuant to his promise not to execute any senator (*SHA Pius* 8.10). There was no similar promise to decurions. When Ulpian says that decurions cannot be sentenced to the mines or hard labour, nor can they be crucified or burnt alive (*D.* 48.19.9.11), he does not mean that they cannot be put to death (by 'regular' means) for *parricidium*.[27]

Decurial privileges were extended to the families of decurions. Marcus' exemption of the descendants of 'persons of the greatest eminence' from plebeian penalties and tortures became, by the Severan period, a general exemption of the parents and children of decurions, including children born before the father achieved decurial rank.[28] But because the changes were casuistic, avoiding, as always, comprehensive systematization,[29] there were problems. Judges sometimes inflicted sentences in excess of the permissible limits, and both the emperors and the jurists found it necessary to reinforce decurial rights. Ulpian says that where a decurion has been given a sentence that should not have been imposed on him, he must be set free; the procedure for doing this had been laid down by Marcus and Verus.[30] And Caracalla had to remind the senate that a decurion could not be sentenced to hard labour (*CJ* 9.47.3).

A puzzling factor is introduced into the equation by Modestinus:

> Those who commit murder with malice aforethought are usually deported if they hold office (*in honore aliquo positi*). If they are of the second grade (*secundo gradu*) they are punished capitally. This can happen more easily to decurions, though only if the emperor is first consulted and orders it – except perhaps where a riot cannot be otherwise controlled.
>
> (Modestinus *De poenis* 3 = D. 48.8.16)

What is 'the second grade' with which decurions are associated in some way? It cannot simply mean *humiliores*. Having laboriously detached them from that category, we can hardly be asked to thrust them back into it. Mommsen thought there was a second grade within the *honestiores*. He took it to be the *equites Romani*, because in the fourth century they held the rank of the second class (*secundi gradus dignitatis*); they were an intermediate group between office-holders and decurions.[31] Apart from some uncertain support from Cardascia, this eminently sound suggestion has been ignored.[32] But in fact it promises to open a new window on differential punishment.

One or two avenues will serve to illustrate how grades operated within the system of punitive privilege. The first is the military sector, starting with military veterans, who are usually seen as the lowest rung of the *honestiores* ladder. The jurist Arrius Menander, writing in Caracalla's reign at the height of the first Severan dynasty's cultivation of a military power-base, expressed himself as follows, 'The privileges of veterans include the prerogative that even in crimes they are distinguished from others in point of penalties. Thus a veteran is neither thrown to the beasts nor beaten with rods' (Menander *De re militari* 3 = D. 49.18.1). Menander's younger contemporary, Marcian, extended the privilege to the children of veterans,[33] and the position was a stable one – more so, perhaps, than that of the decurions. But there was a complication of a different kind, in the shape of the serving soldier.

There is no statement by a jurist specifically equating the serving soldier with the decurions, as was done in the case of veterans,[34] but there are some partial differentials, and these point the way to a broadening of our perception of differential punishment. Menander says that the serving soldier's crimes are divided into military infractions and civil offences, 'Soldiers' crimes are either peculiar to them or common to everyone. Hence their prosecution is either peculiar or common' (Menander *De re militari* 1 = *D.* 49.16.2 pr.). This should be read with Modestinus, who lists the military offences and adds a privilege, 'Soldiers' punishments include castigation, fines, fatigues (*munerum indictio*), transfer, reduction in rank, dishonourable discharge. For they are not to be sent to the mines or tortured'(Modestinus *De poenis* 4 = *D.* 49.16.3.1). The exclusion of the mines and torture (the latter here counting as a definitive punishment)[35] is not only noticed as a check on the powers of military commanders. It is a general privilege available to soldiers, which needed to be reaffirmed because commanders had disregarded it shortly before Modestinus wrote. One of the culprits had been the historian Cassius Dio during his command in Pannonia. Events had forced Alexander to abandon the relaxation of military discipline favoured by the first Severan dynasty, and Dio had carried out the new policy, the reversion to *disciplina Augusti*. The praetorian cohorts had tried to persuade Ulpian, as their prefect, to charge Dio in what would virtually have been a test case on the status of serving soldiers. But Ulpian had refused. And for that the praetorians had condemned him and forced the emperor to ratify their verdict.[36]

Ulpian's cohorts certainly needed clarification of their rights, for even the first Severan period had known inconsistencies. For example, Modestinus says that for quitting the ranks the penalty is to be beaten with rods or transferred to an inferior unit (*D.* 49.16.3.16). It has been claimed that this sets soldiers on a low level, because Callistratus writes that only free men of the lower classes (*tenuiores*) are beaten with rods.[37] But Modestinus is talking about punishments for a military infraction, and he has already listed beating (*castigatio*) as one of the military penalties. This simply illustrates the patchy nature of the soldiers' privileges. The mines and torture might be excluded, but there was no general formulation.

Soldiers were eligible for other privileges. For example, a soldier sentenced to death was allowed to transmit his property to his heirs, either by will or intestacy, provided that he had been convicted of a military crime, not a civil one (*D.* 38.12.1). On the other hand he was sometimes at a disadvantage, being punished for offences for which a civilian would receive a lighter sentence, or even no punishment at all. Menander cites cases where soldiers incurred the death penalty for appearing on the stage or allowing themselves to be sold into slavery (*D.* 48.19.14). Harsh treatment of the servile sale is understandable; it renders the culprit ineligible for service. Perhaps even the penalty for acting makes sense; by sinking to the lowest depths the soldier had dishonoured his profession. But somehow all this reminds us of Macrinus' soldiers and the serving-maid.[38]

The soldier was not the only occupant of the grey area between *honestiores* and *humiliores*. It was in fact a fairly broad terrain. There is an example in Ulpian's discussion of speculation in grain by *dardanarii*. Ulpian says that if they are *negotiantes*, businessmen, they either lose their licences or suffer interdiction or relegation, but if *humiliores* they face hard labour (*D.* 47.11.6 pr.). We have a sub-category here. *Negotiantes* were not *honestiores* as such, but if they engaged in the grain trade they enjoyed some privileges. Their most likely crime was price-fixing or speculation in grain, and it is a fair guess that it was only such offences that earned them the *honestior* penalty. Consideration was also shown to burglars, thieves and cattle-rustlers, but the test was not the same as in the case of grain-dealers. If a burglar or rustler was treated leniently it was because he happened to be an *honestior* anyway, not because he carried on a particular business.[39] People were encouraged to become *negotiantes* in the vital grain industry, but incentives to burglars or rustlers were rare.

Callistratus frames something of a general proposition on the concession of the ornaments of decurial status to non-decurions:

> Generally speaking, all those whom it is not permissible to beat with rods should be shown the same respect for their rank as decurions are shown. It is inconsistent to say that anyone exempted from the rods by imperial rescripts can be sent to the mines.
>
> (*D.* 48.19.28.5)

The rescripts in question had exempted '*honestiores* but not *tenuiores*' from the rods (*ib.* 48.19.28.2). But under Callistratus' general formulation it was not a matter of terminology but of one penal privilege begetting another. If the emperor said that you could not be beaten, the jurist was entitled to say that you could not be sent to the mines.

THE LOWER CUT-OFF POINT:
HUMILIORES AND SLAVES

Broadly stated, the *humiliores* comprised every free citizen who neither possessed *honestior* status nor enjoyed any of its privileges.[40] But there is an immediate complication, in the shape of the slaves. In the Republic the distinction between free and unfree had been adequately maintained; the free citizen who broke the law was tried, but the slave was coerced.[41] But as the Principate went forward the slaves and the humble free tended to coalesce,[42] and the question is what effect this had on crime and punishment. Was there *isonomia*, equalization of penalties, between *humiliores* and slaves?

One ought to be able to return a positive answer to the question. It should be possible to say that when Augustus created the urban prefecture to discipline both slaves and unruly citizens,[43] he started a process that would inevitably lead to equalization. The prefect imposed the same coercive punishments on both segments of his clientele. And when he did exchange *coercitio* for *iudicatio*, he was free of the shackles of the *poena legis* and could continue imposing a common set of punishments. And among those punishments we should be able to identify penalties of servile origin which over time came to be imposed on the humble free as well.[44] We should be able, finally, to argue that although Caracalla's conferment of citizenship on nearly all the free inhabitants of the empire excluded slaves, that was of little consequence once citizenship had ceased to be the determinant of penal status.[45] But although all this fits together quite nicely, hard evidence is not very thick on the ground. Mommsen was firmly of the opinion that even in the Principate the basic penal distinction was between free and slaves,[46] and the question is whether he can be shown to have been wrong.

The specific problem of the interaction between slaves and free *humiliores* does not appear to have been addressed until the Severan period.[47] And when it was addressed it was controversial. Claudius Saturninus declares flatly that 'Slaves and free persons are punished differently for the same crimes' (*D.* 48.19.16.3). Macer may be replying to him[48] when he says that 'Slaves are punished analogously to those of lowly status – *exemplo humiliorum*' (*D.* 48.19.10 pr.). But Macer does not say that they receive the same punishment. He says it is analogous, and he proceeds to enlarge on the analogy, 'For the same reasons that a free person is beaten with rods (*fustibus*), a slave is beaten with lashes (*flagellis*).' But the analogy is not a compelling one, and becomes even less so when we look at the rest of Macer's comparison. He has the free person consigned to hard labour after being beaten, while the slave is returned to his master after being lashed. But the slave also receives a definitive *poena*: he is to remain shackled for the same length of time as a free person would have to undergo hard labour. This is no closer than the analogies by which Venuleius brings the slave under the public criminal laws. But it certainly shares Venuleius' perception of economic reality. Just as the slave cannot satisfy a pecuniary penalty under the *lex Julia de vi privata*, so he should not dislocate the economy by being taken away from his master. But Macer adds a rider: if his master refuses to take him back he is to be sold, but if there are no buyers he is to be consigned to hard labour in perpetuity. Much thought and experimentation had preceded Macer's exposition, but practical difficulties, if nothing else, ruled out any real thought of equalization.[49]

Callistratus refers again to the punishment of slaves in the rather obscure remark that 'In every case of capital punishment (*in omni supplicio*)[50] our ancestors punished slaves more harshly than free persons, and people of ill-repute (= second offenders) more harshly than those of unblemished reputation' (*D*. 48.19.28.16). The reference to 'people of ill-repute' is quite separate from the equalization question. It means second offenders. Callistratus is here discussing a different kind of differential, according to the *persona* of the offender, and he may be feeling the need to find a moral justification for differentiating on that ground. His precedent may have been the XII Tables rule under which the manifest thief was, if free, adjudged to the victim but was, if a slave, thrown from the Tarpeian Rock (Gell. *NA* 11.18.8). But in making the point Callistratus strikes a major blow at equalization.

There is, finally, a passage in Ulpian that some would take as proof of equalization,[51] though in fact it simply confirms the existence of separate punishments for slaves:

> It is accepted that an accused should not suffer the punishment appropriate to his status at the time of sentencing, but that which he would have suffered had he been sentenced at the time when he committed the offence. Consequently, if a slave attains his freedom after committing an offence he should suffer the punishment appropriate to his status at the time of commission. Conversely, if someone has been reduced to a lower status he should suffer the punishment appropriate to his former condition. It is generally agreed that prefects or governors conducting criminal or civil trials under the relevant laws, but *extra ordinem*, should impose discretionary punishments on those whose lack of means negates pecuniary penalties.

(*D*. 48.19.1)

The penalties to which the ex-slave reverts are not described as common, and the obvious assumption is that specifically servile punishments are meant. Nor does the concluding observation establish equalization. A defendant could be indigent (*egens*) in either a criminal or a civil action, and his indigence was not necessarily due to his legal incapacity to own anything. Even *honestiores* sometimes needed assistance to meet their fines.[52] Ulpian is merely looking at the end-result of something that had started in the Republic, when Sulla included would-be robbers in his homicide law because the delictual remedy of a financial assessment – the value of the property plus a threefold penalty – was meaningless in many cases.

How does equalization fare in *Sententiae*? Moving boundary markers earns the mines for a slave, hard labour for *humiliores*, and relegation/ deportation for *honestiores* (*PS* 5.22.2). There is a similar threefold penalty[53] under the *lex Cornelia testamentaria* (5.25.1). There may have been a different position under the *lex Cornelia de sicariis*, for Ulpian says that the *lex* applies even to slaves and peregrines, but this possibly means that he is looking at the status of the victim rather than at that of the offender.[54] The castration chapter of the homicide law poses a minor problem. A rescript of Hadrian imposed the *poena legis* but singled the slave out for the death penalty (*D.* 48.8.4.2). On the other hand, *Sententiae* prescribes capital punishment for the castrator, 'whether slave or free man'; the only differentiation is that *honestiores* are deported (5.23.13).

The penalties for *iniuria* bring in a source that we now glance at for the first time, the *Epitome of Law* of Hermogenian, which was written under Diocletian, hence contemporaneously with *Sententiae*.[55] Hermogenian says that *iniuria* is usually dealt with *extra ordinem*: slaves are lashed and returned to their masters; free persons of humble status (*liberi humilioris loci*)[56] are beaten with rods; others (*ceteri*)[57] are sentenced to temporary exile or interdiction (*D.* 47.10.45). *Sententiae* deals with the slave separately rather than as part of a threefold system: the slave is condemned to the mines if the *iniuria* is *atrox*, but if it is light (*levis*) he is lashed and returned to his master – subject to the *poena* of being temporarily shackled (*PS* 5.4.22). This is the punishment on which Macer bases his formulation of a general analogy between slaves and humble free.

The evidence for equalization is sparse and sporadic at best. It does not come anywhere near a general assimilation of the slave and the *humilior*. The slave's separate identity before the law might be chipped in a few places, but it was never in danger of serious demolition. To have failed to preserve at least a theoretical distinction would have threatened the very foundations of society.[58]

EXTRA ORDINEM PENALTIES: DISCRETIONARY OR MANDATORY?

The battery of alternative punishments raises a question that does not have to be asked in the case of the *poena legis*. Was the judge bound to impose a penalty appropriate to the accused's status? And if so, was he bound, in the case of *humiliores*, to impose the particular form of death or other unpleasantness laid down for the crime in question? In other words, had the penalties thrown up by *cognitio* crystallized into a new kind of *poena legis*?

The thrust of the question can be illustrated by a modern parallel. If a statute prescribes a penalty of five years' imprisonment without the option of a fine, there is no room for judicial discretion.[59] But if the sentence is defined as 'a maximum of five years' imprisonment' there is a discretion. Other combinations, such as the alternatives of imprisonment or a fine, widen the discretion. But whatever the extent of the discretion, it can always be described as part of a *poena legis*. But there are numerous (although steadily shrinking) areas of common-law crime in which the legislature has not intervened at all. In such cases the punishment is always discretionary, though even here there are limits. They are not imposed by statute, but by practice and precedent, but they are no less effective on that account.

On the Roman scene the specific problem is whether the emperor's legislation fettered the judge's discretion, and on that there are two diametrically opposed views. An unfettered judicial discretion was firmly advocated by Levy. He argued that rescripts on punishment were no more than guidelines which the judge was free to follow or not, as he saw fit. The only binding case that Levy was prepared to concede was mandates to individual officials. Apart from mandates, then, the emperor did not make law on penalties. This was not because he did not have the power to do so, but because he did not choose to use that power.[60]

Levy was strenuously opposed by De Robertis. According to him two phases must be distinguished. In the Early Principate the judge had a discretion, but Hadrian began using his normative power. By the Severan period a fully-fledged dual system was in place, but the emperor was the senior partner. Any penalty on which he had issued a constitution was binding on all judges. Only if it was something on which the emperor had not ruled was there still a discretion; such matters can be recognized by the words *solet, plerumque* in the texts. Thus there was effectively a new *poena legis*.[61]

Neither scholar has made anything like a conclusive case, but four of De Robertis' texts are worth looking at:

> Plunderers (*expilatores*) are usually (*solent*) sentenced to hard labour . . . but *honestiores* are (usually) stripped of their status for a time or relegated. As no special penalty is laid down by rescripts, the judge conducting the *cognitio* has a discretion (*liberum arbitrium statuendi*).
>
> (Ulpian *De off. proc.* 8 = *D.* 47.18.1.1)

> If a judge disregards (*neglexerit*) emperors' constitutions he is punished (under the *lex Cornelia testamentaria*).
>
> (Marcian *Inst.* 14 = *D.* 48.10.1.3)

> A judge who gives judgment contrary to sacred constitutions of emperors [or against public law which is cited to him] is deported to an island.
>
> (*PS* 5.25.4)

> *Emperor Alexander to Paulinus.* Even on other grounds charges of *maiestas* are in abeyance in my reign, and still less will I permit you to accuse a judge because you allege that he has given judgment against my constitution.
>
> (*CJ* 9.8.1, April 223)

The first passage confirms one of De Robertis' points, namely that where there is no constitution the judge has a discretion. But the trouble is that a discretion was sometimes written into the constitution itself. The classic case is Hadrian's rescript on boundary-stones – the *splendidiores* decree (*Coll.* 13.3.1–2). The combination of the mandatory and the discretionary was still being used in the Severan period. A typical case is the legislation against astrologers. Ulpian says that the emperors have laid down different punishments according to the character of the offence. If the astrologer is consulted in regard to the emperor's welfare the penalty is 'death or some other severe punishment'; if it concerns the consultant's welfare the penalty is lighter (*Coll.* 15.2.1–3). Ulpian is summarizing; the alternative to death was obviously deportation. It is for the judge to choose between the two. He has to choose between imprisonment and a fine, so to speak. It can by no means be said that alternative punishments always meant that the case was not yet covered by constitutions.

Our other three passages speak for themselves. There was a general rule requiring judges to give judgment in accordance with constitutions. The evidence of Marcian and *Sententiae* is confirmed by Alexander's rescript, in which the issue was whether a judge who disregarded a constitution should be sentenced to death under the *lex maiestatis* instead of interdiction under the *lex Cornelia testamentaria*. Alexander had thus been asked to reassess the gravity of what was already a recognized offence.[62] Later on he reminded a judge that the use of false rescripts called for an exemplary penalty worthy of the offence (*CJ* 9.22.3[4]).

The aforementioned evidence suggests that the normative power of rescripts, at least in the area of sentence,[63] was controversial. The regime was pressing for binding force, but there was strong resistance. Some of the counter-measures won the jurists' approval. Callistratus says that where constitutions have been promulgated (*prolatis*) and a judge gives judgment contrary to their tenor, but does so on the ground that they are not relevant to the issue before him, he is not taken to have pronounced *contra constitutiones* (*D.* 42.1.32). Callistratus is speaking about civil actions, but in principle there is no reason why a criminal judge should not have had access to similar grounds of exoneration. The technique of drawing a distinction between an instant case and an apparently binding precedent in order to avoid the consequences of the latter has been well known to lawyers down the centuries.

The case put by Callistratus raises another question. Callistratus implies that constitutions only came into the picture at all if they had been promulgated, that is, published. This requirement applied to all types of constitution. The edict speaks for itself. The jurists had no hesitation, for example, in accepting Claudius' addition to the *lex Cornelia testamentaria*, including the important rider that ignorance of the edict would be no excuse.[64] The emperor's verdicts in his own court (*decreta*) were presumably made known in some way. Caligula regularly published his sentences, and others did the same. Domitian's *Epistula ad Falerienses* is a case in point.[65] And Fronto reminded Marcus that his judgments had empire-wide efficacy (*M. Caes.* 1.6). This could not have happened without publication.

The difficult case is the rescript. Learned opinion has come to the anomalous conclusion that when the rescript was in the form of a *subscriptio*, a reply to a private consultant, it was regularly posted up in public. But when it was an *epistula* in reply to an official, publication only occurred in a few cases.[66] But the idea of the private being made public and the public being kept private is questionable. Indeed

Callistratus' language may positively require the supposition that *epistulae* were published. He speaks of constitutions being *promulgatae*, and that seems to exclude private rescripts; the usual word for the posting-up of *subscriptiones* is *propositae*.[67] All the day-to-day business in a province depended on what instructions had been given to the governor. What was the point of keeping them secret, at least insofar as matters of public interest were concerned?

Our conclusion is that there is a slight balance in favour of De Robertis' view. Differential penalties in the second and third centuries were largely determined by imperial rulings. There was still ample room for clarification and generalization by the jurists, but the idea that the emperors did no more than lay down guidelines must be rejected. For one thing, if Papinian could speak of a sentence of temporary imprisonment as agreeing with the *sententia* (rather than the strict language) of a rescript of Marcus (*D.* 40.8.8), the jurist was interpreting a rescript just as if it were a *lex*.

But this is not to say that a new *poena legis* had emerged. Things were still in a state of flux – as late as Alexander the emperor was still being challenged. Moreover, too many alternative penalties were still current at the time of *Sententiae*.[68] There were even cases where the jurists could simply not seize the logic of some rescripts.[69] In essence they were in much the same position in this matter as they were when they tried to iron out the conflicts between the old jurisdictions and the new.[70]

But quite apart from individual factors working against a new *poena legis*, there was a general impediment. By substituting discretion for the old *poena legis* they opened a door which they could never hope to close. Law cannot remain static, nor, with the best will in the world, can professional lawyers or bureaucrats provide all the mechanisms of reform that are required. The courts must always have a major role, and it must be a discretionary role. Judges are not computers. Napoleon overlooked this in his haste to abolish the discretionary powers of the old *Parlements*. French law has spent nearly two hundred years trying to repair the damage.

CONCLUSION

Differential penalties may have existed in embryonic form in the Early Principate, but they did not start receiving formal legal recognition until the second century. Comparison of the stable *honestiores–humiliores* of *Pauli Sententiae* with the usage of the classical jurists produces mixed results. The differences are even more palpable by comparison with imperial constitutions, especially Hadrian's. But even *Sententiae*'s terminology is not entirely stable, nor does it attest punishment according to status for all the public criminal laws. Classification as an *honestior* was an important status symbol. Moreover, there were grades within the *honestiores*. Also, some groups, such as serving soldiers, received privileges of *honestiores* without the actual status. At the lower end of the spectrum equalization of penalty between free *humiliores* and slaves is largely a myth. On the efficacy of constitutions in the matter of punishment we lean slightly towards De Robertis as against Levy. But there can be no question of the cumulative effect of constitutions having created a new *poena legis*.

12

ATTITUDES TO PUNISHMENT

INTRODUCTION

Three questions define the theme of this chapter. First, to what extent was Roman society appalled at the death penalty as such? In other words, is there any reason to believe that it was stigmatized as *saevitia* even when one of the regular modes of execution was employed? Second, if society was quite comfortable with the idea of execution as such, did it have any qualms about the more esoteric varieties, that is, about burning offenders alive, throwing them to the beasts or crucifying them? That is to say, is the smooth detachment of, especially, the legal sources a true pointer to public opinion? Our third question, which will be broached at the end of the chapter, runs as follows: if in capital cases the broad distinction between *honestiores* and *humiliores* was that the former were frequently sentenced to interdiction/deportation and the latter to death, why did they need so many nasty alternatives? Did variety serve any practical purpose, or was the whole thing designed more as a deterrent than for actual use? Was the *poenae metus* which struck fear into potential criminals the mainspring of the exercise?

Our investigation is largely restricted to capital penalties. This is not because there was no opposition to sub-capital forms. Even the first *repetundae* law, with the mildest possible penalty, was condemned as a savage law;[1] and Augustus' legislation on marriage and morality evoked a barrage of criticism.[2] But complaints about sub-capital 'cruelty' expressed little more than the dissatisfaction of special interest groups. There is nothing particularly shocking about a fine. And relegation without loss of citizenship was no worse, and perhaps even better, than a fine; some *multae* were so crushing that culprits preferred exile.[3] One might pause at the extreme non-lethal case, consignment to the mines for life which deprived a man of citizenship and made him a slave of the punishment. If the offender happened to be a woman there was a variant under which she was sent to the mines *in ministerium metallicorum*, for the convenience of the convicts. Ulpian adds with unconscious irony that if sentenced in perpetuity she becomes a *serva poenae*, but if for a period she retains her citizenship (*D.* 48.19.8.8). Although specifically not capital (*D.* 48.19.28 pr.), this compares with the worst types of execution in brutality. But there is no need to deal with it separately; if they could tolerate execution they could tolerate comfort women. Ulpian certainly displays complete tolerance. There is no trace of social conscience in his notice of *in metallum*; it is simply a matter of dotting a few i's and crossing a few t's.

Our theme will be pursued in two segments, one covering the Republic and Early Principate, the other the Later Principate. The dividing-line is determined by the logic of events. Perceptions of punishment in the Early Principate were based on the thinking of the Late Republic. A new society with new institutions was coming into being, but it needed time to evolve its own punitive criteria. Meanwhile punishment was still assessed by its conformity with, or departure from, the models inherited from the Republic. The second century saw the consolidation, the professionalization if one likes, of the new.

THE REPUBLIC AND EARLY PRINCIPATE

The primary source for this period is the two legal philosophers, Cicero and Seneca. Both expressed concern about capital punishment, but their positions were not quite the same. Both believed in *humanitas*, but for the most part Cicero was not called upon to distinguish between different forms of execution. As far as free citizens were concerned, most of the regular methods were acceptable to him; the only exception was the penalty of the sack for *parricidium*. Occasionally he expressed his dislike of experimental punishments; vivicombustion worried him, though cutting out a slave's tongue apparently did not.[4] But for the rest his focus was on the avoidance of execution rather than its performance. Repeatedly endorsing a public perception that had already changed the law, he took his stand on interdiction, on the effective transformation of the death penalty into exile. This, rather than empty propaganda about justice and equity, is the supreme Roman achievement in the field of human rights. It may still have been elitist, since only citizens were eligible for it, but it was a great step forward. Polybius knew of nothing to equal it amongst the Greeks. Nor, on Cicero's terms, does the execution of the Catilinarians alter the picture. Having never condemned the death penalty as such, even in the classic statement of his position at the trial of Rabirius, he had ample room for manoeuvre between citizens who qualified for the blessings of *humanitas* and those who had forfeited their citizenship. Not everyone agreed with him. Caesar spoke, and Sallust wrote, on a more liberal attitude towards the conspirators. But it still fell short of outright rejection of the death penalty. The Populares were not so much concerned with the penalty as with its proper authorization, though Sallust may have come closer to total abolition.

Seneca's main concern was somewhat different from Cicero's. He wanted to avoid punishment altogether and turned clemency into a canon of exculpation for that purpose. When he did address punishment he roundly condemned the use of cruel varieties for public entertainment, but he did not make a feature of the alternative of exile as Cicero had done. When the facts justified it Seneca did not object to execution. He was even able to contemplate it with detachment, portraying the magistrate who pronounced sentence of death as simply exterminating a poisonous snake (*De ira* 1.16.3–6.) The simile would not have appealed to Cicero; he even saw the punishment of the Catilinarians as an example of Plato's curative principle (*Cat.* 2.17). But much water had flowed under the bridge since Augustus invoked the doctrine of quick pursuit in order to block escape into exile. Seneca's stance did narrow the gap – if there was one – between other Stoics and himself. When Thrasea Paetus proposed interdiction/deportation instead of death he was motivated as much by the need to preserve the *poena legis* as a shield against tyranny[5] as by *humanitas*; it is true that he says that the executioner and the noose were abolished long ago (TA 14.48.5–7), but whether it was Thrasea or Tacitus who borrowed this from Cicero is a moot point.

The non-lethal form of capital punishment was only one way of giving expression to a general dislike of *saevitia*. The sentiment also found expression in other ways, notably in Pompey's law on *parricidium*. With the advent of the Principate *saevitia* aroused even greater concern. But its position was ambivalent. Unavoidably so, for opposing forces were at work. On the one hand the experimental penalties of, especially, Caligula began hardening into firm rules. But on the other hand the new cognitionary jurisdictions, in particular that of the emperor himself, gave a new impetus to values like *humanitas* and *clementia*. The sources find it difficult to uncover a consistent pattern and resort to quick, media-like 'bites' instead. The cruelties of some emperors no doubt provided Suetonius' publishers with excellent copy, but they leave us uncertain as to where genuine public opinion ends and sensationalism begins.

Tacitus is (predictably) more reliable. Without him we would not know, for example, that Nero's pyrotechnical experiments with the Christians had evoked strong protests on moral grounds, and had prompted attempts to redefine *utilitas publica* in terms more consonant with *humanitas*. Pliny also reflects public opinion when he condemns the live burial of a Vestal even though he admits that she was probably guilty. But even for these more substantial writers it was a matter of occasional examples of *saevitia*, not of any sustained rethinking. The only exception was the *lex maiestatis*, on which Tacitus did manage to string together a series of examples that point – or at any rate are intended by him to point – to a consistent pattern which distinguishes the Early Principate from the Republic.[6]

Apart from the literary sources of a more or less serious sort, the main avenue for the expression of criticism was black comedy. The *Apocolocyntosis* attributed to Seneca was popular because it was in touch with public opinion. The other work attributed to the philosopher, *Octavia*, was, although not in comic vein, the most serious and sustained presentation of the conscience of the nation. But the emphasis was still on the manner of its doing, not on the fact that it was done at all.

Finally, what of the lawyers? The Republican jurists do not present as critics of punishment. There was almost certainly a juristic hand behind Sulla's formalization of *aquae et ignis interdictio*, but we cannot name any names. Legislation on electoral corruption was inspired as much by Servius Sulpicius Rufus as by his friend Cicero,[7] but even when the penalties were intensified they remained sub-capital.[8] The Early Principate offers some capital evidence, but no pattern. Cassius Longinus justified the mass execution of Pedanius' slaves on the grounds of *utilitas publica*, but there were those who thought that the public interest should be tempered by *humanitas*. That both points of view were canvassed in Nero's reign shows that the search for something more than ad hoc reactions to the new *cognitio* was gathering momentum. The same search was responsible for the first clash between the jury system and the urban prefect's jurisdiction. It was also responsible – specifically as a result of Seneca's influence – for Nero's attempts to deflect the odium of capital punishment.

There was something of a reaction against Cassius' uncompromising severity in the Flavian period. The jurist Pegasus resisted Domitian's attempt to confer capital jurisdiction on the urban prefect; there was no room for the sword in Pegasus' understanding of the prefect's function.[9] The sentiment was not confined to juristic prefects. A previous incumbent, Flavius Sabinus, had had a positive horror of the death sentence, though not everyone agreed with him; some considered him too soft (TH 2.63, 3.75). The humane tradition was continued, and to some extent formalized, by Pegasus' successor, Rutilius Gallicus. It earnt him an accolade from the poet Statius which included the almost unique feature of praise for his considerate attitude towards *humiliores*. Domitian himself was even more taken with the *liberum mortis arbitrium* than Nero had been. It was presented as a signal example of liberalism, and it did at least alleviate one of the most feared features of public execution, its affront to personal dignity. But you still had to die. And in any case the concession was a selective one; it did not go beyond the higher brackets of the *honestiores*, those of the first grade, if one likes. As for wholesale executions of slaves, no one tried to abandon Cassius' position. The *s.c. Silanianum* was alive and well, and its unruffled acceptance of economic dislocation is perhaps the first negative response to our suggestion that savagery may have been preached rather than practised.

By the turn of the first century AD the death sentence was still firmly in place. A Flavius Sabinus, and perhaps a Sallust before him, might have thought about its total abolition, but the idea was never seriously pursued. Yet there was a somewhat different perception of the role of the supreme penalty; it was beginning to be hedged around with qualifications. The change in perspective would be accelerated in the second century.

THE SECOND CENTURY: THE GREAT DEBATES

The second century presents us with a unique feature, a debate on punishment theory. The debate is discussed in great detail by Aulus Gellius, who claims to have attended it in person.[10] The debate is located in Antoninus Pius' reign, and is between the jurist Sextus Caecilius Africanus and the philosopher Favorinus; Africanus was a pupil of Salvius Julianus, the last-known head of the Sabinian law school.[11] The debate turns on the supposed cruelty – but also the in-adequacy – of the XII Tables. What has not been sufficiently noticed is that for a proper interpretation of the debate it should be collated with another debate on the XII Tables which is also described by Aulus Gellius. On that occasion Gellius himself has a discussion with a lawyer whom he does not identify by name; at a certain point they are joined by a third person, the poet Iulius Paulus (Gell. 16.10).

In the debate between Africanus and Favorinus the philosopher launches a four-pronged attack on the XII Tables: it is either too obscure, or too harsh, or too lenient, or – perhaps the most important of all – too improbable to be taken literally. In reply the jurist stresses the need to interpret a law in the context of its own time. Old words and customs in a code some 600 years old are admittedly obsolete, but it is through them that the code can be understood. But it must also be remembered that remedies are in a constant state of flux. They depend on contemporary *mores*, on forms of government, on the current public interest (*utilitates praesentes*) and on the kinds of fault needing to be cured.[12] In other words, the debate accurately reflects the fact that the *poena legis* has been displaced by the discretionary remedy. But, adds the jurist, that discretion is constantly being modified by the fluctuations of wind and wave (22). Which is an intelligent anticipation, and refutation, of De Robertis' theory of a new *poena legis*.

What, asks Africanus, is harsh about the XII Tables laws? Is it harsh to inflict a capital penalty on a corrupt judge, or to adjudge a manifest thief to the complainant as his slave, or to kill a thief who comes by night? To this Favorinus replies that although the people originally decreed these penalties, they later considered them too severe and allowed them to fall into disuse (7–10). Favorinus here purports to rely on the doctrine of abrogation by disuse propounded by Africanus' teacher,[13] but at least as far as the corrupt judge is concerned the philosopher is mistaken. Judicial corruption was punished with death or exile in the Severan period (*D.* 48.11.3, 7). The position was the same in *c.* 146, the dramatic date of the debate; in fact it went back to Tiberius.[14]

Favorinus then attacks the XII Tables rule that anyone too ill to walk to court in response to a summons be conveyed on a beast of burden, but not in a covered wagon. Africanus replies to this trivial point with a series of word-interpretations that stress the innate *humanitas* of the rule (11, 24–30). If any part of the debate is not genuine it is surely this battery of word-interpretations, a topic that never ceases to fascinate Aulus Gellius.

Favorinus then turns to excessive leniency, citing the rule which laid down a fixed penalty of twenty-five *asses* for less serious types of *iniuria*. He illustrates the derisory nature of the penalty by the case of Lucius Veratius, who went around slapping people's faces and immediately paying them twenty-five *asses*. This, says the philosopher, persuaded the praetor to make damages assessable in future (13). Again the replacement of the *poena legis* by a discretionary remedy. In reply Africanus points out that the twenty-five *asses* rule was only one of a number of rules on the subject. But the main thrust of his reply concerns the fact that the code had made provision for retaliation (*talio*) by the victim of an *iniuria*.

Favorinus had ridiculed the remedy of *talio*, claiming that exact correspondence between the *iniuria* and the retaliation was impossible. If a limb is broken, how does the victim break a limb in exactly the same way? Even worse, if the *iniuria* was unintentional, how does one retaliate unintentionally? (14–18). Africanus concedes that sometimes *talio* leads to results that are ingenious rather than real, but the purpose of the rule was to restrain violence by the mere fear of retaliation (31–38). We again confront the *poenae metus*, the fear of retribution, that Cicero makes one of the purposes of punishment.[15]

Finally, Favorinus attacks the rule that allowed a plurality of creditors to cut up a debtor's body and divide it amongst themselves. Africanus traces the history of this bizarre institution, identifying several stages at which the debtor could have compounded his obligation. In any case, he says, the ultimate stage has never been reached in practice. One should also have regard, adds Africanus, to the salutary effect of savage penalties. If perjured witnesses were still thrown off the Tarpeian Rock there would be fewer liars in the witness-box. Africanus ends with a comment on the punishment of Mettius Fufetius: it was novel and harsh, but he had broken his pledged word (19, 39–54). The comment discloses a difference of opinion on how far deterrence should go. We recall that the king had justified it 'as a warning to all mankind', but Livy condemns it as the first and last Roman punishment to disregard *humanitas* (L. 1.28.10–11). As Casavola puts it, the conflict was between an exemplary penalty appropriate to archaic society and the contemporary idea of a sanction proportionate to the crime.[16]

We turn now to the other XII Tables debate. Gellius is puzzled by the word *proletarius* and asks an (unnamed) lawyer to explain it. The lawyer says he is trained in law, not in grammar. When Gellius refers him to a XII Tables rule in which the word is used, the lawyer replies that he is not interested in ancient law. Expressions like *proletarii*, twenty-five *asses* and *talio* have disappeared; in fact nearly all the learning in the code was 'put to sleep' by the *lex Aebutia*.[17] 'My only interest is in law, statutes and legal terms that are currently in use.' At this point the poet Iulius Paulus (!) appears and gives a learned discourse on the troublesome word, sketching its history since early times (16.10.1–15).

Gellius has placed two opposing views of the XII Tables before us. The code was being used as a sounding-board to evaluate current thinking.[18] A return to first principles was indicated, not least in the area of the criminal law. *Cognitio* had stimulated new ideas on punishment, and those ideas needed to be probed and evaluated. But in the wide-ranging intellectual climate of the day[19] the investigation had to be cast in two different moulds. On the one hand it needed to focus on the formal parameters of criminal justice; Maecian and Venuleius were attending to that. But there was also a need for theoretical under-pinning, and that called for a different, academically oriented approach. That need was met by Gaius.

Gaius was not interested in the mechanical details of the *De iudiciis publicis* genre,[20] but he was very interested in the XII Tables. His commentary on the code covered no less than six books,[21] compared with the four books of his *Institutes* into which he compressed the whole of his exposition of the private law for students. The six books did include material on the criminal law. One of the fragments runs as follows:

> Anyone who sets fire to a barn or a heap of grain near a house is sentenced to be bound, flogged and burnt alive (*talio!*), provided that he acted knowingly and deliberately. But if he did it by chance, that is, negligently, he is ordered to pay compensation. But if he is a man of straw he is punished, though more lightly.
>
> (Gaius *XII Tables* 4 = D. 47.9.9)

The penalty cited by Gaius is that laid down by the code itself. He ignores later developments which, as we know from Ulpian, started out as interdiction under the *lex Cornelia de sicariis* but later branched out into death or deportation for *honestiores* and *ad bestias* for *humiliores* (*Coll.* 12.5.1). Gaius does not mention the differential because none existed at the time of the code. He is looking at first principles. But he looks at them within a more sophisticated framework, for he assesses degrees of responsibility. On the formal details Gaius is still in 450 BC; but on amplifying jurisprudence he is right up to date. He is reading into the XII Tables rule a principle derived from Hadrian's dictum that the intention, not the outcome, of a crime is the determinant (*D.* 48.8.14).

Gellius' anonymous lawyer had read Gaius' commentary but he did not like the importance given to the XII Tables. Neither did the classical jurists; none of them ever cites Gaius. Nor, for that matter, does Gellius. Which is surprising, given their common interest in word-interpretation. For example, Gaius made an exhaustive analysis of the word *telum*, which interested him either because of its connection with the nocturnal thief or because of its relevance to the *lex Cornelia de sicariis*.[22] He interpreted the word *venenum* for the poisoning section of the same statute, basing himself on an old XII Tables rule.[23] He also used the laws of Solon, as adopted by the XII Tables, to interpret Hadrian's seminal rescript on boundary-stones.[24] Solon also helped him on the *lex Julia de vi publica*, and he interpreted the word *perduelles* and noted that the penalty for *latrones* applied to those who cut down trees.[25]

Gaius' methodology was close to that of Gellius' poet and marks it as an essentially literary work[26] – which is exactly what it ought to have been if it was to fulfil its broad intellectual function. One might take the literary link still further. Ateius Capito, founder of the Sabinian school to which Gaius belonged, had written a pioneering work on the public criminal laws with a distinctly archaic, but at the same time literary, flavour.[27] The work would have appealed to Gaius as a model. It would not have appealed to Maecian or Venuleius, but they were working on a different kind of *De iudiciis publicis*.

There is a curious passage in Gaius' *Institutes*. He describes enslavement for manifest theft as a *poena capitalis* and says that its harshness was frowned on and a pecuniary penalty was substituted (Gai. 3.189). That is of course exactly what Favorinus says. But Africanus, presumably a member of the same school as Gaius, denies that the penalty was too harsh.[28]

To sum up, the XII Tables was used as the prime example of *saevitia*, and of the reaction against it. But the attack does not go as far as outright condemnation of the death penalty. It is simply seen as too harsh in some cases. Moreover, although Gaius takes the same view as Favorinus of the penalty for manifest theft, he is quite neutral on the penalty for arson, only moderating it for the unintentional act. All this amounts to saying that people were beginning to question *saevitia* by criticizing the law itself, not merely by criticizing abuses of the law by particular regimes. They were starting, in other words, to apply *Rechtskritik*[29] to capital punishment. But that approach was still in its early stages; it was in the same state of transition and flux as the new punitive co-ordinates themselves. It remains to be seen whether it assumed any more specific shape over the rest of the Principate.

THE ATTITUDES OF THE SEVERAN JURISTS

If the Severan jurists did express themselves in this matter, if they did expose *saevitia* to systematic *Rechtskritik*, the most likely place to look for it would be *Digest* 48.19 under the rubric *De Poenis*. But this only proves to be the case to a very limited extent. There is nothing like the debate on the XII Tables in Aulus Gellius. The discussion is professional, giving detailed rules for the guidance of judges, but nearly always in a completely detached way.

This is not to say that systematic thought had not been given to punishment. Claudius Saturninus supplies a numerate exposition in which punishments are allocated to four categories – things done, said, written or planned – and each of the four is considered under seven heads, namely motive, person, place, time, quality, quantity and outcome (48.19.16). Each component is amplified and some careful distinctions are drawn. Thus under 'quantity' a thief is distinguished from a rustler by the fact that he has stolen only one pig, whereas a rustler has stolen several (16.7). The author has literary pretensions. He illustrates the qualitative aspect of *iniuria* by a quotation from Demosthenes, and the outcome of accidental killing by a passage in Homer (16.6, 8). But there is only one passing reference to a differential, namely that the penalties for some crimes are intensified when an example is needed, such as where an excessive number of persons engages in highway robbery (16.10).

The position is no different in other fragments in the title, though this may be partly due to clumsy excerpting by the compilers. The title opens with a fragment in which Ulpian carefully examines the effect on punishment of a change of status between the commission of the crime and the passing of sentence (48.19.1); but the compilers ignored the general discussion of status differentials which they must have found in Ulpian. However, they did manage, although belatedly, to incorporate Ulpian's general list of punishments (6.2, 8–9). An interesting item informs us that governors can only sentence to death by the sword; Ulpian expressly excludes the axe, the *telum*, the club, the noose, poison, flogging, torture and a free choice of death, although he does note a rescript of Marcus and Verus allowing the last-mentioned (8.1,3). None of the exclusions are dictated by *humanitas*; it is simply a matter of precise guidelines. We note the absence of the standard *humiliores* penalties. It might be argued that by not including them amongst his exclusions Ulpian implicitly allows the governor to inflict them, but this is weakened by the fact that he does make express mention of vivicombustion, which he says is used against enemies of the state and deserters (8.2). Why Ulpian should have singled out these particular perpetrators of *maiestas* is a mystery; elsewhere in *De officio proconsulis* he gives a full list of acts falling under that crime (*D.* 48.4.1). In any event the point is that enemies and deserters were found amongst both *honestiores* and *humiliores*, so that in the end there are no status differentials in Ulpian's notice.[30]

Ulpian makes one statement that leads us to suspect that, far from being horrified by *saevitia*, he positively favours it. He is discussing what a governor should do when someone says that he has something to tell the emperor about his safety. This device, which had first been used under Augustus,[31] placed the governor in a quandary. Most governors, says Ulpian, are so timid that even though they have already sentenced the accused they suspend execution. Others have no patience with such claims. Others, again, do not always act consistently; they ask the offender what he wishes to tell the emperor, and then decide whether or not to suspend execution. That, concedes Ulpian, is the rational middle way, but Ulpian himself does not support it:

> In my opinion, once offenders have been condemned they have absolutely no right to be heard further. They are simply trying to escape punishment and should be punished more severely for having kept silent about the emperor's safety for so long.
>
> (*D*. 48.19.6 pr.)

This rejection of the perfectly reasonable middle course is a significant pointer to Ulpian's attitudes. It is in full agreement with his thoughts about the punishment of soldiers. He supported a return to the severe discipline of Augustus, refusing to allow serving soldiers the privileges of veterans, and it was for this that the praetorians killed him.[32]

Callistratus discusses grades of punishment and says that they are more or less (*fere*) as follows: the extreme penalty (*summum supplicium*) is condemnation 'to the fork (*furca*)' – being either bound to 'the infertile tree' and beaten to death, or crucified.[33] Then comes vivicombustion, to which Callistratus assigns second place because it came into use later than the *furca*.[34] Decapitation (*capitis amputatio*) completes the list of death penalties. The first non-lethal penalty is the mines, followed by deportation to an island. This completes the capital penalties, after which come penalties that only affect reputation (*existimatio*) – relegation, hard labour, whipping (*D*. 48.19.28 pr.).

There is another passage that also grades punishments, although not as fully as Callistratus. It is in Ulpian's discussion of the penalties for *sacrilegium* (here, as nearly always, theft from a temple):

> I know that many temple-thieves have been condemned to the beasts, some have been burnt alive, others have been suspended on the fork. But the penalty should be moderated to a maximum of *ad bestias*, which should be inflicted on those who band together, break into a temple by night and carry off the god's

offerings. Theft of an article of modest value by day should be punished by the mines or, if the thief occupies a higher status (*in honestiore loco natus*), by deportation to an island.

(*D.* 48.13.7)

Garnsey argues from this passage that *ad bestias* was the least severe of the three modes of execution mentioned, and thus Ulpian provides a scale of severity for capital punishments.[35] But there are weaknesses in this argument. First, Garnsey himself admits that elsewhere (*D.* 48.19.9.11) the order vivicombustion/suspension on the fork is reversed. Second, Ulpian is only discussing *sacrilegium*. Third, the whole passage merely expresses Ulpian's personal opinion; there has clearly not been an imperial pronouncement on the subject. The truth of the matter is that there was no firm order of preference. Callistratus says so (*fere*), and *Sententiae* confirms it with the following variations: *crux/ad bestias; crux* for magicians, *ad bestias/crux* for their accomplices; *vivi exuruntur/ad bestias*; the mines/*crux, ad bestias/vivi exuruntur*; the mines/*crux*.[36]

We conclude, then, that the material on punishment does not give any sign of a socially aware evaluation of the death penalty. Not even the literary pretensions of Claudius Saturninus point to anything deeper; Demosthenes merely speaks eloquently about the insulting effect of a blow, and Homer writes about accidental homicide during a game of dice (48.19.16.6, 8).

'YOUR INTERPRETATION IS ALIEN TO MY SCHOOL OF THOUGHT'

If the juristic evidence does not point to any overall concept, would we fare any better by looking in some other direction? The hitherto unsuspected answer is that the emperors themselves formalized their attitudes to some extent. The key is supplied by some constitutions of Severus Alexander. In 224 he wrote to a consultant as follows:

> You show understanding alien to my school of thought (*alienam sectae meae*) by supposing that you are liable to a charge of *maiestas* if in a moment of anger you swore (by the emperor) always to treat your slave harshly but violated your oath.
>
> (*CJ* 9.8.2)

Alexander had suspended charges of *maiestas*, of whatever nature, for the duration of his reign.[37] That policy is here identified as a feature of *secta mea.* A different expression, but to the identical effect, is used in a rescript issued in 223, 'Charges of *maiestas* are in abeyance *on whatever grounds they are based* in my age (*meo saeculo*). Therefore you are not permitted to charge a judge with treason because he has given judgment against one of our constitutions' (*CJ* 9.8.1).

Measuring criminal liability against a conceptualized yardstick was not confined to *maiestas*. In 230 Alexander replied to a petitioner as follows:

> My school (*secta mea*) does not permit you to mount a charge of forgery or any other capital charge against your mother. But this does not affect a pecuniary remedy. If there is doubt about the document under which your mother claims a *fideicommissum*, the truth of her claim can be tested even without a criminal charge.
>
> (*CJ* 9.22.5)

The above examples are confined to capital crimes, but the same approach is attested for at least one sub-capital category. In 224 the indefatigable Alexander said this:

> It accords with the chastity of my times (*castitati temporum meorum convenit*) to continue with the statutory penalty against a woman condemned under the *lex Julia de pudicitia*.[38] But anyone who knowingly marries or remarries a woman condemned for adultery – if she has somehow escaped a capital penalty (*si quocumque modo poenam capitalem evaserit*) – is punished under the same law for procuring (*lenocinium*).
>
> (*CJ* 9.9.9)

Castitas temporum meorum is an interesting variation on the theme. Here it is not just a general matter of *tempora mea/secta mea*, but of a special policy feature in the shape of chastity. Instead of legends on coins, Alexander was publicizing his virtues by rescripts. And virtue was measured against the yardstick of punishment.

The rescript on adultery had an unexpected sequel. In 385 the emperors issued a rescript granting a general release of condemned criminals to celebrate Easter (*CTh* 9.38.8). Such an indulgence was regularly given in the Later Empire, but five crimes punished by death made up a special canon which was invariably excluded from the amnesty.[39] In the rescript of 385 the emperors commented on the reasons for excluding the canon, and with respect to adultery they asked, 'In a time of chastity (*tempore castitatis*), who could pardon an adulterer?' Someone in the imperial chancellery had seen Alexander's rescript. The inclusion of adultery among the five crimes punished by death was, of course, a post-Principate development; hence the palpable interpolation of 'if she has escaped a capital penalty' in *CJ* 9.9.9. The statutory penalty to which the genuine part of Alexander's rescript refers was unequivocally sub-capital as late as *Sententiae* (*PS* 2.26.14). The death penalty was introduced by Constantine, who laid down that when adultery was proved by clear evidence, 'the judge must sew up alive in a leather sack and burn the sacrilegious violators of marriage as though they were manifest parricides' (*CTh* 11.36.4). The bureaucrats got it slightly wrong – the sack had never been combined with vivicombustion – but they meant well. Eventually the compilers insinuated the necessary interpolation into Alexander's decree.

Alexander's 'buzzwords' were used only sparingly. Although a mother could not be charged capitally under the *lex Cornelia testamentaria*, Alexander allowed a charge under the same law against a stepmother (*CJ* 9.22.4[3]). The case of the mother was narrowly focused; it depended on the son's duty of *pietas*. That is precisely why the ruling qualified for a special tag; *pietas* was a value of special importance – as *castitas* and *maiestas* also were.

Can we identify any antecedents to Alexander's special signals? If those signals simply provided a foundation for rulings of special importance, Alexander will have modified an Antonine technique. Marcus had made the word *humanitas* something of a trademark. On the advice of the jurist Julian, he had given new vigour to its significance as a canon of interpretation.[40] But even Marcus was not the first. The pattern had originated with Seneca, who used *clementia* as a tool of interpretation that led not to an act of mercy, but to a positive verdict of exculpation. The Antonines put *humanitas* to a similar use. For example, Pius had ruled that the production in court of documents that could not be proved should be punished according to the gravity of the offence. Marcus and Verus modified this 'out of their humanity' (*pro sua humanitate*), exonerating those who produced such documents in error (*D.* 48.10.31). The same emperors approved of 'the excellent rationale of humanity' (*egregia ratio humanitatis*) displayed by a governor who, after condemning a slave for homicide, found on further investigation that the slave had only confessed in order not to have to return to his master; the governor had thereupon rescinded his judgment (48.18. 1.27).

Other rulings were very possibly motivated by *humanitas* although the word is not used in the extant notices. An example is Marcus' exoneration of a son who killed his mother while of unsound mind

(48.9.9.2). Another possible case is attested by a full version of a rescript of Hadrian. A frolic at a banquet having resulted in a young man dying after being tossed in a cloak, the governor found that there had been no ill-will between the parties and merely sentenced the offender to five years' banishment from Rome, Italy and the province. Hadrian commends the governor for moderating the penalty according to the degree of fault, and states his well-known proposition to the effect that even in capital crimes it is relevant to ask whether the act was intentional or accidental (*Coll.* 1.11.1–3). The word *humanitas* is not used, nor is it used in the restatements of the proposition by Caracalla, Alexander or Diocletian (*ib.* 1.8, 9, 10). Nor, of course, is it used in Callistratus' brief extraction of a principle from Hadrian's rescript (*D.* 48.8.14). But the idea is there.

In another case Hadrian made *pietas* his criterion. A father having killed his son in a hunting 'accident' after it was discovered that the son had committed adultery with the stepmother, Hadrian deported the father for using his paternal power like a brigand; that power should be governed by *pietas*, not by cruelty (48.9.5). Another ruling on paternal power and the criminal law was given by Pius. A deserting soldier having been sent back to his unit by his father, Pius punished the man by transferring him to an inferior unit, so that the father would not be seen to have sent his son to his death (49.16.13.6). Although no label is attached to this ruling in our sources, it has been cogently argued that the idea of *humanitas* is there, as it is in other parts of Pius' legislation, especially on the treatment of slaves.[41]

An instructive ruling was given by Caracalla in response to a petition from Ulpian (!) of Damascus. Ulpian's mother having been deported, he asked that she be allowed to leave him the necessities of life despite the usual confiscation order; his mother joined him as co-petitioner. The emperor replied that although this was contrary to both custom and the public criminal laws, the request would be granted because it was based on *pietas* (*D.* 48.22.16). As Schulz has shown, *pietas* expressed very similar ideas to *humanitas*.[42]

Humanitas and associated values dominated the thinking of the Antonine emperors; it is not for nothing that Aulus Gellius takes the trouble to analyse the word *humanitas* (Gell. 13.17). These ideas operated as a general rationale covering much the same ground as Seneca's *clementia*: they justified departures from the usual consequences of an act. The approach continued to have some prominence under the first Severan dynasty. But Alexander, largely under Ulpian's infuence,[43] began experimenting with expressions like *sexta mea, meum saeculum* and *castitas temporum meorum.* Ulpian had earlier used *humanitas* in his writings. But all the examples date to before the end of Caracalla's reign,[44] and he used his dominant position over the first half of Alexander's reign to spread his net more widely. In a sense Alexander's reign was a new beginning – or perhaps more precisely, a new attempt to ward off the crisis that nearly destroyed the empire over the fifty years following Alexander's murder. Far from continuing the dynasty of Septimius Severus, Alexander traversed the road already mapped out by Macrinus and Elagabalus. In particular, he cultivated the senate and the great proprietors rather than the soldiers and the middle class. This agreed perfectly with Ulpian's own sentiments.[45] The new slogans were intended to epitomize the new realities, and perhaps to do something more. It may have been only Ulpian's untimely death that prevented the great synthesizer from formulating a new exposition of punishment. The only comprehensive treatise *De poenis* was written by Ulpian's pupil, Modestinus. The fragments do not enable us to determine the approach that informed the work, but it is Modestinus who has alerted us to the existence of grades within the *honestiores* (*D.* 48.8.16).

'CRUEL PUNISHMENTS WERE THREATENED BUT NEVER USED'

We now address the third question that was posed at the beginning of this chapter, namely whether *poenae metus* was the main reason why they had so many unpleasant modes of execution. Africanus' reply to Favorinus in the XII Tables debate suggests one possible answer. He says that the dissection of a debtor by his creditors was made so cruel in order to ensure that it would never have to be used; and, he adds, it never was used. As nothing in Gellius' account is pure invention, we may have here an actual controversy about the overriding purpose of punishment. Was that purpose deterrence, and if so, was it not so much a question of making an example of a few offenders, as of making the punishment so nasty that its mere presence on the statute-book was enough?

These questions are suggested not only by what Africanus said, but also by some of the punishments in the Later Empire. One wonders whether Constantine's bureaucrats drew up the following with straight faces:

> Since the watchfulness of parents over their daughters is often defeated by wicked nurses (who help their charges to make contact

with their lovers), punishment shall threaten those nurses whose care is shown to have been detestable and their errands bribed, and the penalty shall be that the mouths and throats of those who incited evil shall be closed by pouring in molten lead.

(*CTh* 9.24.1.1)

We are not dealing here with treason, but with a common-law crime of everyday occurrence. Yet the penalty is not stated in a casual rescript, but in an edict on rape addressed by the emperor *Ad Populum*, to the people.[46] It was too much for Justinian. He simply stated the penalty for all accomplices as *poena capitalis*, only emphasizing its special character by applying it to both men and women, and to free persons of every status or dignity.[47] But almost as if anticipating our problem, Justinian goes on to say, apropos of the rapist/abductor himself, that he will be deterred by fear of the savagery of the penalty, *metu atrocitatis poenae*.[48]

Do we have anything to support Africanus' postulate of a similar expectation in the Principate? For this we must go to yet another passage in Aulus Gellius (*NA* 7.14). Gellius distinguishes three functions of punishment. The first, which he identifies by its Greek name of *kolasis* or *nouthesia*, is correction and reformation. To Gellius this is only a limited type, for he restricts it to one who does wrong fortuitously; the punishment is intended to make him more careful (7.14.2). Whether this is intended to restrict Plato's curative principle to faults that are not innately evil is a moot point. The second function, continues Gellius, is expounded by those who make a feature of subtle distinctions.[49] It is also limited in scope. It is applied when the dignity and prestige of the victim – *not* of the offender – must be safeguarded by ensuring that failure to punish does not cause him to lose face (7.14.3). The third function is not limited. It is called *paradeigma* and is applied when punishment is needed as an example, so that fear of the known penalty (*metus cognitae poenae*) may deter others from similar wrongdoing which it is in the public interest to prevent – *quae prohiberi publicitus interest*. Therefore, adds Gellius, our ancestors also used the word *exempla* for the heaviest penalties – *maximis gravissimisque poenis*. But, he concludes, punishment should not be stipulated if the offence is not of a kind to need an *exemplum* which inspires fear.[50]

Gellius goes on to note that Plato himself gives only two reasons for punishment, namely that the wrongdoer should either be made better by the punishment or should serve as an example to others so that they may be made better through fear. Plato thus excludes the second category.[51] Be that as it may, the point is that on either view the principal function is deterrence through fear.[52] Gellius excludes offences which do not need an *exemplum*, but he does not say what offences *do* need one. We might think that it means something like the five crimes that were excluded from Easter amnesties in the Later Empire.[53] But this is too narrow a criterion in Gellius' own time if any of Hadrian's rulings are a guide. We may pause to glance at some of them.

Hadrian appears to have applied the criminal sanctions of the *lex Cornelia de falsis* (= *testamentaria*) to commercial transactions. He laid down that anyone who falsified weights or measures should be relegated to an island (*D.* 48.10.32.1. This was an innovation; previously the only penalty had been payment of double the value of the goods (*ib.*). Hadrian's decree was also unusual in another respect: although many shopkeepers were *humiliores* they would be receiving an *honestior* punishment.

There are even greater anomalies in Hadrian's second venture into the law of sale. Anyone who sold something to two different people by separate contracts was to incur the penalty for *falsum*, though in practice only temporary relegation without confiscation was imposed (*D.* 48.10.21). Here, too, an aggrieved buyer had a civil remedy, but it only became available if he faced a serious threat of eviction by someone with a better title, whereas the criminal remedy presumably became available as soon as the facts came to light.

The one case that defies resolution is the cattle-rustlers, *abigei*. Hadrian stated in a rescript that for the first offence they should be given to the sword, *ad gladium dentur*. This, he says, should normally be the highest penalty. But if the culprit has a previous conviction for the same offence he should be sent to the mines (*Coll.* 11.7.1–3). This ruling baffled Ulpian. He says that it seems to imply that consignment to the mines is harsher than the sword. He tentatively suggests that by *gladii poena* Hadrian meant *ludi damnatio*, condemnation to the gladiatorial games. But, concludes Ulpian, this does not work, because of the difference between being sentenced to the sword and sentenced to the games. The former means execution within a year, but those sentenced to the games are not necessarily put to death at all; they may, with time, be restored to freedom (they had become *servi poenae*) or released from the games (*Coll.* 11.7.3–4). Nörr thinks the meaning of the puzzle may be that the *poena gladii* was laid down as the maximum; if the second conviction was of a minor character the mines sufficed.[54] That is one possibility, but one is inclined to join Ulpian in consigning the whole thing to the 'too hard' basket.[55] In any case the point is that *cognitio* was still in a state of great uncertainty and flux. This should be borne in mind when considering what Gellius means by offences that call for a fear-inspiring *exemplum*. There were many grey areas.

We return now to the debate between Africanus and Favorinus, but with the addition of a further piece to the puzzle. As Diliberto has recently shown, Gellius gives an important proof of the genuineness of the debate by ending his account with the observation that in the end Africanus won the support not only of the bystanders, but also of Favorinus (20.1.55). Diliberto argues that Gellius would not have cast his teacher, Favorinus, in a losing role unless it had actually happened.[56] The point is well taken, and leads us to suggest something else, namely that philosophy had yielded to jurisprudence on the question of cruel punishments. Africanus' claim that some punishments spoke for themselves had won acceptance. It was recognized that they sometimes inspired enough fear to act as a deterrent without lifting a finger, so to speak.

In the last resort, however, a distinction must be drawn between *honestiores* and *humiliores* – at least in the Principate.[57] *Honestiores* were largely immune to the *poenae metus*. Their standard punishment of exile was not always a burden.[58] Even death lost some of its sting under the *liberum mortis arbitrium*, and the only penalty that really deterred them was the sack for manifest and confessed parricides. The *poenae metus* weighed mainly on *humiliores*. But even this is not to say that the penalties earmarked for them eliminated crime. We have no statistics, but the volume of juristic material on *humiliores* penalties is itself a statistic. One of the reasons for that volume is that the suppression of crime was not always the main consideration. The demands of the games made a constant supply of victims imperative. Indeed even non-lethal punishments catered for public entertainment. Ulpian lists those who are required to take part in hunting games, or to perform Pyrrhic dances, 'or to provide some other kind of entertainment by mime or other bodily movements' (*D.* 48.19.8.11). But at the end of the day it was the hard core of vivicombustion, the beasts and suspension/crucifixion that provided what the public wanted to see.

CONCLUSION

Attitudes to capital punishment in the Republic did not go as far as outright rejection of the death penalty. And in the Early Principate Seneca accepted that penalty even more easily than Cicero had done. The literary sources present a superficial picture, with the possible exception of Tacitus. As for the lawyers, in the first century AD opinions were divided. The second-century debates described by Aulus Gellius suggest that legal opinion was divided between those who focused on the practicalities of criminal justice and those, notably Gaius, who preferred a theoretical approach. The Severans expounded punitive rules systematically, but they did not theorize about it, although Ulpian might have done so if he had lived. But he is in favour of *saevitia* rather than horrified by it. He was responsible for Alexander's adoption of a new set of catch phrases alongside the Antonine concepts of *humanitas, clementia, pietas*. Whether deterrence, epitomized as *poenae metus*, was the principal function of punishment, did not trouble *honestiores* overmuch. But to *humiliores* fear of punishment was a very real thing.

13

IN RETROSPECT

At this point we step back and ask ourselves two questions. What have we said? And have we said it successfully? Not all the matters discussed can be incorporated in our answer, but an assessment of some of the highlights will help to draw the threads together.

If any topic can be said to have dominated the discussion, it is the alternations between fixed and discretionary penalties. Mommsen's rigid dogma of *nulla poena sine lege* is, if taken literally, an assertion of the absolute supremacy of the *poena legis* under all circumstances and at all times. Is it right or wrong? There is no unequivocal answer either way. It depends on the preconceptions with which one starts out, and here our evidence points in both directions. On the one hand we have said, and supported by ample evidence, that the fixed penalty is the meat in the sandwich, being flanked on both sides by discretionary assessments. But we have also said that the punishment inflicted on Mettius Fufetius was criticized because it was discretionary, because it lacked a legislative credential. And there is much evidence over the ensuing centuries to support this. Cicero made it the focal point of his defence of Rabirius. In the Principate the hardline Stoics virtually staked their lives on it. Africanus asserted it successfully against Favorinus. And the entire sub-genre of parody and pastiche ridiculed its violation.

The safest answer seems to be that there was an ongoing dispute about punishment. And one of the factors that fuelled the dispute was *humanitas* and its associated values. From the moment that the first condemned wrongdoer escaped into exile, the supremacy of the ordained penalty was under challenge. Roman society confronted a dilemma. Equity could be absorbed into the private law without much discomfort, but at the criminal level it threatened the very foundations. Cicero made a point of this when he presented the augurs as the guarantors of stability. And in order to protect the stability of the state

161

he made *utilitas publica* the decisive criterion. But he did not jettison *humanitas* in order to do this. He simply interpreted it in a manner consistent with the public interest. In this regard we may even have to qualify our statement about equity being perfectly comfortable in the private law. In spite of what Cicero says in *De officiis*, abstract notions of justice are no more consistent or eternal in the praetor's edict than they are in the battery of criminal punishments. In the last resort the public interest determined remedies in contract or delict as much as it did in crime. Seneca realized this when he made *clementia* an active canon of exoneration based on *bonum et aequum*.

In a very real sense the troubled punitive scene right across the period was due to the flexibility impressed on *humanitas* by the need to reconcile its prescriptions with the public interest. The meaning of *humanitas* was in the discretion of the interpreter. Cicero was able to defend Rabirius and execute the Catilinarians in the same year. Augustus was criticized for having destroyed Brutus and Cassius; his claim that the *poena legis*, *utilitas publica* and *pietas* had coincided did not satisfy everyone. Yet many years later he was praised for circumventing the penalty for *parricidium* by *humanitas*. Nero saw no conflict between what Seneca had taught him and *utilitas publica* when he staged a cruel entertainment with the Christians; many people were outraged, but not everyone. And Justinian had no hesitation in expressly claiming *humanitas* as the inspiration of his decision to raise the penalty for adultery to death, because it would deter others from risking their immortal souls. There is no need to labour the point. Even the Antonines refrained from interfering with the *s.c. Silanianum*.

On more specific levels we need do no more than comment briefly on some of our findings. The allocation of *aquae et ignis interdictio* to the text of at least two of Sulla's laws, and the conversion of what had previously been left to the individual magistrate's discretion into a statutory duty, is felt to be secure. The effect of this finding on Sulla's image need not be gone into here. The more active role postulated for the magistrate in a jury trial may have wider implications. It supports Kunkel's belief that the jury-courts evolved out of the pre-quaestionary process of a magistrate (or head of a family) sitting in judgment with a *consilium*; in those cases the president was certainly not a figurehead. The need to deflect the odium of death sentences is a pointer to public dislike of capital punishment as such, but in the end it must be seen as a minority view; Seneca's attack on nasty modes of execution failed to lessen the lure of the arena. And the *liberum mortis arbitrium* was elitist at best, besides being a fraud as used by Claudius, though Domitian's concession of it to some of the Vestals improves its image. The latter's use of live burial as shock therapy was no doubt an application of *poenae metus*, but it went further than that. The number of women needing to be deterred was extremely small, and the purpose was the larger one of publicizing moral reform in general. But even that had a precedent. In his notice of voluntary exile Polybius says that punishment is one of the two bonds that hold society together (Pol. 6.14.4-8).

Of the important topics discussed in chapters 10 to 12, a last word must be said about attitudes to punishment, in the course of which we searched for opposition to capital punishment as such. Once Cicero has to be ruled out in spite of the ringing tones of his speech for Rabirius, we are left, for the Republic, with little more than what Sallust says Caesar said (*Cat.* 51.40–43). Caesar may have been pressing for abolition, but on our analysis he simply wanted to counter the danger posed by Catiline without contravening the *lex Sempronia* by adjudicating *de capite civium*. The debates in the senate under Tiberius and Nero do not take it much further. Lepidus and Thrasea pressed for the *poena legis*, but if that had happened to be death they would not have complained. Tacitus roundly condemns the *lex maiestatis*, but he never quite gets around to condemning capital punishment as such. In the second century Pius may have merely marooned a senatorial parricide, but the concession was limited to senators (*SHA Pius* 8.10). Marcus may have burnt the record to avoid having his relegation of a prefect used against him; he may also have asked the senate not to inflict the death penalty on Avidius Cassius' accomplices (CD 71.28.3, 30.1–2). But he used relentless severity against those (non-senators) who were clearly guilty of serious crimes (*SHA Marc.* 24.1). This is hardly surprising in the light of Favorinus' very specialized attack on the cruelty of the XII Tables. And the Severan jurists show much ability to systematize the rules of punishment, but no emotion whatever.

The bottom line is that there were very few bleeding hearts in Ancient Rome. Even in the very best period, the Late Republic, the most law-minded people of antiquity made the law their only criterion. Then, in the Principate, the rapid re-emergence of the death penalty hardly caused a ripple. We do not hear of any protests when Augustus had Caepio and Murena cut down on their way into exile. He had both precedent and *utilitas publica* on his side. Objections to the mass execution of Pedanius' slaves came from special interest groups. *Honestior* status may have been gradually extended beyond the senatorial order, but more civilized penalties were merely an affirmation of the new realities of social, economic and – in the Severan period – military power. Even the

Antonines, far from checking the gulf between *honestiores* and *humiliores*, took the initiative in giving it legislative definition. It was not by accident that the criminal law missed out on the accolade that greeted its private counterpart over the long centuries following the fall of Rome.

NOTES

1 INTRODUCTION

1 See chapter 4 under the headings '*Humanitas* and *Utilitas Publica*' and 'The conspiracy of Catiline'.
2 A useful account of Plato's *Laws* is provided by Stalley 1983. See also M. M. Mackenzie, *Plato on Punishment*, Berkeley 1981; T. J. Saunders, *Plato's Penal Code*, Oxford 1991. On Aristotle see H. G. Apostle, *Aristotle: The Nicomachean Ethics*, Dordrecht 1975. And on Theophrastus, A. Szegedy-Maszak, *The Nomoi of Theophrastus*, New York 1981.
3 See Bauman 1980.
4 The connection between Cicero's theory and practice on the specific question of *humanitas* and *utilitas rei publicae* is explored in chapter 4. On *De legibus* in general see Rawson 1973; Perelli 1990.
5 The major prefects are discussed in chapter 9. Provincial governors will be dealt with *passim*. A systematic exposition would require a book.

2 TRIAL BY MAGISTRATE AND PEOPLE

1 Dion. Hal. 2.25.6. Romulus 'allowed' rather than ordained it because jurisdiction was exercised by the family court. On Numa and Tullius see Servius ad Verg. *Ecl.* 4.43; L. 1.26.5–6.
2 Plin. *NH* 18.12; *D.* 47.9.9; Cic. *Rep.* 4.12; Cornutus ad Persius 1.137; Plin. *NH* 28.17.
3 See Mommsen 1887–8, 1.149–50, 2.109–l0, 3.351–4; 1899, 163–71, 473–8. See also Strachan-Davidson 1912, 1.127–45; Jones 1972, 1–39. For a useful summary (although he disagrees sharply with Mommsen) see Kunkel 1962, 9–17.
4 L. 3 56.1–58.6, 45.8, 55.4; Cic. *Orat.* 2.199, *Rep.* 2.53–5, *Rab. perd.* 11.
5 Critical assessments of Mommsen include Greenidge 1901, 305–31; Brecht 1939; Heuss 1944; Bleicken 1959; Kunkel 1962, 9–17 and *passim*; Martin 1970; Bauman 1973a; Cloud 1994, 501–3. Also of interest: Staveley 1954; De Martino 1972–4, 1.204–8, 314–16; Garofalo 1989, 53–68; Amirante 1991, 77–117. One pertinent criticism (cf. Heuss 1944, 80, 107) is that the sources do anything but support the idea that *provocatio* protected plebeians

against patrician oppression. Protection is usually claimed by patricians. L. 3.58.1–6 (despite 3.56.1,13); 1.26.5–6; 8.30.2–32.10; 37.51.3–5; 40.42.8–10; Fest. 462–4. The only plebeian claimant is in L. 2.55.4–11.

6 Kunkel 1962, 18–36. See also the neglected comments of Greenidge 1901, 304–31, especially 327–31. Also (critical of Kunkel) Jolowicz 1972, 308–16. The suggestion by B. Santalucia in Diliberto 1993, 9–28, that the jurisdiction was created by the XII Tables in one move rather than de facto and over time, does not convince.

7 For a concise summary of the tribunician process see Cic. *Dom.* 45. Also Mommsen 1899, 161–71; Greenidge 1901, 344–9; Bleicken 1968, *passim*; Jones 1972, 6–15.

8 Did *leges* regulate the definitions of crimes prior to the introduction of the jury-courts? Mommsen 1899, 57 firmly believed that there was always a *lex* – for definitions, procedures and penalties. Siber 1936 conceded a narrow original *lex* but gave the main thrust to magisterial (tribunician) interpretation. To Strachan-Davidson 1912, 105–8, 113 and Brecht 1938, 193 no *lex* was required; it was simply a question of what the tribune could persuade the people to punish as a crime.

9 Sources and discussion in Bauman 1967, 28–9; 1992, 19–20.

10 For a full discussion of this penalty see chapter 3 under the heading '*Humanitas*: The Alternative Capital Penalty'.

11 On this and what follows see, in more detail, Bauman 1974a.

12 Sources and discussion in Bauman 1967, 28–9; 1992, 19–20.

13 So Schadewalt 1973, 44, in the course of a lucid exposition of *humanitas*. For other useful discussions see Heinemann 1931; Schulz 1936, 189–222; Maschi 1948; Honig 1960, *passim*; Riccobono 1965; Büchner 1967; Lapicki 1969; Bauman 1980, 173–9, 182–218. And, marginally, Wubbe 1968.

14 Aulus Gellius *NA* 13.17.1 rejects the *philanthropia* component and focuses on *paideia*, which he defines as education and training in the liberal arts. But the dominant modern view is expressed in the text.

15 See *TLL, OLD* s.vv. See also the works in n. 13.

16 Polybius' *phylē* confuses the centuriate and tribal assemblies. But Dio 37.28.2 also has trouble with the centuries, for which the best he can do is *ekklēsiazontōn*.

17 Cic. *Caec.* 100. The passage has been attacked on technical grounds, but is acceptable to Levy 1963, 2.10–11, 337 n. 97, 340, 347; and De Martino 1972–74, 2.111, citing L. 26.3.12. I have been unable to find any reference to the passage in Crifo 1961 or 1984. For some interesting points see Sherwin-White 1973, 34–5, 126, arguing that the right of exile was first formally recognized in 211 BC. Cf. L. 26.3.12.

18 So Mommsen 1899, 70–3, ascribing three purposes to voluntary exile: to avoid a civil debt; to avoid a criminal fine; to avoid execution. Kunkel 1962, 67 n., 1974, 87 only considers the capital case. Jones 1972, 77 assumes both capital and pecuniary cases.

19 There is no reason to assume a fixed period (under the Republic), despite B. Levick, *Hist.* 28 (1979), 365. In Postumius Pyrgensis' case the period was fixed by reference to the date of the trial. L. 25.4.9. The sureties (*vades*) given in the paradigm case of Capitolinus were called up on the day of the trial when the accused failed to appear. L. 3.13.9–10. The trial date

was probably inserted as the marker in the stipulations taken from the sureties. In post-verdict departures a date was probably agreed with the offender and the sureties.

20 L. 29.9.10, 21.1, 22.9, 34.44.6.
21 Sources: Ascon. p. 25 St; Cic. *Fin.* 2.54. Mommsen 1899, 71 n. 1, 197 n. 2, 633 n. 4 thought he was brought back for a subsequent crime. But if he had completed his escape into exile he would no longer have been subject to Roman Law.
22 Strachan-Davidson 1912, 1.160–4; Jones 1972, 14, 77; Kunkel 1974, 87.
23 Kunkel 1962, 67 n. 253; Jones 1972, 14–15.
24 On federate treaties see De Martino 1972–74, 108–12; On *ius mutandae civitatis* see Sherwin-White 1973, 34.
25 So Gell. 6.19; his verbatim citation of two tribunician decrees lends credence to his account. Livy 38.60 makes it a special commission under a praetor.
26 On the private law *legis actio sacramento* see Jolowicz 1972, 180–2.
27 Kunkel 1962, 34–6, 51–70, 91–130; *SZ* (1967), 382–5; 1974, 38–45, 111–16. Kunkel's principal sources: Probus 4.5; Fest. 466 L (344 M) s.v. *sacramento tradere*; XII Tables 8.9, 8.23 (*FIRA* 1.56, 62); L. 3.11–13, 23.14.2–3; Dion. Hal. 10.5–8; Cic. *Fam.* 7.12; Serv. ad Verg. *Ecl.* 4.43; Apul. *Met.* 3.3.8. To these I would add L. 39.18.6. For a critical review of the theory see Jolowicz 1972, 308–13, 315–17. See also Eder 1969, 101–19. I am not sure that Kunkel has advanced the only cogent reason for postulating a common-law criminal jurisdiction. It was needed not only because of the political character of *iudicia populi*, but also because it was quite impracticable to keep the popular assembly in virtually permanent session.
28 On this episode see, in detail with sources, Bauman 1990; 1992, 35–9.
29 Bauman 1992, 38–9 on the trials of 184, 180, 154. Jones 1972, 28–9 on these and others over the period.
30 On the *tresviri* in general see Mommsen 1887–88, 2.594–601; 1899, 298. Also Strachan-Davidson 1912, 1.53, 2.24 n., 151 n.; Jones 1972, 2, 26–7; Cloud 1994, 500–1. On their criminal adjudications see Kunkel 1962, 71–9; 1974, 87. Doubts about their possession of actual jurisdiction in Jones 1972, 26–7; Robinson 1981, 214. See also Robinson 215–16 on whether slaves were tried by Republican jury-courts at all. I cannot agree, however, that the *iudices* who condemned the slave in VM 8.4.2 were the *tresviri* or their *consilium* or the slave-owner's *consilium*. One does not see the verdicts of either the *tresviri* or the *dominus* being identified by reference to the *consilium* rather than to the president.
31 Gell. 3.3.15; Hieron. *a. Abr.* 1805.
32 The *liberum mortis arbitrium* became a recognized penalty for lucky (*sic*) members of the elite in the Principate. See p. 74 below.
33 See Broughton 1952, 2.593–4.
34 See chapter 3 under '*Humanitas*: The Alternative Capital Penalty'.
35 On Cicero see chapter 4 under 'The trial of Rabirius'. On Sallust, chapter 3 under '*Humanitas*: The Alternative Penalty'. On Livy see the first section of this chapter.
36 The best account of the Roman death sentence is still that of Mommsen 1899, 911–44, though Cantarella 1991 must be given serious attention.

37 TA 5.9.3; CD 58.11.5. Cf. Mommsen 1899, 530.
38 Brasiello 1937, 246–71. Graphically, if over-enthusiastically, elaborated by Grodzynski 1984, 362.
39 Despite Garnsey 1970, 122–5. See the sixth section of chapter 12.
40 Sen. Rhet. *Controv.* 9.25 (pp. 382–95 M); VM 2.9.3.
41 See Bauman 1992, 22–8.

3 TRIAL BY JURY

1 See for example Gallini 1970.
2 See Bauman 1990; 1992, 35–9.
3 L. 42.8.1–96, 10.9–15, 21.1–5.
4 See L. 43.2.1–12 (considered by Eder 1969, 34 to be the first true *repetundae* process); L. 43.7.5–8.9; L. *Per.* 49, *Per. Oxy.* 49.
5 The attempt by Richardson 1987 to make a remedy for *Roman citizens* the primary purpose of the law fails to convince. The citizen had quite enough remedies already, in particular the *condictio*. Mommsen 1899, 708 thinks the law made *condictio* available to non-citizens, which makes better sense. The events leading up to the *lex Calpurnia* focus exclusively on subject peoples. There are no exploited citizens. Also, how did the tralatician references to the *lex Calpurnia* get into the *lex Acilia* (*vv.* 23, 74, *FIRA* 1.90, 100) if one law was talking about apples, the other about oranges? See also Cic. *Brut.* 106, *Off.* 2.75.
6 On the case for denying that the Calpurnian *quaestio* was a criminal court see Eder 1969, 58–74. Also Mommsen 1899, 190 n. 4; Kunkel 1974, 49–50. A criminal court is accepted by Jones 1972, 48–9; Jolowicz 1972, 308. That view is to be preferred. See Cic. *Brutus* 106, *De officiis* 2.75. On *infamia* in general see Greenidge 1894; Kaser 1956. On civil disabilities from the *lex Acilia* to the *lex Julia* see especially Eder 1969, 133, 136 n. 1, 178 n. 1, 181 n. 2. See also *FIRA* 1.90; (Auct.) *Ad Herennium* 1.20; Plin. *Ep.* 2.11.12. The generalization by A. N. Sherwin-White, *PBSR* 1949, 7 is not cogent.
7 On the cessation of the last of them, the *quaestio de adulteriis*, see p. 171 n. 46 below.
8 The course of a *repetundae* trial is sufficiently described by Strachan-Davidson 1912, 2.6–15.
9 Under the *lex maiestatis* it had to be shown that the act had been committed in order to diminish the majesty of the Roman people. This imported a subjective element which was not required under the *repetundae* law. On Scaurus' case See Bauman 1983, 390–4.
10 See Kunkel 1974, 66–7, inferring the double penalty in Caesar's law from the practice in the Principate. The leading case is C. Silanus, on which see Bauman 1974b, 92–9.
11 On the *lex Appuleia maiestatis* see Bauman 1967, 38–58. On other early *quaestiones perpetuae* see Kunkel 1962, 64–7; 1974, 52–6. See also Jones 1972, 54–6.
12 On the homicide law see Cloud 1969; Bauman 1980, 116–17, 120–3. On the forgery law see Pugliese 1982, 756–8; Marino 1988. On Sulla's laws in

general see Kunkel 1974, 56–67. One of those laws, the *lex Cornelia de iniuriis*, occupies a gray area between crime and delict. Although including a number of features of the criminal courts, it gave a private action to the injured party. The Severan jurist Aemilius Macer does not include it in his list of *iudicia publica*. *D*. 48.1.1. See Kunkel 1974, 58–9; Pugliese 1982, 724 n. 3.

13 See Cloud 1971; Jones 1972, 57; Kunkel 1974, 61–7.

14 See the section on 'Mixed penalties: *adulterium*', p. 32.

15 On the general procedural law and the *maiestas* law see Bauman 1980, 106 n. 1; 1967, 266–92. On the others see Jones 1972, 91; Kunkel 1974, 90–102.

16 The most lucid account is in Greenidge 1901, 456–504. See also Mommsen 1899, 366–451; Kunkel 1974, 74–90; Jones 1972, 58–73.

17 That is, senators, *equites* and *tribuni aerarii*. This was the final shape of the Republican album of jurors. Further decuries were added in the Principate.

18 Cic. *Rosc. Amer*. 30, 38, 61–3, 68–72.

19 E.g. Mommsen 1899, 421–3; Strachan-Davidson 1912, 2.125.

20 Ascon. p. 40 St. Elaborated by Bauman 1992, 56.

21 For our purpose it does not make much difference if Sallust gives the substance of what Caesar actually said or his own version of what was appropriate, Thucydides' *ta deonta*. The former is likely enough, but in any case the passage reflects enlightened opinion in the mid-first century BC.

22 In *Cat*. 51.22, 40 Sallust refers to 'the *lex Porcia* and other laws that allow exile'. The 'other laws' are not laws of *provocatio*; the *lex Porcia* was the last law on that subject. See Bauman 1973a. The 'other laws' are later, which means laws of Sulla. But Sallust preferred not to identify anything to Sulla's credit. In the *Catiline* he is uniformly hostile to Sulla. E.g. 5.6, 11.4–5, 28.4, 37.9, 51.34. Cf. *Hist*. 1.55.1, 7, 16–21; 3.48.1, 9; *In Cic*. 3.6. Strachan-Davidson 1912, 2.63–4 seizes some points correctly.

23 Strachan-Davidson 1912, 2.40–7. Cf. Mommsen 1899, 907. See also the observations of Brasiello 1937, 97–9.

24 E.g. Cic. *Dom*. 72; (Auct.) *Herenn*. 2.45; *D*. 48.1.2 (see below). Despite *Cluent*. 29, Cicero does not depart decisively from his position in *Pro Caecina* 100. He ranges to and fro depending on what the occasion requires.

25 Kunkel 1974, 87–90. Levy 1963 332–51, 442–6 is less drastic, reserving his attack for Sulla's laws and accepting interdiction in Caesar's; His argument is addressed under 'Mixed penalties: *parricidium*', p.30.

26 Despite Mommsen 1899, 840 n. 4 this is the *lex* that Ulpian is discussing. See Strachan-Davidson 1912, 2.23; Kunkel 1974, 87; Garnsey 1970, 109.

27 *Coll*. 12.5.1 read with *D*. 47.9.12.1

28 See for example *Coll*. 15.2.1 on the senate's decree of 17 AD against astrologers: 'A decree of the senate *is extant* by which it is provided that astrologers . . . be interdicted from water and fire and that their properties be confiscated.'

29 E.g. Gai. 1.128; *Coll*. 12.4.1; *D*. 48.13.3, 48.19.2.1; *PS* 5.29.1.

30 *D*. 48.10.33 (Modestinus) supports the ascription of interdiction to the *lex Cornelia testamentaria* (= *de falsis*). A third possible case is *peculatus*. *D*. 48.13.3.

31 See 'Mixed penalties: *parricidium*', p.30.
32 For a full discussion see Garnsey 1970, 111–22.
33 On this see Parpaglia 1987.
34 On the *lex Calpurnia* see CD 36.38.1 with Mommsen 1899, 873–5; Jones 1972, 57, 127 n.l. On Cicero's law see *Mur.* 3, 5, 46–7, 67, 89; *Sest.* 133; *Vat.* 37; CD 37.29.1. Rotondi 1912, 370 thinks the penalty under Cornelius' law was exile, in which case Cornelius may have anticipated Cicero. Cicero defended Cornelius on a charge of *maiestas* arising out of the passage of his law in 66. Bauman 1967, 71–5. On the Tullian exile's retention of his full status cf. the three degrees of *capitis deminutio* listed by Buckland 1963, 135. None of the three fits the Tullian case.
35 So Mommsen 1899, 874 but only as a weak suggestion.
36 Despite Mommsen 1899, 874, we cannot take Caesar *BC* 3.1, with its plebiscites recalling those exiled under Pompey's law, as a proof that the exile was permanent; recall in 48 was less than ten years after the law's enactment. On Pompey's law as a whole see Ascon. p. 34 St; App. *BC* 2.23–4 (misunderstood by Jones 1972, 57); Plut. *Cat. Min.* 48.3.
37 CD 54.16.1; SA 34.1; *D.* 48.14.1–4. Kunkel 1974, 91 postulates a penalty of a fine.
38 *D.* 48.7.1 pr., 15.7, 12.2.2.
39 We are here concerned with whether imprisonment was a formal *poena legis* in any public criminal law. We know that it was used against unruly citizens by a magistrate exercising *coercitio*, but that was not *adiudicatio*; the public criminal laws applied only to the latter. When punishments like imprisonment were imposed in the Principate they were considered of dubious validity. *D.* 48.3.1, *CJ.* 9.47.6. Cf. Garnsey 1970, 147–52. Eisenhut 1972 seeks to make imprisonment a definitive penalty and places great weight on the Catilinarian debate, but that was not held under any public criminal law. For a succinct account of the problem see Mayer-Maly 1964.
40 See Kunkel 1962, 37–45, 139 n. 476; 1974, 64; Cloud 1971; A. Magdelain, in Thomas 1984, 549–71; Cantarella 1991, 171–210; Lassen 1992. Also, briefly, Mommsen 1899, 612–13, 643–6; Levy 1963, 343.
41 Very ancient: Mommsen 1899, 922–3. Late third century BC: Cloud 1971, 27–36. The latter is almost certainly correct. See also chapter 6 n. 28.
42 L. *Per.* 68; Oros. 5.16.23–4; (Auct.) *Herenn.* 1.23; Cic. *Inv.* 2.149. On Cicero and Sex. Roscius see the references in n. 18.
43 This is the thrust of Levy's argument. Cf. n. 25 above. Levy thinks that the penalty had to be inferred from the clause constituting the *quaestio de sicariis*, that is, the clause requiring the court to *quaerere de capite eius*. As *capite puniri* primarily means to suffer the death penalty, Levy reads that meaning into the *lex*. But this makes the homicide law an exceptional case, given that the penalty was regularly included in the enabling statute. But then the testamentary forgery and *peculatus* laws were also exceptional. Cf. n. 30 above. For our main reply to Levy see the text.
44 With however a question mark against *Pauli Sententiae*'s identification of the *lex Pompeia* as the source of the *poena cullei*. In support of the solution offered here see also *CTh* 11.36.4, discussed in the fifth section of chapter 11.

45 SA 33.1, where the language, although slightly clumsy, makes it clear that both the *manifestus* and the *confessus* are at risk of the sack. Seneca cites another case under Augustus. A certain Tarius uncovered a plot by his son against his life, tried him in his domestic tribunal to which he summoned Augustus, and sent the youth into comfortable exile at Massilia. The lenient alternative to the sack was proposed by Augustus. Sen. *Clem.* 1.15.1–7. The case proves the existence of the *poena cullei*, but neither its inclusion or non-inclusion in the *quaestio perpetua*.

46 The jurists were critical of the law's inability to maintain a consistent distinction between *adulterium* and *stuprum*. D. 48.5.6.1, 50.16.101. Those texts might be examples of *Rechtskritik*, although Nörr 1974 does not cite them as such in his pioneering study. On the survival and workload of the *quaestio de adulteriis* see Bauman 1968.

47 Treggiari 1991, 290 and n. 172 notes some disabilities flowing from condemnation but sees them only as specific disqualifications.

48 For a clear account see Cantarella 1972. See also Kunkel 1962, 122–3. Treggiari 1991, 282–5 is of interest although she goes astray on the husband's right, making it an Augustan innovation with no traditional roots. We have the word of Cato the Censor for the existence of the husband's right in the early second century BC: 'If you should catch your wife in adultery you would kill her without trial, with impunity.' H. Malcovati (ed.), *Oratorum Romanorum Fragmenta*, 3 ed., Turin 1967, fr. 221–2.

49 The base categories enumerated in the texts include a pimp, an actor, a dancer, a singer, a contracted gladiator, a hired beast fighter, a convicted criminal, a freedman of the husband or wife, or a slave. D. 48.5.25 pr., *Coll.* 4.3. Cf. *PS* 2.26.4. On the detailed rules see Cantarella 1972.

50 *Coll.* 4.3.5; D. 48.5.25.1. Cf. *Coll.* 4.12.5, D. 48.5.12.10.

51 Adultery never attracted the death penalty in the Principate. Cf. chapter 12, fifth section.

4 CICERO ON PUNISHMENT

1 On this work see De Plinval 1969; Rawson 1973; Perelli 1990, 113–36. It was almost certainly written in 52–1 BC rather than in the mid-forties. See Rawson, 335–8. *De officiis*, our other major source for Cicero's theoretical thinking on crime and punishment, was written in 44. It is Cicero's last work but one. Only *Topica* was still to come.

2 The expression *utilitas publica* is substantially equivalent to *rei publicae utilitas*, which is the form most favoured by Cicero, and also to *utilitas communis/omnium/hominum/civium/civitatis/populi*. Cf. Gaudemet 1951, 467–8 and *passim*.

3 On this step reference should also be made to Ducos 1984a, 341–81, under the heading '*La crainte du châtiment*'. It is the first serious attempt to assess Cicero's thinking on punishment.

4 Cf. n. 2.

5 See the works listed in chapter 2 n. 13. See also *TLL* s.v. *humanitas*.

6 The theme of the *poena legis* is developed further in this chapter (below) and throughout the work.

7 See for example Aria's encouragement of her husband to follow her example and stab himself with the words, 'You see, it doesn't hurt.' On the incident see Sherwin-White 1966, 248–9.

8 See also chapter 6 n. 29.

9 See *Leg.* 1.40, 2.19, 25, 43, 44. Also the citation of Cicero's *Republic* by Lactantius *Div. Inst.* 6.8, on which see Perelli 1990, 115–16. On *luctus animi* see *TLL* s.v; *OLD* s.v. For a graphic description see TA 2.29.1. On Menenius and Augustus see L. 2.52.5; SA 32.2.

10 *Leg.* 1.40–1, *Off.* 3.38 on the ephemeral temporal punishment; *Leg.* 2.19, 25 on the superior power of divine punishment.

11 So Rawson 1973, 348. If we want a 'local' rather than a general motivation we can also point to P. Clodius' law of 58 which prevented augural obstructions from holding up the business of the assembly. Sources in Broughton 1952, 2.196.

12 *Leg.* 2.31, 3.27. Cf. Cic. *Pis.* 8, 10; *Vat.* 18, 23; *Prov. Con.* 46; *Sest.* 33, 114; *Post red.* 11; *Har. Resp.* 58. See also Perelli 1990, 127–8.

13 Cf. Bauman 1983, 135–41.

14 *Rep.* 5.1–2. Seneca puts a similar sentiment in Nero's mouth. *Clem.* 1.1.4.

15 That *cavere* in a legal context denotes a provision in a *lex* hardly needs documentation. See for example *D.* 48.9.1, 48.7.1.

16 See for example *Rep.* 1.3: the citizen compels everyone by the authority of magistrates and the penalties of the laws to obey rules which philosophers are only able to impress on a few by their dissertations. See also *Rep.* 3.18, 5.6; *Verr.* 2.1.124. Cf. Ducos 1984a, 342–3.

17 On this see Ducos 1984a, 344–5, though she errs in attributing a single penalty for all crimes to Dracon. That canard preserved by Plutarch loses sight of the vital distinction between intentional and unintentional wrongdoing that Dracon was the first to spell out. See my 'The interface of Greek and Roman law: Contract, Delict and Crime'. RIDA 43 (1996).

18 See especially *De finibus* 4.74, 77. Cf. Ducos 1984a, 345–6.

19 See for example Boyancé 1970. He does not so much as mention the word *humanitas*, let alone its criminal law implications. Ciulei 1972 is similarly limited.

20 See for example Hadrian's legislation on the subject. Bauman 1989, 278–80, 72–3.

21 He was thinking about it in the 80s, in *De inventione* 2.101: In all things the intent (*voluntas*) should be looked to. He cannot be condemned because he is free of fault (*culpa*). Nothing is more disgraceful than that one who is free of fault should not be free of punishment. Cf. *ib.* 2.86. He was still thinking of it nearly forty years later. *Topica* 63–4.

22 On this as the original form of Sulla's homicide law see Cloud 1969; Bauman 1980, 120–3. On intention in general see Genin 1968, *passim*; Gioffredi 1970, 63–109.

23 Kunkel 1974, 57 thinks that was included in the original *lex*.

24 See for example the cases of unlawful killing by a husband in chapter 3. Also below *passim*.

25 *Off.* 1.27; *Top.* 64.

26 *Nomoi* 866d–867b with *De officiis* 1.28.

27 See *TLL* s.v. *humanitas*, coll. 1079–81.
28 Quintilian *Inst. Orat.* 7.4.18, 5.13.5.
29 On this case se Bauman 1967, 142–8.
30 See Jossa 1964, especially 279–88.
31 On tbe Epaminondas episode see Nepos *Epam.* 7–8. See also Cic. *Tusc.* 1.4; *Orat.* 3.139.
32 See for example *Deiot.* 30, 32; *Cael.* 26; *Mil.* 22; *Verr.* 2.5.187; *Flacc.* 24, 57, 62.
33 On these events see Bauman 1967, 33, 49–50; 1976, 60–5; 1983, 333–7. On the precedent for the decree against Saturninus, and on the prosecution and acquittal of the consul Opimius for acting thereunder, see Ungern-Sternberg 1970, 55–71. The sole purpose of decrees of this sort was to calm a disturbance; when that was achieved the decree lapsed. Cloud 1994, 495 mistakenly has the senate pass a decree 'to enable the magistrates to *execute* citizens'. That might follow, but it was not the primary purpose. Cicero did not put his first decree against the Catilinarians to such a use. See below, p. 45.
34 Bauman 1973b, *passim*; 1983, 337–40.
35 The more liberal wing of Late Republican politics. Not democratic, but populist.
36 At the trial of Opimius, on which see Ungern-Sternberg 1970, 68–71.
37 On the acquittal see Cic. *Rap. perd.* 18. He was tried either by a *iudicium populi* or by a jury-court under Sulla's homicide law. *Rab. perd.* 18, 7, 8 do not make it possible to say which it was. But a jury-court may be the better guess.
38 I here summarize, with some amplifications, Bauman 1969. The case raises so many anomalies that a received view may never emerge. In any case our primary concern is with certain passages in Cicero's speech whose interpretation is largely independent of the anomalies. The mini-corpus on the case includes Mommsen 1887–8, 2.615–18, 1899, 155 n. 1; Greenidge 1901, 354–9; Strachan-Davidson 1912, 1.188–204; Brecht 1938, 170–89; Ungern-Sternberg 1970, 81–5; Jones 1972, 40–4; W. B. Tyrrell, *SZ* 91 (1974), 106–25; J. D. Cloud, *Liverpool Classical Monthly* 2 (1977), 205–13; A. Primmer, *Sitzungsberichte d. Akad. d. Wissenschaft in Wien., Phil.-Hist. Kl.* 169 (1985), 1–68; C. Loutsch, *REL* 64 (1986), 28–31; Cantarella 1991, 178, 186–7, 198. The theory of L. Havas, *Acta Classica Univ. Scient. Debreceniensis* 12 (1976), 19–27, that the trial was not instigated by Caesar, but by Varro on Pompey's behalf, and that Rabirius was a willing participant against an indemnity, need not be taken seriously. Nothing of value on the criminal side is offered by B. Liou-Gille, *Lat.* 53 (1994), 3–38.
39 The paradigm case is the trial of Horatius in the regal period. L. 1.26.2–6, on which see Cantarella 1991, 171–210. On the identification of suspension on the *infelix arbor* as death by being beaten, not by crucificion, see W. Oldfather, *TAPA* 39 (1908), 49–72; and, most recently, Cantarella 1991, 175–206.
40 CD 37.27.3. I previously argued that Suetonius is right about tbe second trial, Dio having mistakenly allocated the flag incident to the second trial instead of to the first. But I am now inclined to take Dio's account more seriously. *Rab. perd.* 18 has Rabirius acquitted at the first trial on the

merits, not because of a disruption of the proceedings. When Suetonius says that nothing so helped Rabirius as the people's dislike of the harshness of the *duumviri* (SJ 12), is he not reflecting his own reaction when he read Cicero's speech? That is what Cicero wanted people to feel, but as he had already eliminated the duumviral penalty from the case, he was really arguing against himself.

41 This is a safe inference from the extract from the speech set out below. Cicero's language, *meo consilio, virtute, auctoritate . . . senatus me agente* clearly makes him the author of a *senatus consultum*, not a consul using his veto (despite Strachan-Davidson 1912, 1.197–8). There will have been an interval between Rabirius' exercise of *provocatio* and the comitial trial during which Cicero had ample time to consult the senate. Labienus probably held three sessions of an *anquisitio* before committing Rabirius for trial by the people.

42 *Rab. perd.* 10, 12–13, 15, 16, 17, 32.

43 The most recent accounts of the conspiracy are by T. P. Wiseman, *CAH* 9, 2 ed. 1994, 353–8 and R. Stewart, *Lat.* 54 (1995), 62–78. I have not seen A. Drummond, *Law, Politics and Power*, Franz Steiner, Stuttgart 1995.

44 On the *lex Sempronia* see for example Ungern-Sternberg 1970, 48–54, 104–8; Kunkel 1974, 25–6, 271–3.

45 Cf. Merrill 1918, 44–52; Brecht 1938, 205–9; De Martino 1972–4, 3.16.3.

46 He again raises the question of Catiline joining Manlius' forces in Etruria in *Cat.* 1.5–6, 23–4.

47 Cf. Kunkel 1974, 17–22, 273–5; Bauman 1974b, 177–90, 192–4, 195–7, 202–3, 215–17; 1981, *passim.* The very existence of the doctrine is queried by J. A. Crook, *Camb. Philol. Journ.* 1987, 38–52, but he leaves too many of the examples unexplained. To the evidence already adduced in favour of the doctrine add the interpretation (below) of Sall. *Cat.* 52.36, where *confessi* are dealt with by analogy with *manifesti* – *not* the other way around. See also nn. 48, 49.

48 This is a typical pointer to the manifest case. Cf. TA 11.30.4–5 with Bauman 1974b, 182.

49 This is the *confessus*, here as elsewhere in second position after the *manifestus.*

50 All five of Cicero's applications of that theory are in speeches connected with Catiline. *Cat.* 2.11 (*bis*), 2.17, 3.14; *Sull.* 28.

51 *Eos . . . senatus iudicaverat contra rem publicam fecisse.* On that type of declaration see Mommsen 1887–8, 4.1067–9; Bauman 1980, 124–6. It was not a criminal adjudication; it was not even equivalent to a *hostis* declaration. Bleicken 1962, 24; Ungern-Sternberg 1970, 92–3 with n. 40; Kunkel 1974, 272–3 with n. 6. The declaration was primarily an interpretation enabling a given set of facts to be brought under a given public criminal law. But it also served as an indemnity to anyone who acted under a *s.c. ultimum* or other emergency decree. It is in that sense that it is used here.

52 Bleicken 1962, 17–27, thinks that where a *hostis* declaration was involved the senate gave a finding of fact in regard to the guilt of the person concerned. That underpinning of the *hostis* declaration amounted, though

only in cases of treason, to adjudicating as a court. This theory is strongly opposed by Kunkel 1974, 268–75, 327, and rightly. It is true that Catiline was declared a *hostis* when it became known that in Etruria he had assumed magisterial insignia and taken command of troops raised by Manlius. Sall. *Cat.* 36.1–3; CD 37.33.3. But in order to qualify as an adjudication the senate's debate needed to be focused on a *crimen*, a charge under one of the public criminal laws. When it became a criminal court proper in the Principate its debates and verdicts were always so focused. In 63 the only *lex* that might have applied was the *lex Cornelia maiestatis*, but there is no trace of it in the Catilinarian affair.

53 Cic. *Cat.* 4.7–8; Sall. *Cat.* 51.43; CD 37.36.2. On the divergent tradition which wrongly has the imprisonment only continue until Catiline is defeated see Ungern-Sternberg 1970, 102 n. 95. That tradition is a doublet of Tiberius Nero's proposal.

54 Sall. *Cat.* 51.18, 22. 40.

55 App. *BC* 2.5–6; Plut. *Caes.* 7.5, *Cat. Min.* 22.4.

56 Plut. *Cic.* 21.3, *Cat. Min.* 22.5.

57 Sall. *Cat.* 52.1–36. The brief summary in Plut. *Cat. Min.* 1–2 includes an allegation that Caesar was using *humanitas* (*philanthropia*) to subvert the state. Ungern-Sternberg 1970, 94–5 lists a number of items attested by other sources but absent from Sallust's account. But these do not warrant the rejection of the speech. In particular the motion at the end of the speech (below, p. 48) reflects careful juristic formulation. See also n. 59.

58 The conspirators in Rome had tried to arouse the Gallic Allobroges to revolt. The incriminating letters that came into Cicero's possession related to this attempt.

59 I am unable to agree with Ungern-Sternberg 1970, 94 that Cato avoids all confrontation with opposing juristic arguments. The analogy here drawn is distinctly juristic.

60 Sources in Broughton 1952, 2.174.

61 Vell. 2.45.1; CD 38.14. Cf. Greenidge 1901, 359; Rotondi 1912, 394.

62 Greenidge 1901, 359–66; Rotondi 1912, 395. The allegedly false *senatus consultum* (Cic. *Dom.* 50) was the subject of vigorous controversy. Cicero attempts to refute it in his defence of P. Sulla in 62 (on a charge of conspiring with Catiline!); he details all the precautions he had taken to ensure an accurate transcript of the proceedings and the distribution of copies throughout the empire. *Pro Sulla* 41–4.

63 He addressed the senate, the people and the pontifical college. Whether or not the speeches are genuine, they add very little to his thinking on punishment.

5 THE NEW COURTS: AUGUSTUS AND TIBERIUS

1 Also known as *c. extra ordinem*. The use of this as a technical term has been criticized. See references in Fanizza 1982, 96 n. 221. But convenience prescribes its continued use.

2 At the turn of the first century AD Pliny cited as axiomatic the maxim *licere senatui et mitigare leges et intendere* – 'the senate has power to mitigate or

intensify the laws'. Plin. *EP.* 4.9.17. On this passage and its antecedents see Bauman 1980, 151–3. The superior power was the emperor, who over time exercised more and more control over the senate in this regard. The emperor's delegates, the urban and praetorian prefects, did not have the power of mitigation or intensification at all. See below.

3 See for example *D.* 48.1.1, 48.4–15. For the theory of Dupont and Brasiello, according to which the *cognitio extraordinaria* eventually brought about the abandonment of the link with the *leges iudiciorum publicorum*, and for a refutation of that theory, see Bauman 1980, 219–27.

4 See for example *Coll.* 12.5.1.

5 On this see De Robertis 1939a; Levy 1963, 433–508. Discussion in chapter 11 *passim.*

6 Despite Jones 1972, 91–3. For a refutation of his view that *iudicii publici exercitio* was conferred on senate and emperor by a *lex* see Bauman 1980, 147 n. 260. For other views on the origin of the *cognitio extraordinaria* see *ibid.* 146–7. And for a theory as to the origin of the emperor's jurisdiction see Bauman 1967, 203–4, 231–3. For other views as to the origin of this jurisdiction see the literature cited in Bauman 1980, 163, nn. 42–4.

7 Bauman 1968, 77–85.

8 This is deduced for at least one court, the *quaestio de adulteriis* which was the main victim of congestion, by CD 55.10.16: Augustus laid down a specific period and decreed that there was to be no investigation of anything done prior to that. The period was five years. D. 48.5.30.5–7.

9 See Bauman 1968, 88–93. See also chapter 9 below on the prefectorial jurisdictions.

10 Either Diocletian or Constantine abolished appeals against judgments of the praetorian prefect. *D.* 1.11.1; *CTh* 11.30.16. This made him an independent, hence lawmaking, jurisdiction. The urban prefect did not receive a similar power. Cf. *D.* 1.12.

11 Cf. Cic. *Sull.* 41–3.

12 I here summarize, with additions, the relevant features of Bauman 1974b, 25–51.

13 On *deportatio* see Mommsen 1899, 974–80; Garnsey 1970, 113–15; Pugliese 1982, 765–6. Mommsen thinks the intensification of interdiction began under Tiberius. But Augustus had made inroads into free access to any treaty state. In 12 AD exiles were excluded from the mainland and from any island within fifty miles of the coast, with a few exceptions. Garnsey thinks *deportatio* as a technical term did not establish itself until the early second century. But it was in use from Tiberius' time, and was in fact intensified by him when he deprived the *deportatus* of the right to make a will. Strachan-Davidson 1912, 2.55–7 with CD 57.22.5.

14 Plato 862a–863a, 942a, 958a.

15 A possible predecessor can be distinguished. In 26 BC Cornelius Gallus, prefect of Egypt, was punished by Augustus by renunciation of friendship and exclusion from the imperial provinces. But proceedings in the jury-court were also set on foot (much to the annoyance of Augustus), and the senate fixed a hybrid penalty: he was to be exiled but his property was to be handed over to Augustus instead of to the state treasury. But the senate was only interpreting a public criminal law, it was not actually trying the

case itself. Bauman 1980, 147–9. On possible trials see Bleicken 1962, 32–5; Kunkel 1974, 326–30. The only strong contender is L. Valerius Messala Volesus, whose trial for *repetundae* in 13 AD was probably by the senate rather than by the *quaestio*. Bleiken 1962, 35. Contra Kunkel 1974, 328. In any case this was later than Cassius Severus' trial.

16 For full discussions of this *cause célèbre* see Bauman 1967, 198–242; 1992, 105–19.

17 Vell. 2.100.5; Sen. *Clem.* 1.10.3.

18 Silanus left Rome of his own accord. In 20 AD he applied for permission to return, but Tiberius ruled that this was not necessary; Silanus had not been exiled under the public criminal laws and was entitled to return as of right. TA 3.24.1, 5–7.

19 Tiberius referred the case to her family's domestic court. But her lover, Manlius, was tried by the senate – understandably, since the family court had no jurisdiction over him. TA 2.50. On Tiberius's sparing use of personal *cognitio* altogether see below, n. 27.

20 Their deaths are attested by CD 54.3.5, Vell. 2.91.2. They do not say that they were killed while in flight, but Macrobius *Sat.* 1.11.21 says Caepio was pursued after his condemnation. And Strabo 14.5.4 says Murena's friend Athenaeus was captured in flight.

21 On that precept see chapter 7 under 'Seneca on clemency'.

22 It empowered the *quaestio maiestatis*, authorized trials *in absentia* and raised confiscation to total forfeiture. Mommsen 1899, 199 n. 3; Rotondi 1912, 435. Kunkel 1974, 78 points out that trials *in absentia* were only allowed where the accused stayed away contumaciously. The *quaestio* that tried Caepio and Murena was aware of that. CD 54.3.5.

23 See Bauman 1982b.

24 Sen. *Clem.* 1.9.2–12 makes the conspirator L. Cinna and dates it to when Augustus was 'past his fortieth year' and staying in Gaul. This is usually taken as Augustus' sojourn over 16–13 BC. Volkmann 1969, 84; Kunkel 1974, 182. But Livia was not with Augustus in Gaul at that time. CD 54.19.3. If Gaul was the venue – and Seneca must have had some reason for nominating it – it will have to be 10 or 8 BC. In Dio 55.14.1–22.2 the conspirator is Cn. Cornelius Cinna Magnus, the date is 4 AD, and the location is Rome. Dio's date is too close to Cinna Magnus' consulship of 5 *AD*. His venue explains Livia's presence but may not be true. But he names the conspirator correctly.

25 It is rejected by Fitzler-Seeck, *RE* 10.370–1 and Speyer 1956. Kunkel 1974, 181–3 is less sceptical.

26 See chapter 3 under 'Mixed Penalties: *Parricidium*'.

27 TA 3.10.3–4, 12.4. His only known use of *cognitio* was on Capri, but only two cases are attested. Bauman 1989, 72 and n. 94. Dio 57.7.2–6 is badly confused.

28 TA 1.75.1; ST 33; CD 57.7.6.

29 ST 33; TA 4.38.1.

30 On which see T. Honoré, *Emperors and Lawyers*, London 1981, viii–ix, 7.

31 Cf. Bauman 1974b, 221–3.

32 As throughout this study, our main focus will be on trials bearing significantly on punishment. For complete accounts see Marsh 1931; Rogers

1935. See also Bauman 1974b, *passim*. For a survey of the types of charge adjudicated on by the senate see Bleicken 1962, 53–4.

33 To some extent the earliest example was that of Libo Drusus in 16. Charged with *maiestas* and occult practices, he killed himself in the middle of the trial. Tiberius declared on oath that he would have pardoned him if he had not been in such a hurry to take his life. TA 2.31.4. Tiberius made his statement on oath in order to make it something of a precedent on clemency. But Piso's trlal (below) is one of Tacitus' major episodes and will have occupied that position at the time.

34 TA 3.12.4–10; ST 28. For a precis of the speech see Bauman 1974b, 109.

35 TA 3.15.4–6, 17.1–2, 17.8, 18.1. Furneaux 1896, 562 thinks L. Calpurnius Cn. f. Piso, *cos*. 27, is the son who took a new *praenomen*.

36 E.g. Libo Drusus. See n. 33.

37 TA 3.49–51.1; CD 57.20.3. See also Bauman 1974b, 63–4.

38 TA 3.51.2–3; CD 57.20.4.

39 TA 3.66–9. On tbe Republican and Augustan precedents see Bauman 1974b, 94–5.

40 The clearest attestation of the rule is TA 6.29.2. The defence of this position by C. W. Chilton, *JRS* 45 (1955), 73–81 against the attack by R. S. Rogers, *JRS* 49 (1959), 90–4, undoubtedly succeeded, but the whole debate was unnecessary in view of the demonstration by E. Volterra, *RIDA* 2 (1949), 488–90 that posthumous *maiestas* charges were first introduced by Marcus Aurelius in the second century. On the supposed distinction in the *lex Julia maiestatis* between *perduellio* which generated posthumous charges and other forms of the crime that did not, see Bauman 1967, 287–8.

41 On Silius' case see TA 4.18–20. For the emphasis on *maiestas* in the case and the illusory inclusion of *repetundae*, and also for the arguments supporting the various propositions in the text, see Bauman 1974, 116–19. On the background to the case see Bauman 1992, 145–7, 176–7.

42 See for example *PS* 5.4.8–9. See also below *passim*.

43 The senate had taken over the jury-court practice under which successful accusers had been rewarded even in the Republic. But it was only in the Principate that the delators turned this into a cottage industry, acquiring wealth from the defined share of confiscated property that accrued to them. Under Claudius, P. Suillius earned as much as 40,000 sesterces per case. TA 11.5.2. Their technique of beating up business by creating indictable opportunities through networks of agents and informers is seen by the sources as one of the great evils of the treason trials, but the emperors considered them an indispensable cog in the machine. When no accuser was forthcoming regular criminal process could not take place. TA 15.69.1. But it should be said in their favour that they were not responsible for the intensification of the *poena legis* to death. They got the same share either way. On the system see Mommsen 1899, 366–75, 381–6, 253 n. 7, 504–11, 830 n. 2; Kunkel 1974, 13, 49–50, 74–8, 82–4, 96, 283. See also Greenidge 1901, 459–60, 467–71, 475–6; Marsh 1931, 107–10; Jones 1972, 110–11.

44 TA 6.19.1; CD 58.22.2–3 (with embellishments).

45 Cf. Mommsen 1899, 688 n. 4. Precipitation from the Tarpeian Rock (on

the Arx of the Capitol in Rome – Cantarella 1991, 241) rules out a trial by Tiberius on Capri. Whether Suetonius' description of the precipitation of the condemned from the cliffs of Capri (ST 52.2) is true – he claims to have been shown the spot as a tourist – or is an elaboration of Sex. Marius' case cannot be determined.

46 *D.* 48.18.5, 48.5.39 pr., 2. Less clearly *PS* 2.26.15.
47 See the detailed analysis of this mode of execution by Cantarella 1991, 238–63.
48 E.g. TA 1.72.3, 73.1, 74.3; 2.50.1; 3.37.1, 38.1, 67.3; 4.19.5, 34.3, 36.1; 6.18.1, 38.4.
49 E.g. 1.74.7; 3.33.4, 38.1, 67.2, 70.1; 4.19.5.
50 TA 4.13.2, 28.1–30.2; CD 57.24.8.
51 TA 4.31.2–3, 5–6 (where *e re publica* is an assertion of *utilitas publica*).
52 On this case see Bauman 1974b, 99–103. See also Marsh 1931, 290–3; Rogers 1935, 86–7 (but with caution in view of their fixation on 'preliminary charges preceding more serious accusations').
53 TA 4.52.1–2, 5–6, 66.1; CD 59.19.1.
54 On Agrippina and her party see Bauman 1992, 143–5, 154–6. The trials of her supporters include Silius, Sosia and Claudia Pulchra.
55 On the delators see n. 43.
56 Cf. Bauman 1974b, 113–24.
57 Julia was transferred from the island of Pandateria to Rhegium on the mainland in 3 AD. CD 55.13.1. Agrippina was interned at Herculaneum. Sen. *De ira* 3.21.5. Nero's place of internment is not known. On the rearrangement of TA 5.3.3–4.2 in order to uncover the first (non-capital) trial in 27 see Meise 1969, 237–44; Bauman 1992, 150–1.
58 TA 4.67.6. The agents advised them to flee to the German armies or to embrace the statue of Augustus in the Forum and to call for assistance. Cf. ST 53.2.
59 TA 4.68–70; CD 58.1b–3; ST 61.2; Plin. *NH* 8.145.
60 On the second trial see Bauman 1974b, 122–3; 1992, 151–3.
61 TA 6.19.2–5, where the victims are accused of *societas cum Seiano*, elsewhere rendered as *Seiani amicitia*; the use of both expressions in indictments was designed to support an inference of complicity in Sejanus' conspiracy (whatever that was). This use of metonymy was not uncommon. See for example *quod in Africa fuerit* (Cic. *Lig.* 1.1, 3.9, *Schol. Gron.* p. 84) for Q. Ligarius' support of the Pompeians against Caesar. Tacitus' *omnis sexus, omnis aetas, inlustres ignobiles* is also important; the punitive differentials between *honestiores* and *humiliores*, already appearing in Tacitus' day, had specifically not influenced Tiberius in 33. The *immensa strages* is broadly confirmed by CD 58.21.5 and ST 61.4. But Dio's restriction of the victims to accusers (who had presumably failed to secure convictions) is a retrojection of the punishment of delators under later reigns (on which see Bauman 1974b, 192–4). Suetonius' version is misunderstood by Rogers 1935, 147; he does not say that there were only twenty victims, but that twenty were cast out on the Gemonian Steps and thrown into the Tiber in a single day – in other words, a record amongst several days' tallies.
62 TA 6.18.1–5, where *aqua atque igni interdictum* with reference to Sancia is simply a variant for the, by this time, standard intensification of the

poena legis to deportation. In Pompeia Macrina's case another variant, *exilium*, is used.

63 Both she and her brother were accused by the same man, Q. Pomponius 'who undertook these cases (*haec*) . . . in order to win the emperor's favour'.

64 TA 6.10.1; CD 58.4.5–6.

65 Cic. *Rab. perd.* 24; VM 8.1 damn. 2. It was probably at this time that the rule known to the jurists, whereunder suicide in order to avoid a conviction could not be mourned, was formulated. *D* 3.2.11.3, on which see Bauman 1989, 72–3, 278–80.

66 TA 6.8–9.1; CD 58.19.1, 3–5.

67 TA 6.9.1; CD 58.19.5, where E. Cary's rendering of *prosepitimēse* as 'rebuked' is one of the great understatements of classical translation. On *calumnia* in general see Greenidge 1901, 468–70; Jones 1972, 62–4, 73, 118; Kunkel 1974, 76, 90, 204, 240, 310, 316, 329.

68 On Albucilla's case see Rogers 1935, 162–4; Bauman 1974b, 130–4, 175–6.

6 THE MATURING *COGNITIO*: CALIGULA AND CLAUDIUS

1 Officially Gaius, but generally known by his nickname.

2 CD 59.18.2, where *ephesimoi* may mean appeals but is more probably the emperor's assumption of jurisdiction of first instance on request, thus doing what Tiberius had refused to do.

3 Augustus had created a fourth decury and Caligula added a fifth. Bauman 1968, 83. When Galba was asked to provide a sixth he refused and lengthened the court year instead. Suet. *Galb.* 14.3.

4 Bauman 1974b, 204–10.

5 CD 59.8.2–3, 8.8, 10.2–4, 10.7, 11.6, 13.2–7, 18.2–3, 19.1–7, 20.6, 22.6, 25.6, 26.4; SG 23.3, 24.2, 26.1–2, 27, 28, 29.2, 30.1, 32.1–3, 35.1, 38.1–3, 39.1, 41.2, 53.2; Jos. *Ant.* 19.12–14, 24–6, 32–6, 43. See also, on Seneca's views, chapter 7, n. 8.

6 CD 59.10.4 also has a cage. It may have been copied from the punishment reputedly inflicted on Callisthenes by Alexander. Diog. Laert. 5.5.

7 Cf. Mommsen 1899, 947 n. 4, 949–53; Garnsey 1970, 132 and n. 4.

8 See for example *D.* 28.3.6.10, reading *poena non [sumpta] sua* with Mommsen; *D.* 48.19.9.11.

9 Mommsen 1899, 925–8; Garnsey 1970, 129–31.

10 *D.* 48.8.11.2, 40.1.24 pr. Cf. Mommsen 1899, 926 n. 2; Rotondi 1912, 468; Garnsey 1970, 130 n. 7.

11 Cf. the felicitous 'vivicombustione' of Cantarella 1991, 224. Latin terms: *vivicomburium, crematio, vivus exuril incendi, igni necari*. The most convenient equivalent is 'vivicombustion'. *Crematio* primarily implies burning the dead.

12 *D.* 47.9.9. If the act was accidental the penalty was commuted to pecuniary compensation.

13 Deserters were burnt alive or hanged; *humiliores* guilty of *maiestas* received

ad bestias or vivicombustion; magicians were burnt alive, but their assistants suffered *ad bestias* or crucifixion. *D.* 48.19.38.1; *PS* 5.29.1, 23.17. Slaves who plotted against their masters were burnt alive; Callistratus adds as a general proposition that plebeians and persons of lowly status sometimes suffer the same penalty. *D.* 48.19.28.11.

14 Bauman 1989, 278. Cantarella 1991, 225–36 takes the story too seriously.

15 Bauman 1989, 130–1, 133, 138–9, discussing SG 34.2.

16 Suetonius notices Caligula's attack on the lawyers in only one place, SG 34.2.

17 On the emperor's *consilium* in its judicial mode see Kunkel 1974, 178–254. Crook 1955, 39–40 adduces some evidence for a *consilium* but does not press it; he concedes that Caligula did not hold court in public. In fact CD 60.4.3 is decisive: the practice of sitting with a *consilium* was in abeyance from Tiberius' withdrawal to Capri until Claudius' accession.

18 References and discussion in Bauman 1989, 134–7.

19 On trials held privately and alone see n. 17. On the absence of the accused see CD 59.18.2. On judging his own cause see the case of the Atellan farce-writer (above) and the posthumous *maiestas* confiscations (below).

20 Instituting the emperor was usually a compliment that he gracefully declined, letting the inheritance go to the substitutes, who were the intended heirs all along. Whether Caligula looked at it in this way is debatable.

21 Bauman 1974b, 138 with SG 38.2–3.

22 See SC 11, 12, 14, 15, 22, 23, 25, 29.1–2; CD 60.3.1–4.4, 5.7, 6.3, 13–16, 17.7, 18.4, 25.8, 28.6, 29.4–6a, 33.6, 8; *Apocolocyntosis* 6, 7, 10–14; Jos. *Ant.* 20.132. Tacitus Books 11–12 focuses so intently on Messalina's bigamous marriage and Valerius Asiaticus' trial that he hardly has time for anything else. See however TA 12.22, 41, 52, 59, 64; and on professional accusers 11.5–7, 12.42. It should be noted however that we only have Book 11 in a very incomplete form. In general see Stroux 1929; May 1936; Bleicken 1962, 104–15; Wolf 1991. On his public sittings see Bleicken *loc. cit.* with CD 60.4.3.

23 See Bauman 1974b, 194–204.

24 Cf. Bauman *loc. cit.* On the hostile tradition see SC 29.1–2; CD 60.14–16 (including16.7, citing Homer *Il.* 24.369 for the assertion that 'one must take revenge when someone injures one'); *Apocolocyntosis* 9.7, 10.2–11.6, 14–15. The doctrine of manifest guilt was still in full operation in the second century. *SHA Vit. Marc.* 24.1. See also Jones 1972, 118.

25 On verdicts by acclamation see Colin 1965; Bauman 1974b, 195–6, 177–88; 1995, 389–90. On the proceedings against Messalina and her lovers see TA 11.26.1, 27, 31–2, 35–8; SC 26.2, 29.3, 36, 39.1; CD 60.30.6a–31.5. See also Bauman 1974, 177–88; 1992, 176–9.

26 So May 1936, 244–5. Followed by J. W. Basore, *Seneca: Moral Essays*, Loeb edn 1928, 1.420 n.

27 His statement that men of insight ignored this crime as incredible is a reflection of Cicero's assertion (*Rosc. Amer.* 70) that Solon had not fixed a punishment for it because no one would commit such a crime. On Plato's position see *Nomoi* 869, 872, 873.

28 On the penalty see Cantarella 1991, 204–6, especially 205. On the date see Cloud 1971, 27–36. Cantarella, 274–9 goes somewhat further back.

She rejects Malleolus' primacy for parricide but concedes it for matricide. She notes the earlier sacking of L. Ostius in 202 BC, but puts the origin of that penalty slightly earlier in the third century.

29 The preservation of dignity was of paramount importance. Garnsey 1970, 1 cites it as a non-Platonian motive devised by the Romans. The same appears to hold good for the wrongdoer's dignity. Cf. Garnsey, 132–5 including *D.* 5.13.5.3 (Callistratus): communal esteem (*existimatio*) is extinguished when freedom is taken away, as by interdiction or, in the case of a plebeian, by consignment to the mines.

30 It is no more than arguable (cf. n. 34 i.f.), but may be close to the mark.

31 See Bauman 1969, 2, 3–4, 22–35, citing L. 1.26.5, 6.20.2; Fest. 380 L; *D.* 1.2.2.23. Add Flor. 1.3.7, Dion. Hal. 3.22.3. But not (despite Cantarella 1991, 173) Flor. 1.1.3 or VM 6.3.6, 8.1.1 abs.

32 On Claudius' fears and his use of both *parricidium* and manifest and confessed guilt see Bauman 1974b, 194–204; 1992, 170. When he used *parricidium* he was, of course, proceeding under a public criminal law. That is why he brought in scourging as an alternative *poena legis*. He may have retained the sack for the *manifestus* and *confessus*, as Pompey's law had (implicitly) done. Cf. chapter 3 under 'Mixed penalties: *parricidium*'. Or he may have made the choice between scourging and the sack discretionary, depending on gravity.

33 On its position vis-a-vis the sack see n. 32

34 Cantarella 1991, 205 with SN 49.2–3. There is some confusion in Modestinus *D.* 48.9.9, writing in the first half of the third century. He says that the penalty is traditional (*more maiorum*), but adds that the culprit is first beaten with rods and then sewn into the sack. But there is no mention of scourging in Cicero's description of the sack. *Inv.* 2.149. Modestinus may be confused. He is not alone. I offer little more than a possible scenario.

35 See n. 34.

36 See Bauman 1974b, 141–3; 1992, 203–4.

37 E.g. when Claudius convicted someone of forgery and a spectator called out that the man's hands should be cut off, he sent for the executioner. SC 15.2. Or when he was trying a case involving citizenship and the advocates could not agree whether the defendant should appear in a toga or a Greek mantle, Claudius demonstrated his *aequitas* by telling the man to change his clothes according as he was accused or defended. *Ibid.*

38 Thus when a woman refused to acknowledge her son he forced her to admit it by ordering her to marry the youth. SC 15.2.

39 See Stroux 1929. Dio 60.28.6 gives a more balanced version. Generally Dio's assessment of Claudius' *cognitio* is less hostile than that of Suetonius. Cf. CD 60.4.3–4 with SC 15.1, 29, 37. But CD 60.13–16 is hostile. One wonders whether the exchanges between Claudius and the parties and their counsel do not simply anticipate those between Caracalla and counsel in the Dmeir inscription, on which see Kunkel 1974, 255–66.

40 See for example *J. Nov.* 30.11, where Justinian ordains the death penalty for adultery on the grounds of *humanitas*, 'for the threat will save many immortal souls'.

41 See chapter 7 under 'Nero and the Stoics'.

42 The attack is mainly in *Apocolocyntosis*, on which see below. See also SC 38.2, 29.2.

43 See for example the case of Ap. Iunius Silanus. Messalina and Narcissus having told Claudius of their dream in which Silanus killed Claudius, when Claudius was informed soon after that Silanus was trying to force his way into the palace (he had in fact come to attend an audience) he took it as proof of manifest guilt and ordered Silanus' immediate execution. SC 37.2; CD 60.14.2–4.

44 See TA 11.1–3, 13.43.3; CD 60.29.4–6a.

45 On these 'self-condemnations', including the right of burial, see TA 6.29.1–2. Specifically on the preservation of dignity see *D* 48.19.16.6. As it happened Asiaticus did not save his property; the trick used against him included the fraudulent seizure o the Gardens of Lucullus which Messalina coveted. TA 11.1.1, 37–8.

46 TA 16.33.2; *D*. 48.9.8.1.

47 Bauman 1989, 278–80, 72–3.

48 His authorship is apparently attested by CD 60.35.3, unless Dio is not referring to the work that has come down to us and seems to have also been known as *Ludus de Morte Claudii*. For some opinions see Kraft, *Hist.* 15 (1966), 96–122; Rozelaar 1976, 259–62; Grimal 1979, 107–19; Griffin 1984, 96–7. A new interpretation is offered by Roncali 1989, 11–30.

49 On the probable position then see chapter 2 under '*Humanitas* and punishment: voluntary exile'.

50 For the little that is known about this (apparently) general statute regulating all the jury-courts see Girard, 1913; Kunkel 1974, 37–8, 45, 83, 90, 97, 415.

51 Roncali 1989, 97 n. 85. The senatorial trial was confined to the murders of Claudius' family members. The jury-court trial is general.

52 SC 29.2 in a passage strongly attacking Claudius' freedmen-secretaries.

7 NERO AND THE STOICS

1 Stoicism was by no means a homogeneous monolith. See for example MacMullen 1966, 47–8; Brunt 1975, 30 n. 149 and *passim*; Griffin 1976, 140–1, 153–60, 256–314, 131 n., 154 n.; Warmington 1981, 142–54; Cizek 1982, 230–43 (detecting three different Stoic circles); Bauman 1989, *passim*. See especially Griffin 1976, 159 on the conflict between Seneca's *clementia* and the regular Stoic conception of justice.

2 See the last section of this chapter.

3 On this work see Fillion-Lahille 1989, 1616–38.

4 See especially on the Pedanius case, below.

5 *Clem.* 1.14. The idea was known to Tiberius when he condemned the hasty execution of Clutorius Priscus. Cf. also Cic. *Off.* 1.89. See also Strabo 6.4.2 p. 288 C on Augustus.

6 *Perversa induenda vestis*, which perhaps means that he put it on back to front. It is reminiscent of the judge's black cap in the era of modern capital punishment.

7 *De ira* 1.15–16. See also *Clem.* 1.2.1–2, 1.17.2, 1.11.1, 1.17.1; *De ira* 1.6.2–4, 1.15.1–2, 1.16.3–4, 3.10. Seneca's fourth stage of imprisonment is not intended as a definitive punishment. He may be thinking of the occasional sentences of imprisonment proposed by Plato, on which see Stalley 1983, 138.

8 Seneca is tacitly attacking Claudius, the emperor who had exiled him. Cf. SC 34.1.

9 *De ira* 3.3.6; *Clem.* 1.13.2, 1.5.2, 1.25.1; *Ep.* 14.4–5, 7.2.4, 90.45, 95.30. On the cruelty of Caligula see *De ira* 1.20.8–9, 2.33.3–4, 3.18–19, 3.21.5.

10 André 1979.

11 See the third section of this chapter.

12 Calpurnius Siculus 1.59–60, 69–73. I follow the majority opinion which locates the poet in Nero's reign rather than 150 years later. Not much jurisdiction was being returned to the jury-courts in the Severan period.

13 On this episode see Robinson 1981, 233–5; Nörr 1983; Wolf 1988; Bauman 1989, 92–107. The text is TA 14.42–45.

14 On the presumption of complicity see Bauman 1989, 99 and n. 130. Wolf 1988, 11–12 thinks the law made failure to prevent a specific crime. But in that case Hadrian's interpretation (below) would not have been necessary. Robinson 1981, 234 thinks the *s.c. Silanianum* had no Republican antecedents; Republican practice was purely arbitrary. I believe, however, that there was a firm practice which the *Silanianum* simply restated. Bauman 1989, 98–9. If, as Robinson argues, it had depended on the heir's views in the Republic, there would never have been an execution. No one wanted to inherit a *hereditas damnosa*, such as Pedanius' heirs faced after losing 400 slaves.

15 Wolf 1988, 16 thinks they were tried by a praetor. But the *publica quaestio* of *D.* 29.5.1 pr. includes trials in the senate, and in TA 14.42.2 the protestors besiege the senate-house, not the praetor's tribunal. See also Bauman 1989, 97 n. 119.

16 Bauman 1989, 101–2, discussing *FIRA* 1.322–4.

17 *Ibid.* 102–7, arguing that the people affected were the smaller proprietors who depended on a small but efficient slave force. They could look to only limited support in the senate, where the *latifundia* interests who were indifferent to the slave's individual welfare predominated.

18 The law had been extended to slaves manumitted by the murdered owner's will, slaves who escaped but were recaptured, slaves belonging to the deceased's wife and, where the wife was killed, slaves belonging to the husband. TA 13.32.1; *D.* 29.5.1.5, 27; *PS* 3.5.5–6.

19 Grimal 1979, 180–3; Manning 1989, 1525–8, 1536–41.

20 *Clem.* 1.24.1, *Ep.* 47.5. It was a warning, but also had a bearing on *utilitas publica*.

21 It has a whole title in the *Digest* and another in the *Code. D.* 29.5; *CJ* 6.35.

22 See Robinson 1981, 234–5.

23 Bauman 1974b, 211–13; 1992, 196–8.

24 SN 39.3, saying that the sentence was exceptionally mild, either because Nero was indifferent to insults or because he did not want to encourage them by showing annoyance.

25 The reference was to Nero's murder of Agrippina in 59.

26 TA 14.48.4. It was based on the XII Tables rule prescribing death for magical spells and, by extension, defamatory statements.

27 The accuser was Tigellinus' son-in-law, Cossutianus Capito.

28 *Clem.* 2.5.2-3, where Seneca defends the Stoics against the charge that they allow neither pity nor pardon.

29 See the references in n. 1, especially Griffin 1976.

30 Cf. the case of the bungling praetor who failed to register the jury's verdict. Cic. *Fam.* 8.8.3.

31 See chapter 8 under 'Clemency and the deflection of odium'.

32 *Clem.* 2.1.1-2. SN 10.1-2 has a slightly edited version.

33 Burrus' judicial function needs a word of explanation. Jones 1972, 98 dates the praetorian prefect's jurisdiction from Trajan's reign. But Burrus represents a transitional stage between the purely evidence-gathering function of earlier prefects like Sejanus and Macro, and the second century. Burrus did not have independent capital jurisdiction. He had a general mandate from Nero, but its application to particular cases was in the prefect's discretion. This was already halfway to adjudication proper, but Burrus did not want to be a smokescreen for Nero indefinitely. He wanted a special mandate for each case. It would identify the real author of the execution and would at the same time show what degrees of culpability were not considered proper cases for *clementia*.

34 See chapter 8 under 'Clemency and the deflection of odium'.

35 The *odio humani generis* of TA 15.44.5 is capable of either meaning, but despite Furneaux 1907, *ad loc.* the more likely rendering is 'hated by the human race'.

36 The most likely work, *De clementia*, has only one example – 1.12.3. Neither in *Clem.* 1.3.2 nor in *De beneficiis* 4.14.4 does *utilitas* mean the public interest.

37 See *Off.* 3.30-1, 3.24; *Fin.* 3.64. Where the conflict between *u. publica* and *honestum* cannot be reconciled this is because there is only an illusion of the public interest, *publicae utilitatis species. Off.* 3.47.

38 TA 4.38.1, 3.12.4; ST 33.

39 See chapter 5 under 'Augustus and punishment'.

40 That his motives also included his penchant for the spectacular (on which see Cizek 1982, 123-7) is likely enough. Was he fostering *hilaritas*, jovial relations between emperor and populace?

41 For a summary of current views see Cizek 1982, 311 n. 3.

42 TA 16.21.1, on which see Bauman 1989, 112-13.

43 On Thrasea's trial see Bauman 1974b, 153-7; 1989, 111-13. It is all conveniently brought together in TA 16.21-35. See also SN 37.1; CD 62.26.3-4.

44 TA 4.60.1. Furneaux 1907, 307 n. thinks the sentence was a *memoriae damnatio*.

45 That it was all part of a single sentence is suggested by TA 14.63.2, 64.2: *Pandateria Octaviam claudit . . . paucis interiectis diebus mori iubetur.* Cf. *Octavia* 974-5: *devectam rate procul in remotum litus interimi iube.*

46 TA 14.64.3-4. Suffocation in a hot bath was not a special atrocity. It was used against Seneca. TA 15.63.4-7. It was one way of assisting someone who was unable to carry out *liberum mortis arbitrium*.

47 By, for example, Rozelaar 1976, 598–607. F. J. Miller, *Seneca's Tragedies*, Loeb edn 1917, 2.405 rejects Seneca's authorship because of a prophecy in the play describing Nero's death. Similarly Griffin 1984, 100.

48 Women could not be charged with aspiring to supreme power. TA 6.10.1. Thus the underpinning for a *hostis* declaration was lacking.

49 Bauman 1974b, 188–90, 215–17.

50 See also perhaps *De ira* 2.2.3, 3.18.2 on Catiline.

8 DOMITIAN AND MORALITY

1 One of the major questions, his use of the urban prefect, will be included in the overall discussion of that official's jurisdiction. See chapter 9 under 'The urban prefect: From Vitellius to Domitian'.

2 Tac. *Agr.* 45. The attacks on the Stoics do not include punitive novelties and will not be specially discussed. For surveys of the cases see Gsell 1893, 275–86; Arias 1945; B. W. Jones 1992, 180–90. We cannot be specific about Tacitus' overall attitude without the lost Books of his *Historiae*. But he may have been sharply critical of Domitian. See TH 1.2. See also Grelle 1980, 342 n. 11.

3 See the works cited in n. 2.

4 Technically 'incest' in the sense of the Vestals being daughters of the community and sisters of any men with whom they consorted. But Vestal unchastity was interpreted more extensively; she did not escape liability by consorting with a non-Roman. Crispinus who committed incest with a Vestal began life as an Egyptian slave, although he did rise to membership of Domitian's *consilium*. Juv. 4.8–10.

5 See Koch 1958; Beard 1980; Cornell 1981; Fraschetti 1984; Cantarella 1991, 136–40.

6 On these developments see Bauman 1992, 52–8, 61–3. See also E. Rawson, *Phoenix* 28 (1974), 193–212.

7 Scott 1936, 187 assumes that she had been tried (and acquitted) by Vespasian or Titus, but Suetonius' statement that Vestal unchastity had been condoned (*neglecta*) by those rulers, and that it was Domitian who punished it severely and in various ways (SD 8.3) rules that out. See also below on the circumstances of Cornelia's acquittal.

8 Plin. *Ep.* 4.11.1, 11; SD 8.3–4; CD 67.3.3[2]–4[1]; Juv. 4.8–10; Philostr. *Apollonius* 7.6; TH 1.2. See also Grelle 1980, 347 n. 28. Beating to death was of course the traditional penalty for other crimes as well. Cf. Cantarella 1991, 171–210, especially 211–22. But whether death or exile, the men's punishment was completely secular; they had not betrayed Vesta.

9 On the lapse of time see Fraschetti 1984, 119 (89 AD); Bauman 1989, 154–5 (93); Cantarella 1991, 137 (91). I now incline to an earlier date than 93, probably 89. See below. There are some doubts about the date of the first series of trials (Grelle 1980, 345 n. 21), but the variations are slight.

10 The parade through the streets can be inferred from Pliny's version (*Ep.* 4.11.7–9) and is clearly implied by Plutarch *Num.* 10.4–7: she was placed

on a litter, covered so that her cries could not be heard, and carried through the Forum, with the people silently making way and following the litter in depressed silence. Plutarch's *Lives* were written after Domitian's reign. He was often in Rome in the Flavian period.

11 The *confessus*, Licinianus, was interdicted from water and fire. This enabled him to avoid the rods and the Comitium. Plin. *Ep.* 4.11.1, 11. Suetonius confirms both his lighter sentence and the lethal flogging of the others in the Comitium. SD 8.4.

12 There is much talk about Vespasian's strict policy on morality – for example E. T. Salmon, *A History of the Roman World: 30 BC to AD 138*, 6th edn, London 1968, 216 – but not much hard evidence. Suetonius has Vestal incest condoned by Vespasian and Titus. SD 8.3. He expresses surprise at Vespasian, though it was only to be expected from Titus: *a patre quoque suo et fratre neglecta*, where *quoque* has the force of *etiam*. On Titus' morals see ST 6.1, 7.1.

13 On this see Grelle 1980, 341–5, 356–8. A by-product of the edict was that Labeo's classification of the castration of a slave as a latent defect under the aedilician actions was reinstated after its rejection by Titus' friend, Caelius Sabinus. Gell. *NA* 4.2.2–7, 6.4.

14 Contra Grelle 1980, 345 n. 19. But Domitian's edict had to be sanctioned somehow. Extending a criminal *lex* by edict was common enough. E.g. *D.* 48.10.15 pr. In fact castration was subsumed under the *lex de sicariis* by *senatus consultum* (*D.* 48.8.3.4), and the only question is whose senate it was. There is nothing against the view that it was Domitian's, which incorporated his edict in its own decree. The same thing had happened under Augustus in regard to the *lex maiestatis*. Bauman 1974, 35–48.

15 On charges under the *lex Scantinia* see SD 8.3 On the adultery charges see CD 67.12.1–2, which also notes that a woman was put to death for undressing in front of an image of Domitian. Our topic does not require us to address the incomprehensible relationship between Domitian and his niece Julia. For a recent discussion see B. W. Jones 1992, 34–40, though his suggestion that Domitian did not divorce his wife Domitia but merely exiled her is neither probable in itself, nor would it throw much light on the Julia affair. On the divorce and the killing of Paris see below.

16 See SD 8.3.

17 Domitian did not become censor until April 85. B. W. Jones 1992, 106. By that time the first series of Vestal trials was already two years in the past.

18 On the *correctio morum* as a whole see Grelle 1980, 346–7, 348–52, including *princeps pudicus* and other laudatory references in Martial and Statius. Also his note on *pulchra clementia* in Stat. *Silv.* 3.4.73, though he cannot mean that in Statius' context the word has the same connotation of absolution rather than pardon that it has in Seneca. Grelle does not consider *corrector morum* an official title. He thinks, probably correctly, that the revival of the *lex Julia de adulteriis* was seen by the Flavian poets as the main inspiration of the *correctio*. On the attitude of the poets see also Gsell 1893, 83 n. 5, 84–5. But he goes too far when he takes Martial's *Julia lex renata* (6.7) and Juvenal's *leges revocabat amaras* (2.30) as evidence of re-enactment, as distinct from more vigorous enforcement. In TA

1.72.3 *legem maiestatis reduxerat* does not mean that Tiberius re-enacted the law. Bauman 1974b, 221–3.

19 See chapter 4 under 'Cicero in theoretical mode'.

20 See Stalley 1983, 40–4.

21 Horace portrays a lover of low degree hiding in terror when the husband comes home unexpectedly. *Sat.* 1.2.41–6.

22 Bauman 1992, 55–8.

23 On Julia and the Bacchanals see chapter 5 under 'Augustus and punishment', chapter 3 under 'The decline of the *Iudicia Populi*'. On Albucilla in 37 AD see Bauman 1974b, 130–4.

24 Bauman 1992, 57–9.

25 If other precccupations interfered with their primary function of tending the eternal flame it spelled disaster; it portended the fall of Rome.

26 Cf. Bauman 1992, 54.

27 On the inclusion of *incestum* see Treggiari 1991, 281.

28 Dio's anecdote about Helvius Agrippa (above) may imply that the unfortunate Pontiff died at a senatorial trial, in which case it would refer to the first series of trials. But merely to witness the senate imposing the (by then) routine penalties of *liberum mortis arbitrium* and deportation could hardly have given Helvius a heart attack. Suetonius paints a favourable picture of the senate's jurisdiction. SD 8.1–2. In any case Domitian would not have left the vital question of Vestal unchastity to the senate. Dio has confused the two series of trials. Pliny specially notes that the Pontiffs were despatched to witness the live burial of Cornelia. *Ep.* 4.11.9.

29 Cf. Garnsey 1970, 115–17.

30 See the summary of known cases in Fraschetti 1984, 102–9.

31 That it was the watershed of the reign is denied by B. W. Jones 1992, 144–9, but see the works cited by him at p. 229 n. 15. See also Bauman 1989, 172, 178.

32 Licinianus had concealed a freedwoman of Cornelia's on his estate. He was arrested and on the advice of friends confessed. Plin. *Ep.* 4.11.11. But the problem of proof that his confession resolved was not Cornelia's guilt but his own. Pliny locates the incident *after* his account of the fate of Cornelia and the Roman knight. See also n. 33 below.

33 Cf. n. 32. In Suetonius, Licinianus confessed while the case was still undetermined and examination and torture had produced no result. SD 8.4.

34 C. R. Whittaker, *Herodian*, Loeb edn 1969, 405 n. 7 ad Herod. 4.6.4. Whittaker is less successful with his suggestion that Dio deliberately created Caracalla as a second Domitian. If the four Vestals whom he names had not in fact been brought up for unchastity at all Dio would have been deluged with claims for damages.

35 Where there was a small temple of Vesta. Juv. 4.61.

36 See for example the incident of the spectator whose criticism of Domitian's bias against Thracian gladiators had him dragged from his seat and thrown to the dogs in the arena. SD 10.1; Plin. *Pan.* 33.3–4. Discussion in Bauman 1974b, 163–5.

9 PREFECTS AND CRIMINAL TRIALS

1 Its workload was exceeded only by that of the adultery court. A survey by page count of the *Digest* material on the public criminal Laws (*D.* 48.4–15) in the major Mommsen–Krueger edition gives the following results: *lex Julia de adulteriis coercendis,* 11½ pp.; *lex Cornelia testamentaria,* 7 pp.; *lex Cornelia de sicariis,* 2½ pp. etc. As is well known, the greater part of the material consists of jurists' *responsa* or emperors' rescripts, both for use in real-life situations. It is time for ideas about the rarity of testamentary prosecutions to be laid to rest.

2 Our text is a composite of Tacitus' notices of the Domitius Balbus case and the Valerius Ponticus case. TA 14.40–1. His language apropos of Ponticus makes it clear that the two are linked. Mommsen 1899, 273 n. 3 thinks Ponticus got into trouble over a poisoning case. But in 1887–8, 1065 n. 3 he identifies it as a case of testamentary forgery. Sachers 1954, 2521 perpetuates Mommsen's mistaken version. Garnsey 1970, 27 gets it right.

3 On the early history of the office see Vitucci 1956, 9–40. More briefly Sachers 1954, 2513–14. There is an interesting discussion in De Martino 1972–4, 4.641–7.

4 See SN 17, crediting Nero with the first protection against forgers. The most important, and controversial, item is that prohibiting the writer of another's will from including a legacy to himself. Suetonius' attribution of it to Nero is indirectly supported by *PS* 5.25.6. But the problem of disentangling Nero's measures from Claudius' edict and the *s.c. Libonianum* remains. For a full discussion see Marino 1988.

5 Marino 1988, 635–6 suggests that the *lex Cornelia testamentaria nummaria* (= *de falsis*) contained two distinct chapters, one dealing with the falsification of wills and seals and the other with false coinage. But it may have been even more comprehensive than that. When Marino 1988, 640 and n. 33 sees the *lex* as the criminal counterpart of the praetor's *bonorum possessio secundum tabulas,* he comes close to more than a casual link between the two.

6 Remittals were common enough. E.g. emperor to senate: TA 3.10.6; praetor to urban prefect: *D.* 26.10.1.8, 2; provincial governor to praetorian prefect: *CJ* 4.65.4.1.

7 TA 14.40–1: *pari ignominia Valerius Ponticus adficitur.*

8 The statutory penalty under the *lex Cornelia* was *aquae et ignis interdictio.* *D.* 48.10.33.

9 See chapter 7 under 'Nero and clemency: the deflection of odium'.

10 On the *ius gladii* see Mommsen 1887–8, 2.270–1, 968; 1899, 243–5. On its inclusion in Domitian's proposals see Bauman 1989, 152–3.

11 Cf. chapter 8 under 'Domitian and the Vestals'.

12 For the detailed exposition of this see Bauman 1989, 147–53. On a possible reorganization of the urban prefecture at this time see *ib.* 152–3, 156–7.

13 The civilian orientation of the lawyers hardly needs documentation. See however Bauman 1983 on Ap. Claudius Caecus; 1985 on Servius Sulpicius Rufus; 1989 on Cassius Longinus (despite his stance – on slaves – in the Pedanius case).

14 Rutilius is noted briefly by Schiller 1949, 326; Vitucci 1956, 69. He is not noticed by Sachers 1954 or Jones 1972.

15 Statius *Silvae* 1.4.43–8.

16 I am unable to support Vitucci 1956, 69 when he takes *nec proturbare curules* to mean that Rutilius did not abstain from competing, he merely refrained from interfering with the regular jurisdictions under his *alta potestas*. But how could he have interfered? Himself the emperor's subordinate, how could he have had any authority over duly elected magistrates? The passage can only mean rivalry between the two jurisdictions. Such rivalry, as between emperor and senate for example, was as old as the Principate. See SA 66.2 with Bauman 1967, 180–3.

17 The *lex Papia Poppaea*, read with Augustus' earlier *lex Julia*, encouraged marriage and procreation, and penalized the unmarried and the childless. In common with the public criminal Laws, its enforcement depended on informers, but details of the penalties and process are not available. For what can be said about this law see Spruit 1969; Treggiari 1991, 60–80.

18 Cf. Stat. *Silv.* 1.42.24–5: *centum dedisti iudicium mentemque viris.*

19 Mommsen 1899, 220 and n. 5. Garnsey 1970, 59 n. 1 takes Mommsen to be referring to the senatorial court. Kunkel 1974, 102 flatly rejects Mommsen's view, holding that *Marc.* 24.2 merely means that Marcus tried certain capital cases himself instead of delegating them. Kunkel believes (correctly) that capital cases still came before jury-courts, but he does not restrict them to *humiliores* as we are doing. See below, p. 104.

20 Marcus' Stoicism is generally recognized as the moving spirit behind his legislation. One of the best accounts is still that of Noyen 1954–5.

21 *SHA Marc.* 23.1: *proscriptus est.* The reference is to an *aquae et ignis interdictio.* Cf. Cic. *Dom.* 43–4, *Sest.* 65. D. Magie, Loeb edn of *SHA*, 1.189 gets close enough with 'outlaw'.

22 There is no evidence to fill the gap between Rutilius Gallicus and Marcus' prefects. What is known about Antoninus Pius (above) does not assist.

23 Garnsey 1970, 96–8 is quite clear about the prefect trying members of all classes. To his reasons for making the bulk of the prefect's clientele members of the lower orders, we may add that the office had been created by Augustus to discipline unruly plebeians and slaves. TA 6.11.3. On the other hand there must have been a substantial complement of persons of higher status. The all-important testamentary side of the prefect's work guarantees that.

24 *SHA Marc.* 23.1 does not present the infliction of interdiction as a general practice amongst urban prefects. A single incumbent was responsible.

25 On Iunius Rusticus see R. Hanslik, *Kl.P.* 2 (1967), 1558–9 with TA 16.26.6. By the time of his prefecture a man whose father had been tribune in 66 will have been of an advanced age and set in his beliefs.

26 *D.* 1.12, from Ulpian's monograph on the prefecture. On this consolidation by Severus see Vitucci 1956, 53–5; Garnsey 1970, 93–4.

27 On the adultery court see Bauman 1968. On the *lex Fabia* see below, p. 110.

28 On these see Mommsen 1899, 193–6; Garnsey 1970, 94–5. See also below, p. 113.

29 Elagabalus' reform is inferred from the statement in *SHA Alex.* 15.1 that

Alexander abolished the jurors whom Elagabalus had drawn 'from the lowest levels'.

30 On the death of Ulpian and its date see Bauman 1995. On his reorganization of the criminal courts see *ib.* with Bauman 1968.

31 *SHA Alex.* 15.1 probably signals the abolition of the jury system as a whole, not merely of Elagabalus' sixth decury. *Ib.* 33.1 attests the appointment of fourteen curators. That attestation need not be queried; the prefect now had the entire criminal court system on his shoulders.

32 See Bauman 1974, 180–5. There was a partial precedent, in the shape of popular demands for the punishment of Caligula's murderers, but it did not involve the praetorians. *Ib.* 195–6.

33 *Ib.* 159. He also sought condemnations from the general public, thus continuing the Claudian precedent in that respect as well. Cf. n. 32.

34 CD 68.3.3; Joann. Antioch. fr. 110 M. 1–6.

35 On the death of Papinian see Bauman 1995, 390. Cf. especially CD 77.4.12.1a–2. With a nice sense of propriety Caracalla rebuked the cohorts for killing him with an axe instead of a sword.

36 On the murder see CD 77.2.2–6; Herod. 4.4.3. On Papinian's refusal to write a speech for Caracalla excusing the murder see *SHA Carac.* 8.4–6.

37 See Bauman 1995, 386, 396.

38 See for example Bauman 1974, 113–24, 130–4; 1992, 143–53, 158. Even under Nero this was the more important part of the prefect's duties. See for example Bauman 1992, 196–8. See also TA 14.60.4 on Tigellinus' part in the attack on Octavia. On the prefect's role as a custodian of suspects see Ensslin 1954, 2414.

39 Burrus' trial of the robbers may have been held in public – his anxiety to shift the responsibility suggests that – but the case in Trajan's reign is the first to be specifically so described.

40 Despite Jones 1972, 98. See the list of Trajan's prefects in Ensslin 1954, 2423. On Suburanus see Passerini 1939, 295.

41 Ensslin, *loc. cit.*

42 Pliny *Ep.* 7.6.9 describes how he rebutted the clumsy arguments of his young opponent by saying nothing, for which he received an ovation.

43 Despite Mommsen 1887–8, 2.990. For a contrary view see Durry 1938, 175; Passerini 1939, 261.

44 As all praetorian prefects were, with the exception of Vespasian's son Titus.

45 *Corp. Gloss. Lat.* 3.32, pp. 387–8.

46 All prefects are meant. D. Magie, *SHA*, Loeb edn 1.162 n. 5 makes the praetorian prefects the sole subject of the exercise. Kunkel 1974, 209 inclines in the same direction. But if legal expertise was a recommendation, Q. Cervidius Scaevola was *praefectus vigilum*, and L. Volusius Maecianus was *praefectus Aegypti*. Cf. Kunkel 1967, 217, 174. On Scaevola see also *SHA Marc.* 11.10.

47 See *CTh* 4.17.3, 4; *CJ* 7.44.

48 Hence perhaps the rare note of disapproval in *SHA Marc.* 29.

49 *SHA Marc.* 10.6. Cf. 25.6, 26.13, 29.4. See also CD 72.30, 71.28.2.

50 Presumably the Athenian charge of tyranny was converted into a Roman equivalent under the *lex maiestatis*. Hadrian had revised Athenian criminal law so as to bring it into line with Roman law. Bauman 1989, 284–5.

51 As, for example Narcissus had done with Claudius.
52 As not infrequently, there were two incumbents. Cleander is one of the possible names. Cf. Ensslin 1954, 2424.
53 For a useful discussion see Greenidge 1901, 468–70.
54 Bauman 1974, 192–4.
55 *SHA Pert.* 7.1; *PS* 1.5.2, 5.4.11.
56 Mommsen 1887–8, 2.972 n. 1, 991 n. 2 only allows Alexander's reform to apply to when the praetorian prefects sat on the emperor's *consilium*, not when they judged in their own tribunal. But this requires them to have been given second-class senatorial status.
57 E.g. by Mommsen 1887–8, 2.969; Passerini 1939, 236–7; (by implication) Ensslin 1954, 2414–15.
58 For some of the literature see Bauman 1989, 103–4, nn. 150, 151, 152. See also below p. 110.
59 For example in the Bacchanalian affair, on which see chapter 3 under 'The decline of the *iudicia populi*' with n. 2 of that chapter.
60 And thus fell under the first chapter of the *lex Fabia. Coll.* 14.3.4.
61 Many of whom were slaves falling under the second chapter of the *lex.*
62 CD 76.10. Dio locates the sentence subsequent to the exchange – 'later, under edict' – but whether this means confirmation by Severus or a *ius edicendi* possessed by the prefect is not clear.
63 The elastic word *latro* covered his activities. Dio's equivalents are *lēistērion, eleisteusas.* CD 76.10.1, 7. The Maternus movement under Commodus was on very much the same lines, and in Herodian's account of Maternus the word is *lēistēs.* Herod. 1.10.1, 7. On the background to the Maternus movement see C. R. Whittaker, *Herodian,* Loeb edn 1969, 1.61 nn. 2, 3, 62 n. 1. Note also that the case of Burrus and the robbers uses the word *latro.* Sen. *Clem.* 2.1.2.
64 This is suggested by Herodian's statement that they were no longer classed simply as robbers, but as enemies. Herod. 1.10.1.
65 On what had to be recorded see *CTh* 4.17.2 read with 4.17.1, 3, 4.
66 He was the first reference point in the *Law of Citations* of 426 AD, on which see Jolowicz 1972, 452–3.
67 See generally the works cited in n. 57.
68 *D.* 32.1.4. Thus the deferment of the loss until the acquisition of the citizenship of the sheltering state, as described by Cicero in the case of voluntary exile, no longer applied. The change may have been made as early as Sulla, although the Principate is more likely.
69 *CJ* 4.65.4.1, where *parentum meum* may reflect Ulpian's friendship with Alexander's mother, Julia Mamaea; or it may reflect Ulpian's virtual regency during Alexander's minority.
70 See for example *D.* 47.11–22. Cf. Mommsen 1899, 194 nn. 3, 4; 195.
71 Dupont 1953–5, 1.120–3; U. Brasiello, *Iura* 5 (1954), 378. It is argued that under the impact of *cognitio* Constantine began moving, for example, from the *lex Julia de adulteriis* towards the *crimen adulterii,* from the *lex Cornelia de sicariis* towards *homicidium,* thus breaking free of the shackles of the *leges.*
72 For the case against the *crimen* theory see Bauman 1980, 219–27.
73 CJ 1.26.2. Despite *D. id. Aug. Severo et Quintiano conss.,* the rescript was

not issued by Alexander. He died in March 235, some five months before the Ides of August. Maximinus may have found the decree amongst his predecessor's papers. The groundwork may well have been done by Ulpian before his death.

74 Constantine's decree (*CTh* 11.30.16) may merely be a restatement. Arcadius Charisius was able to say that by his time appeals from the prefect's judgments, although previously known, were forbidden by imperial edict. *D.* 1.11. Arcadius is dated to Diocletian by Jolowicz 1972, 394 n. 9 and Spruit 1992, 199. Kunkel 1967, 263 n. 565 merely makes him postclassical. Schulz 1963, 246 and Wenger 1953, 523 do not exclude a date at the turn of the third century.

10 THE GROWTH OF CRIMINAL JURISPRUDENCE: *DE IUDICIIS PUBLICIS*

1 Criminal *responsa* appear only sporadically in the Republic and merely serve to illustrate rules of private law. See for example *D.* 48.22.3, a comment on the testamentary consequences of exile.

2 On the *lex de sicariis* see Cloud 1969; Bauman 1980, 116–24. On the question of a *telum*, Plutarch *TG* 19.5–6 says the mob which assassinated Tiberius Gracchus used broken benches and stones but nothing of iron. In the second round of mayhem, against Gaius Gracchus, the carnage was the work of Cretan archers. Plut. *CG* 16.3–4. The controversy about the meaning of *telum* reached the Antonine jurist, Gaius, who rejects the claim that it only means a missile despatched by a bow and has it include objects thrown by hand, such as a stone or a piece of wood or iron. *D.* 50.16.233.2. Cf. *PS* 5.23.2. As for intent, that is discussed by Cicero in *Pro Milone* 11, arguing that carrying a weapon for the purpose of self-defence is not culpable.

3 If the jurist Aulus Ofilius wrote a commentary on the *leges* in twenty books this view might have to be revised. But that is unlikely. See Bauman 1985, 83–4.

4 The many examples of genuine cases in *Ad Herennium* include 1.20, 21, 23, 2.17. Fictitious: 1.18, 27, 2.28. Genuine cases in *De inventione*: 2.522, 78–9, 105, 111, 144, 149. Fictitious: 1.11, 18–19, 2.14–15, 95, 118. Interpretative: 1.70, 2.55–6. Punitive: 1.46, 2.58–9, 141. These are only examples selected at random.

5 On Capito and his work see Bauman 1980, 129; 1989, 27–35; Fanizza 1982, 4–5.

6 The fragments are in Gell. 10.6, 4.14. They bore respectively on *maiestas minuta* and magisterial inviolability.

7 Fanizza 1982, 8–9 n. 14 cites *D.* 2.13.3, 3.2.22 which attest a *De poenis* by Mauricianus and a *De iudiciis publicis* by Marcellus. Mommsen replaced Mauricianus by Modestinus and Marcellus by Macer. Lenel accepts Mauricianus but allocates the fragment to his *Ad legem Iuliam et Papiam*; he replaces Marcellus by Marcianus. *Quot homines.*

8 For the fragments see Lenel 1.587–8, 2.1214–16 (covering both *De iudiciis publicis* and the criminal fragments of Venuleius *De officio proconsulis*). On *De poenis paganorum* see Fanizza 1982, 13, 16 n. 34.

9 *D*. 29.5.14, where *de impubere sumi iussit supplicium* was taken by Brasiello to mean interrogation under torture rather than definitive capital punishment. Both were covered by the *s.c. Silanianum*, but Garnsey 1970, 123 and nn. 3, 4 effectively argues for a definitive penalty. Fanizza 1982, 41 supports Garnsey, although at 85 nn. 200, 201 she cites Pius' rescript exempting *impuberes* from examination under torture. *D*. 48.18.15.1. In *D*. 29.5.1.28 *ultimum supplicium pati debet* clearly means execution. There is of course the senator who said during the Catilinarian debate that by 'ultimate penalty' he meant the ultimate penalty for a Roman senator, namely imprisonment. Plut. *Cic.* 21.3. But this was simply a dodge to get behind Caesar's proposal of imprisonment.

10 On which see Mommsen 1899, 75–7; Gioffredi 1970, 85-90; Spruit 1975; Fanizza 1982, 85.

11 On his career see Fanizza 1982, 104–14. See also Millar 1977, 103, citing *D*. 37.14.17 pr. Of particular importance are his posts as *a libellis* to Pius at the end of Hadrian's reign, as *a studiis, procurator bibliothecarum* and *a libellis et censibus* during Pius' own reign, and *praefectus Aegypti* for most of the joint reign of Marcus and Verus. Maecian probably died after being designated as consul for 166 but before holding the office. Fanizza 114.

12 *D*. 48.9.9.2 (Modestinus), 1.18.13.1 (Ulpian), 1.18.14 (Macer). Modestinus and Ulpian date the case to Marcus and Verus, when Maecian was probably still alive. Macer dates it to Marcus and Commodus when he was probably dead.

13 Fanizza 1982, 16–18.

14 Lenel 2.1214–15 (frs. 32, 35).

15 The ban was imposed in case the will manumitted any of the slaves.

16 For some suggestions see Bauman 1974–5, 48; Fanizza 1982, 23–32.

17 Fragments in Lenel, 1.565–70, 675–80, 1180–1 (= pp. 511–13, 547–9, 718–19).

18 Marcian commented on the *leges* in his *Institutiones*; two of the most important laws, *Cornelia de sicariis* and *Cornelia de falsis*, are discussed in greater detail here than in his *De iudiciis publicis*. Cf. Lenel 1.169–71, 175–6, 190–1. Perhaps, like Venuleius, he wrote for different readerships.

19 Measured by the volume of material used by Justinian's compilers, guidance to governors in the criminal area was more important than the rest of the work put together. It makes up three-quarters of the extant material. The principal topics are: the public criminal laws; *crimina extraordinaria*; procedure; penalties; examinations under torture.

20 The approximate dates of the two works are 213 and 217. T. Honoré, *Ulpian*, Oxford 1982, 156, 186.

21 Of Alexander's eight extant rescripts on the subject, four were issued in 223, two in 224 and two over 225–6 – all while Ulpian was still alive on the writer's dating of his death. See Bauman 1968, 88–93; 1995 *passim*.

22 See Lenel 1.1–27, 1.6–22 (= pp. 803–9, 951–4).

23 On this work see below.

24 The 521 fragments in Lenel 1.181–266 include a mere six on the criminal law, namely frs. 342, 431, 434, 435, 448, 484. But see pp. 148–9 below.

25 On this genre see Schulz 1963, 243–6.

26 *D.* 48.15.4, where Gaius' main interest in the *lex Fabia* is in placing one who receives a free person by way of gift or dowry in the same position as the parties to a sale or exchange. On a fragment of his commentary on the *lex Julia et Papia* see below, p. 122.

27 As for example by Schulz 1963, 124–40; Casavola 1980, *passim*; Bretone 1982, 24–55, 205–32. See also, more generally, Starr 1965, *passim*.

28 Fanizza 1982, xi–xii, 10–11, 18–19, 93–123 (especially 93–104).

29 That is, the general judiciary law known as the *lex Julia iudiciorum publicorum* and the individual *leges* for the *quaestiones perpetuae*. On the former see Girard 1913.

30 E.g. *PS* 5.23.1; 24; 25.1, 2, 5, 7; 26.1–3; 29; 30b.2; 2.26.1–3, 14.

31 This can only be identified by positioning within titles, as all references to rescripts, decrees of the senate and opinions of jurists have been ironed out, but positioning is a sufficient guide. See e.g. *PS* 5.23.2–6, 7, 8–10, 13–16, 18, 19; 25.4, 8, 10, 12; 26.4; 29.2.

32 *PS* 5.23.12. Cf. Paul *De publicis iudiciis D.* 48.8.7. In principle the case is similar to those discussed by Venuleius in *D.* 48.2.12. I here attempt to resolve the anomaly posed by Pugliese 1982, 749–50.

33 Fanizza 1982, 93–123 (especially 93–104).

34 Maecian has one *lex* and one *senatus consultum*. Venuleius has eight *leges*, four *senatus consulta* and two constitutions. Fragments as in n. 8.

35 E.g. Marcian *De iud. pub.*, Lenel 1.675–80: *leges*, frs. 187–8, 194–5; *constitutiones*, frs. 188, 190, 192, 194.1, 195 pr., 198 (*quat.*); *senatus consulta*, 202.1. Marcian *Institut.*, Lenel 1.670–4: *leges*, 162-5, 167, 168 (*bis*), 169, 171, 172 (*bis*), 173, 175, 177–9; *constitutiones*, 166, 168, 169 (*ter*), 171, 174, 175 (*quat.*), 178–9; *senatus consulta*, 171 (*bis*), 175. Macer *De iud. pub.*, Lenel 1.565–70: *leges*, 15–17, 19, 22–7, 34; *constitutiones*, 22, 31, 36 (*bis*), 42–4; *senatus consulta*, 24, 36. Paul *De pub. iud.*, Lenel 1.1180–1: *leges*, 1266–7; *constitutiones*, 1265, 1268; *senatus consulta*, 1267; *responsa prudentium*, 1267. The criminal books of Ulpian *De off. proc.* exhibit an overwhelming preponderance of constitutions – 40, as against 14 *leges* and 4 *senatus consulta*. Lenel 2.975–91. The work is also noted for its verbatim quotation of constitutions. E.g. Lenel frs. 2196–9. And on *cognitio* see Marcian *De iud. pub.*, frs. 199–204; Macer *De iud. pub.*, frs. 18, 27, 36; Paul *De pub. iud.* frs. 1265, 1268.

36 We possess statements of his on the following: robbery from a deceased estate which is tried by the urban prefect or a governor; an ungrateful freedman who is tried by a procurator; governors, especially irenarchs in Asia, must be meticulous when trying *latrones*; and the *praefectus annonae* is authorized, in the interests of *utilitas publica*, to receive charges concerning the corn supply from women, infamous persons, soldiers and slaves, none of whom are competent accusers in jury-courts. Lenel frs. 201, 203–5, 192. The last-mentioned (= *D.* 48.2.13) fell theoretically under a public criminal law, the *lex Julia de annona* (cf. *D.* 48.1.1), but the procedure in that prefect's court is not known. Mommsen 1899, 852; Kunkel 1974, 92. It will have been closer to the urban prefect than to a jury-court. Papinian's inferral of a general right of accusation for women in *maiestas* cases from Fulvia's role in the Catilinarian affair (*D.* 48.4.8) is, one hopes, the work of the compilers rather than of the jurist. Fulvia did no more than disclose the

conspiracy to Cicero (Bauman 1992, 67–9); and the conspirators were not charged with *maiestas*.

37 *CJ* 9.8.6 pr. Why the compilers noticed this fragment in time for the *Code* but not for the *Digest* is not clear. Other examples of the emperor's *cognitio* do appear in the *Digest*, but not under *De iud. pub.* E.g. Marcian *Institut.* fr. 175; Ulpian *Off. proc.* frs. 2192, 2213. The jurists occasionally note senatorial trials as well. E.g. *D.* 48.10.5, 4.8.

38 See Schulz 1963, 154, 340. Fragments in Lenel 1. 67, 71, 877–80 (pp. 961, 963, 1111–12).

39 All the fragments (n. 38) deal with private-law matters.

40 Cf. *Coll.* 12.5.1. When imposed by a governer interdiction covered the province as well as Rome and Italy. Mommsen 1899, 972; Kunkel 1974, 176.

41 See Bleicken 1962, 166–76. Cf. Kunkel 1974, 178–254, 341–2, 106–7 (citing *ILS* 6286); Pugliese 1982, 743–4 with n. 42, 747 n. 48. We also note Paul's specimen indictment for adultery: *apud praetorem vel proconsulem. D.* 48.2.3.

42 Which he does not always do. Cf. Bleicken, *loc. cit.* on when he sits alone. The prefectorial procedure eliminated some of the cumbersome features of a jury trlal. The best description of the latter is still Greenidge 1901, 486–504.

43 Presumably the usual *fecisse videtur* followed by the automatic imposition of the *poena legis* applies here. Cf. Bleicken 1962, 172.

44 Bleicken 1962, 172 and n. 4 cites Cyrene Edict 4.66 and *lex Acilia* 57 as examples of the use of *consilium* to denote the jury. Cf. Kunkel 1974, 164–6. But neither author says – nor could they have said – that there was no difference between a *consilium* as usually understood and a jury. In fact Kunkel 236 n. 127 makes it clear that the two institutions are quite different.

45 See *PS* 5.13–22 (thematic), 23–30b (individual *leges*), 31–7 (military penalties and appeals). The adultery law is separate, in 2.26.

46 The case for a post-classical origin is argued in detail by Levy 1963, 1.99, 122, 220, 231, 245, 284; 2.496. Cf. Schulz 1963, 176–9; Garnsey 1970, 221; Jolowicz 1972, 452, 457; Schiller 1978, 46–8; Rilinger 1988, *passim*; Spruit 1992, 212–15. The view that the work is of Severan provenance is taken by Cardascia 1950, 324 and *passim*. But apart from anything else, his claim that the *honestiores–humiliores* dichotomy was not legal but only social is unrealistic. As to whether the work was not so much cut from the whole cloth by the post-classical compiler, but was reworked from something with a similar title that Paul himself had written, opinions are similarly divided.

47 See for example the mutual invectives of Sallust and Cicero usually printed with Sallust's works.

48 Fanizza 1982, 100–1.

49 In fact it might not mean death at all. See *Coll.* 11.7.3–4, which is noted in n. 36, chapter 12.

50 On the meaning of *servus poenae* see Mommsen 1899, 947–8; Garnsey 1970, 132, 165; Jones 1972, 108; U. Zilletti, *SDHI* 34 (1968), 32. Although often linked to a sentence of hard labour in the mines, the Macer fragment shows that it was of more general application.

51 As for example in the *iudicia populi* when the tribune's choice of assembly was determined by whether the penalty that he proposed was capital or sub-capital.

11 THE GROWTH OF CRIMINAL JURISPRUDENCE: *DE POENIS*

1 On Modestinus see Wenger 1953, 521–2; Kunkel 1967, 259–61; Jolowicz 1972, 394. Fragments in Lenel 1.726–32. See also Brassloff, *RE* 8. 668–75.

2 They were on the following: the penalties under all the laws; the penalties imposed on civilians; military punishments; and the release of property to the children of the condemned. Cf. Schulz 1963, 256–7.

3 Lenel 2.1207 n. 1 confidently makes the two Saturnini the same person. Cf. Peter, *Mélanges Philippe Meylan*, Lausanne 1963, 1.273. But see Fanizza 1982, 10 n. 21, 16 n. 34, discussing R. Bonini, *Riv. It. Sci. Giur.* 10 (1959–62), 130, 175. De Robertis 1939b, 65 dates Claudius Saturninus to the turn of the first century. According to some the Saturninus of *D.* 48.19.16 is the *commentator* noticed by Tertullian. A. Masi, *Iura* 28 (1977), 143. Kunkel 1967, 184–5 tacitly rejects the identification with Venuleius but is more interested in Claudius Saturninus' possible membership of a family which was prominent in the second century. One hopes that Kunkel's reference (184 n. 331) to Q. Volusius Saturninus *cos.* 92 AD does not mean that Maecian is a factor in the Saturninus equation. At all events our support for non-identification is not fervent. Our main interest is in what *De poenis paganorum* can tell us about punitive thinking.

4 Suetonius SD 10.1 attests the former; Pliny *Pan.* 33.3–4 has the latter. Oddly enough, they were the most common forms of lower-class execution later on.

5 See for example De Robertis 1939a, 1939b, 1942a, 1942b; Cardascia 1950, 1953; Levy 1963, 2.433–508; Garnsey 1970; Rilinger 1988. Cardascia 1950, 307 observes that a full treatment would require a book.

6 Cf. chapter 7 under 'The urban prefect in Nero's reign'.

7 If the upper classes are above the *poena legis*, how do they manage to end up with the statutory penalty of deportation? Attempts to uncover interpolations are criticized by Garnsey 1970, 109 n. 1 and Pugliese 1982 769 n. 112. But something is wrong. *Altiores* is particularly suspicious. Cf. Brasiello 1937, 202–5; Cardascia 1950, 325 n. 7. Rilinger 1988, 203 is not persuasive when he suggests that by the Severan period death had become the '*Regelstrafe*'. He does not mean the *poena legis* by this. He means that in practice death had become so firmly entrenched that it had virtually superseded interdiction/deportation. But it had not become firmly entrenched; *honestiores* were above it.

8 The text is arrived at by combining Ulpian *Coll.* 12.5.1 and *D.* 47.9.12.1. On differences between the two versions see Cardascia 1950, 468–9; Garnsey 1970, 156 n. 1; Pugliese 1982, 781–2; Rilinger 1988, 258–9.

9 Cf. Chapter 10 under 'Motivation and ideology' on the different treatment accorded to the *leges* and *cognitio* by the jurists.

10 For a full exposition of Hadrian's part in the formation of punitive differentials see Garnsey 1970, 153–72. Cardascia 1950, 306 n. 1 thinks the earliest text is Pius' rescript on adultery (*D.* 48.5.39.8 on which see below). But at the most it is the earliest on a public criminal law.

11 Hadrian's approach is not unlike Macer's definition of eligible accusers: 'We will perceive who can accuse if we know who cannot.' *D.* 48.2.8.

12 Hadrian makes no mention of a law of Nerva which laid down that if a slave acted with wrongful intent and without the owner's knowledge, he was to be put to death unless the owner preferred to pay a fine. *D.* 47.21.3.1.

13 *PS* 5.22.2, under the rubric *De seditiosis.*

14 The best count gives twenty-five *honestiores* to *Sententiae* and perhaps seven to the jurists; and twenty-three *humiliores* against perhaps seven. Cardascia 1950, 324–6, but with our addition of *D.* 48.13.7 pr., 47.14.1.3, 48.8.3.5 for *honestiores*; and *D.* 47.9.12, 47.12.11, 48.19.28.11, 48.5.39.8, 47.10.45, *Coll.* 12.5.1 for close equivalents in the jurists' tally of *humiliores*, such as *humiliore loco, humillimo loco, humilioris fortunae, humilis personae, humilis loci.* For some interesting statistics on Ulpian's terminology see Rilinger 1988, 37 n. 18.

15 *PS.* 5.4.10. Under the rubric *De iniuriis* the compendium deals with both civil and criminal remedies. The assessent in the text is of civil damages.

16 Cf. for example Gai. 3.220–5 with Paul frs. 881–2, Lenel 1.1112–13.

17 *PS* 5.19, 20, 21, 23, 22, 26, 25, 29, 21A, 30B.

18 *PS* 5.24 imposes *vivi exuruntur* or *ad bestias* on all offenders, regardless of status. Perfectly credible. See below on Hadrian's ruling on decurions, *D.* 48.19.15.

19 *PS* 5.24, 27, 28, 30A.

20 Pius' rescript in *D.* 48.5.39.8 concerns the husband's punishment for homicide, not that of the wife for adultery. *Sententiae* 2.26 treats adultery separately from the other *leges*, which are handled in Book 5.

21 See n. 14.

22 Cf. chapter 10 under 'The *De iudiciis publicis* genre'.

23 E.g. *D.* 47.12.11; 48.19.38 pr., 1–4; 48.8.17; 48.6.11; 48.19.38.5; 48.10.19; 48.19.38.6; 48.19.37.7; 8; 48.19.38.9; 48.19.38.11, 12. Even *Collatio*, compiled in the early fourth century, made extracts from *Sententiae* either the lead item or an amplification of what Ulpian had said: 1.2, 4.12, 5.2, 7.2, 8.3–6, 14.2.

24 Cf. Mommsen 1899, 1033–7; Garnsey 1970, 234–51.

25 On Hadrian's rescript see especially Garnsey 1970, 84, 155–7; Rilinger 1988, 195–8 and *passim.* Cardascia 1950, 331 is more succinct.

26 *D.* 48.22.6.2, where *propter capitalia crimina* must mean the generalization of Hadrian's rule. Ulpian states the general rule before the case of Priscus and introduces the latter with *denique*, but it is likely that the general rule was framed in the course of that trial. *Propter capitalia crimina* means something more general than the *lex Cornelia de sicariis.* It would have been otiose to limit the phrase to a particular *lex*, charges under which were always capital.

27 Cf. Hadrian's ruling on the decurions (above). See also Cardascia 1950, 331 n. 3.

28 D. 48.19.9.12–15; *CJ* 9.41.11.

29 Cf. chapter 10 under 'Motivation and ideology' i.f.

30 *D*. 48.19.9.11; 48.19.27 pr.

31 Mommsen 1899, 1034 with n. 1, 1035 with nn. 3, 4, citing *CTh* 6.37.1 (not 36.1), *CJ* 12.31.1, Cyprian *Ep*. 80.

32 Cardascia 1950, 327 makes decurions second-rank *honestiores*, but at 311 n. 5, 326 n. 8 he thinks Modestinus is merely using a variant of *humiliores*. Cf. Garnsey 1970, 155 n. 1, 223, 228, 242 n. 6; he does not consider the second rank aspect. Rilinger 1988, 204 n. 107 thinks that everyone except Mommsen accepts the variant of *humiliores* view. But he mistakenly cites Levy 1963, 2.358, 445 n. 53, 488. In fact Levy expresses no opinion.

33 *D*. 49.18.3. Cf. *CJ* 9.47.5.

34 Marcian *loc. cit.*: 'Veterans and their children have the same *honor* as decurions.'

35 On this type of torture see Garnsey 1970, 141–7; Brunt 1980, 259–65 (including the reasonable suggestion, 263, that Priscus' confession before Marcus *ante quaestionem*, *D*.48.22.6.2, means 'before slave witnesses were examined'). See also Robinson 1981, 223–7.

36 I here summarize and apply some of the findings in Bauman 1995.

37 De Robertis 1939b, 69 n. 1 with *D*. 48.19.28.2; Cardascia 1950, 328 and n. 2.

38 Cf. chapter 6 under 'Black comedy and punishment'.

39 On these groups see *D*. 47.18.1.1–2, 47.14.1.3.

40 De Robertis 1939b, 87 makes the *humiliores* penalties the norm and the *honestiores* the exception, but this is preposterous.

41 See Robinson 1981, 214–17 for the cogent argument that slaves were not tried by the jury-courts in the Republic; the only public authority concerned with them was the *tresviri nocturni*.

42 On the process generally see Bauman 1989, 102–7 with the literature listed at 103 nn. 150, 151 and 106 n. 164.

43 TA 6.11.3 puts it as 'slaves and that part of the citizenry whose audacity made them unruly unless they were restrained by force'. If there was an erosion of the dividing-line this reform marks the start of it. One can no doubt say that Roman society was always elitist (cf. Garnsey 1970, *passim*). Cicero advised pettifogging lawyers to look to the disreputable elements for their clients. Ps.-Ascon. 201 St. But Augustus took the first step towards institutionalizing elitism.

44 See Garnsey 1970, 126–33; Robinson 1981, 227–33. The clearest case is crucifixion. Burning alive is less specifically servile in origin. The XII tables had prescribed it for arson. Mommsen 1899, 836–7. *Ad bestias* against free persons was not unknown in the Republic. Garnsey 1970, 129–30. Tacitus speaks of a place where *serviles poenae* were carried out. TA 15.60.2. Cf. Garnsey, 261 n. 1.

45 Of the voluminous literature on Caracalla's *Constitutio Antoniniana* of c. 212 it suffices to cite Sherwin-White 1973, 279–87, 380–93; 1972, 55–8. On the reduced importance of citizenship see for example *FIRA* 1.103 on Commodus' peasants who complained, apparently in vain, of being beaten by the estate manager although they were citizens. Cf. Garnsey 1970, 261, 264.

46 Mommsen 1899, 1032.
47 Maecian and Venuleius looked only at the slave *qua* slave. See chapter 10 under 'The *De Iudiciis Publicis* genre'.
48 This depends on Saturninus' dates. Most investigators date him to the second or third century. Perhaps he can be placed in the Severan period, roughly contemporaneous with Callistratus. His discourse on capital penalties (*D.* 48.19.16) reflects a general similarity of method to that of, especially, Ulpian and Callistratus in 48.19.
49 Callistratus confirms the exposure of the humble free to the rods; he probably also commented on the slave's exposure to a similar penalty. In *D.* 48.19.28.2 he does not include slaves alongside free *tenuiores*, but in 28.4 he says it is usual to return slaves to their masters after they have been beaten.
50 *Supplicium* is clearly the extreme penalty here. The fragment is part of Callistratus' discourse on capital penalties, not on torture.
51 See De Robertis 1939b, 65-7.
52 See for example the case of Camillus. L. 5.32.8-9.
53 The '*Dreierschema*' is one of the main points in the attack by Rilinger 1988 on the existence of any coherent system of status-based differentials.
54 Robinson 1981, 229 argues the reverse. But the passage on which she relies (*Coll.* 1.3.2) is not free of ambiguity. Ulpian first cites the 'intention' formulation of the *lex Cornelia* – 'walking around with a weapon for the purpose of' – and then continues: 'It likewise punishes the person who kills someone, nor does it add anything concerning the status. Thus this law seems also to apply to a slave and an alien – *conpescit item eum, qui hominem occidit, nec adiecit cuius condicionis hominem, ut et ad servum et peregrinum pertinere haec lex videatur.*' Here the first *hominem*, the victim, seems to be the same entity as the second *hominem* whose *condicio* is being considered. It may thus be the *persona* of the victim that is in issue. On the other hand there is no evidence of any penal differentials under Sulla's law, whether in respect of *persona* or anything else.
55 On Hermogenian see Jolowicz 1972, 464. See also Wenger 1953, 522-3, 535.
56 If Hermogenian was exactly contemporaneous with the author of *Sententiae*, his terminology is noticeably different from the latter's. But that may be because he has to put his expression in the genitive after *liberi*.
57 Cf. the equally non-specific *alii* in Hadrian's rescript on boundary-stones.
58 De Robertis 1939b, 90-107 establishes separate penalties for slaves and free in the Later Empire, but asks why Justinian preserved the *honestiores–humiliores* distinction. De Robertis is forced to ask this by his mistaken postulate of a sandwich: free and slaves in the Republic; evolution of *humiliores* which incorporated slaves in the Principate; reversion to free and slaves in the Later Empire. Justinian preserved *honestiores–humiliores* because that subdivision within the free still existed alongside the free–slaves division.
59 I omit suspended sentences, which would simply obscure the point that I wish to make.
60 Levy 1963, 2.459-90.
61 De Robertis 1939a, 1939b, 1942a, 1942b. Garnsey 1970, 103-78 gives a different meaning to the dual-penalty system: it means the *honestiores–humiliores* duality.

62 His refusal to do so set the tone for the future. In the Later Empire the judge was only fined. *CTh* 1.2.7.

63 It is not proposed to address the general question of the normative efficacy of constitutions. For some of the literature see Bauman 1980, 156 n. 15. The evidence is conveniently assembled by Schiller 1978, 506–11. A practical approach may be to assume that when a ruling was published (below) it had normative efficacy, at least in the province with which it was concerned. The distinction between an *exemplum* and a binding legal rule drawn by v.Schwind 1940, 144–5 and frequently adopted by later writers obscures more than it clarifies. When the emperor ordered publication of a ruling did he wait hopefully for acceptance by the jurists before marking it down as a success? The ruling had, after all, been drafted by his jurists.

64 *D.* 48.10.15 pr. Cf. 48.10.14.2. On the publication of edicts generally see v.Schwind 1940, 157–64.

65 See *FIRA* 1.423. In the Severan period Paul, and before that Pliny's friend Titus Aristo, made collections of decisions (Schulz 1963, 154), but that was not promulgation.

66 Wilcken 1920, 14–27; v.Schwind 1940, 167–74. On rescripts generally see Wilcken, *passim*; Wenger 1953, 427–32; Jolowicz 1972, 371; Schiller 1978, 488–501; Spruit 1992, 134–9.

67 Wilcken 1920, 14; *VIR, OLD* s.v. *propono*.

68 E.g. *PS* 5.21.1, 4; 22.1, 2; 23.1, 17; 24; 25.1; 29.1; 30B.1.

69 E.g. Ulpian's problems with Hadrian's rescript on rustlers. See *Coll.* 11.7.1–4, 8.3 with Nörr 1974, 12. See also Garnsey 1970, 157–8. See also chapter 12, sixth section.

70 See chapter 10 under 'Motivation and ideology' i.f.

12 ATTITUDES TO PUNISHMENT

1 *Saeva lex:* 607–8 Warmington.

2 For some of the details see Nörr 1974, 76–8, 105–6.

3 See for example the fifth section of chapter 2.

4 See the second section of chapter 6.

5 Cf. Griffin 1976, 200–1; Bauman 1989, 96–7.

6 The evidence is conveniently collected by Nörr 1974, 64–5. For fuller discussions see Rogers 1935, *passim*; Bauman 1974, *passim*. For a somewhat different approach see M. Ducos, *REL* 68 (1990), 99–111.

7 See Bauman 1985, 21–2.

8 See chapter 3, fifth section.

9 See Bauman 1989, 147–50, 152–3, arguing that the matter was raised during Domitian's reorganization of the prefect's functions.

10 Aulus Gellius *NA* 20.1. On the debate see Kunkel 1967, 172–3; Nörr 1974, 66–9; Casavola 1980, 1–125; Ducos 1984a; Diliberto 1993, 146–70. The authenticity of Gellius' account is accepted by Casavola, 92–7; Ducos 288 and n. 1. On Diliberto's analysis see the last section of this chapter. It is not certain that the debate about authenticity needs to be taken any further. Whatever its specific credentials, the account portrays an important aspect of mid-second-century thinking.

11 On Africanus, and the identification of Gellius' jurist with him, see Kunkel 1967, 172–3 with n. 295. See also Jolowicz 1972, 386 and the references in n. 10.

12 Gell. 20.1.5–6, 22. Levy 1963, 2.330 notes only a relatively minor point in the debate, instead of drawing out the substantial support for the continued discretion of the judge that it could have given him.

13 Cf. Julian *Digesta* 84 = *D.* 1.3.32.1: *Leges* are abrogated not only by vote of the legislator but also, with the tacit consent of all, by disuse. The most recent application of this doctrine was in 1914, when the South African Appellate Division held that Augustus' adultery law had been abrogated by disuse, See Green v. Fitzgerald 1914 AD 88. It appears from the report that the law had still been in force in the Cape Colony in the early nineteenth century.

14 TA 4.31.5. That the penalty as stated by *Sententiae* is only exile does not affect the position, for it applies only to the *iudex pedaneus* who tried minor cases. *PS* 5.28.1.

15 See the second section of chapter 4.

16 See Casavola 1980, 25–33, especially 27, 32.

17 Gell. 16.10.7–8. On the *lex Aebutia* which substituted the formulary system for the *legis actiones* in all tribunals except the Centumviral Court see Jolowicz 1972, 218–25.

18 This theme is worked out in detail by Casavola 1980, 1–73. See also Ducos 1984a; Nörr 1976. But it has not been broached in the particular way adopted here.

19 See the references in n. 18. The jurists were prominent, perhaps predominately so, in this intellectual ferment. See for example Nörr 1976.

20 He does not exploit it in his *Institutes*. His notice of the effect of interdiction on citizenship and *patria potestas* in 1.189–90 merely aims at the private-law repercussions.

21 Fragments in Lenel, 1.242–6 (frs. 418–45).

22 On his analysis of this word see my 'Roman Law and Nationalism in the XII Tables and Justinian' (in the press). See also Lenel, fr. 425.

23 See Lenel, fr. 436.

24 Lenel, fr. 437.

25 Lenel, frs. 435, 426, 428.

26 On Gaius' literary bent in his criticisms see Nörr 1974, 92–7.

27 See the second section of chapter 10. The work was part of Capito's *Coniectanea*, a literary miscellany. Gell. 4.14.1. *De iudiciis publicis* was the ninth book of that work.

28 See Gell 20.1.7–10.

29 The term and the exploration of its significance are the work of Nörr 1974. Nörr's focus is on the private law, with occasional glances at criminal law. An attempt is made here to apply some of Nörr's criteria to the criminal law.

30 *D.* 48.19.8.2 is not noticed by Mommsen 1899 or Garnsey 1970. Levy 1963 only notices it on some other point.

31 By the Stlacci, whom Augustus ordered to be sent to him in chains. His investigation having shown that there was nothing in it, Augustus released them. *Cyrene Edict* I = *FIRA* 1.407.

32 See Bauman 1995, 388–9, 392–6.
33 Mommsen 1899, 918–21 appears to equate the *furca* with crucifixion, although his reasoning is not altogether clear. Garnsey 1970, 128 appears to consider the *furca* a separate punishment from crucifixion, but a preparation for the latter.
34 On the *furca* at the trial of Horatius see L. 1.16.6.
35 Garnsey 1970, 125, 129.
36 See *PS* 5.23.1, 15; 23.17; 24; 25.1; 29.1; 30B.1. As for Callistratus, vivicombustion does not appear in his list, but is noticed later in the fragment. *D.* 48.19.28.11–12. One hopes that Ulpian's omission of *ad bestias* from his list of punishments that cannot be inflicted on decurions (*D.* 48.19.9.11) does not mean that *ad bestias* could be used against them. Ulpian says (*Coll.* 11.7.3–4) that those sentenced to the Games are not necessarily put to death at all. They may after certain periods of time be restored to freedom (they had become *servi poenae*) or released from the Games. But this probably means only gladiatorial games. See the last section of this chapter.
37 On the suspensions of the *lex maiestatis* up to Marcus see Bauman 1974, 18–20, 23, 56–7, 84–5, 157, 167, 171, 178, 191–223, 227. Alexander speaks for himself in the two *maiestas* rescripts in the text.
38 Apparently an alternative title of Augustus' *lex Julia de adulteriis*. No second law by Augustus is known.
39 See Bauman 1980, 193.
40 On Julian's standing with Marcus over the first years of the latter's reign see Bauman 1989, 245. The *locus classicus* on his use of *humanitas* is *D.* 28.2.13 pr. His phrase, *humanitate suggerente*, was adopted by Ulpian *D.* 49.4.1 pr. and in *J. Inst.* 3.2.7, 3.6.10. The best account of Marcus' legal activity is still Noyen 1954. Some of the material is discussed by Birley 1982. It receives no attention at all from G. R. Stanton, *ANRW* II 2 (1975), 478–549.
41 See Hüttl 1936, 86–7. I have not seen Marotta, *Multa de iure sanxit*, Milan 1988.
42 Schulz 1936, 191, 198. Cf. Riccobono 1965, 603–4.
43 This is generally recognized. The controversial part is how long that influence lasted. For the literature on a short spell ending in 223 see Bauman 1995. For a recent attempt to revive the longer estimate, placing Ulpian's death in 228, see *ibid.*
44 See *D.* 49.4.1 pr.; 44.4.7.1; 4.6.38.1; 48.18.1.27; 48.20.5.1. All the works from which these fragments come are dated to Caracalla's reign at the latest by T. Honoré, *Ulpian*, Oxford 1982, *passim*.
45 On Ulpian's lack of sympathy with the soldiers see Bauman 1995. On Alexander, the statement in the text is offered as a talking-point, in the belief that in the unlikely event of a consensus ever emerging about that shadow amongst the half-seen, it will be close to the lines suggested. Perhaps a computer will one day be persuaded to reconcile Dio, Herodian, the *Augustan History* and the legal texts (Alexander's legislative programme was the most comprehensive of any emperor until Diocletian – including 26 constitutions in which Dio is named as eponymous consul with the emperor). In the modern literature there are some valuable remarks by

MacMullen 1976, including vii–ix, 1–23, 195–213. A random selection of other works would include R. V. N. Hopkins, *The Life of Alexander Severus*, Cambridge 1907; K. Hönn, *Quellen-untersuchungen z.d. Viten des Heliogabalus und des Severus Alexander*, Leipzig 1911; A. Jardé, *Étude critique sur la vie et le regne de Sévère Alexandre*, Paris 1925; M. Rostovtzeff, *The Social and Economic History of the Roman Empire*, 2nd edn, Oxford 1957; G. Walser and T. Peckáry, *Die Krise des römischen Reiches*, Berlin 1962, 15–17; Millar 1964; E. M. Shtaerman, *Die Krise d. Sklavenhalterordnung im Westen d. römischen Reiches*, tr. W. Seyfarth, Berlin 1964; R. Hanslik, *Kl.P.* 1 (1964), 769–70; Whittaker 1970; X. Loriot, *ANRW* II 2 (1975), 657–787; G. Walser, *ANRW* II 2 (1975), 614–56; P. Petit, *Pax Romana*, tr. J. Willis, London 1976 (with bibliography, pp. 254–319); M. Mazza, in *Istituzioni Giuridiche e Realtà Politiche nel Tardo Impero*, G. G. Archi (ed.), Milan 1976, 1–62; Liebs 1980; Wells 1984. See also the works listed in Bauman 1995, first footnote.

46 On such edicts see Dupont 1971.
47 *CJ* 9.13.1.3a, laying down the penalty for *ceteros omnes qui conscii et ministri* etc. The only exception to the generalized *poena capitalis* is slave accomplices who are burnt alive 'as Constantine's law (*CTh* 9.24.2) rightly provided'. *CJ* 9.13.1.4.
48 *CJ* 9.13.1.3b. This is only given by Justinian as an example. He in no way implies that culprits other than the rapist/abductor will not be similarly deterred.
49 On this see Diliberto 1993, 129–34.
50 *NA* 7.14.4. Gellius excludes punishment under the first two categories when there is, respectively, no hope of correction or no reason to fear loss of prestige for the victim.
51 Gell. 7.14.5–9, pointing out that Plato uses *timoria* as a general word for punishment. Cf. Plato *Gorg.* 81 p. 525b.
52 Cf. Diliberto 1993, 128.
53 That is, homicide, adultery, treason, magic and sorcery, and rape. *CTh* 9.38.4. Cf. 9.38.3, 6, 7, 8; *Sirm.* 8. In any event, of course, adultery would not have been included in Gellius' day.
54 Nörr 1974, 125,131.
55 The notices of the passage by Levy 1963, 2.474 and Garnsey 1970, *passim* do not include any discussion of the problem that worried Ulpian.
56 Diliberto 1993, 146–72.
57 Justinian (above) expressly made the *poenae metus* for rape/abduction applicable to all levels of society. But that was in the Later Empire.
58 Caesar added confiscation to exile because the rich were encouraged to commit crimes by the fact that they were exiled with their property intact. SJ 42.2. Later on Cassius Severus was comfortable enough in his first exile to continue his defamatory attacks. When Anicetus had to be exiled after perjuring himself to establish the charges of adultery against Octavia, he was exiled to Sardinia where he lived out his days in comfort. TA 14.62.1–6; SN 35.2.

SELECT BIBLIOGRAPHY

Works not frequently cited and, with a few exceptions, ancient sources and articles in standard reference works are sufficiently identified in the notes and the abbreviations and are not listed here.

Alexander, M. C. (1990) *Trials in the Late Roman Republic, 149 BC to 50 BC*, Toronto.

Amirante, L. (1991) *Studi di Storia Costituzionale Romana*, Naples.

André, J. M. (1979) 'Sénèque et la peine de mort', *REL* 57: 278–97.

Archi, G. G. (1957) 'Rescrits impériaux et littérature jurisprudentielle dans le développement du droit criminel', *RIDA* 4: 221–37.

Arias, P. E. (1945) *Domiziano*, Catania.

Avonzo, F. d.M. (1957) *La funzione giurisdizionale del senato romano*, Milan.

Bardon, H. (1980) 'L'opinion publique dans l'Histoire Auguste', *Conferenze Storico-Giuridiche dell'Istituto di Storia del diritto e filologia del diritto*, Perugia: 11–25.

Barrett, A. A. (1989) *Caligula*, London.

Bauman, R. A. (1966) 'Tiberius and Murena', *Hist.* 15: 420–32.

—— (1967) *The Crimen Maiestatis in the Roman Republic and Augustan Principate*, Johannesburg (repr. 1970).

—— (1968) 'Some remarks on the structure and survival of the *Quaestio de Adulteriis*', *Antichthon* 2: 68–93.

—— (1969) 'The Duumviri in the Roman criminal law and in the Horatius legend', *Hist. Einzelschr.* 12.

—— (1973a) 'The *lex Valeria de provocatione* of 300 BC', *Hist.* 22: 34–47.

—— (1973b) 'The *hostis* declarations of 88 and 87 BC', *Ath.* 51: 270–93.

—— (1974a) 'Criminal prosecutions by the aediles', *Lat.* 33: 245–64.

—— (1974b) *Impietas in Principem: A study of treason against the Roman emperor with special reference to the first century AD*, Munich.

—— (1974/5) 'I libri "de iudiciis publicis"', *Index* 5: 39–48.

—— (1976) 'The Gracchi and Saturninus', *Journ. of History* 7: 53–68.

—— (1977) 'The résumé of legislation in the early *Vitae* of the *Historia Augusta*', *SZ* 94: 43–75.

—— (1980) 'The 'Leges iudiciorum publicorum' and their interpretation in the Republic, Principate and Later Empire', *ANRW* II 13: 103–233.

Bauman, R. A. (1981) 'La crisi del "Diritto"', *Labeo* 27: 208–16.
—— (1982a) 'The résumé of legislation in Suetonius', *SZ* 99: 81–127.
—— (1982b) 'Hangman, call a halt!', *Hermes* 110: 102–10.
—— (1983) *Lawyers in Roman Republican Politics*, Munich.
—— (1984) 'Family law and Roman politics', in *Sodalitas: Scritti in onore di Antonio Guarino*, Naples: 1283–1300.
—— (1985) *Lawyers in Roman Transitional Politics*, Munich.
—— (1989) *Lawyers and Politics in the Early Roman Empire*, Munich.
—— (1990) 'The suppression of the Bacchanals: Five questions', *Hist.* 39: 334–48.
—— (1992) *Women and Politics in Anicent Rome*, London.
—— (1993) 'The Rape of Lucretia, *Quod metus causa* and the Criminal Law', *Lat.* 550–66.
—— (1994) 'The Language of Roman Statutes', in J. Neville Turner and Pamela Williams (eds), *The Happy Couple: Law and Literature*, Sydney: 6–13.
—— (1995) 'The Death of Ulpian, the Irresistible Force and the Immovable Object', *SZ* 112: 385–99.
Beard, M. (1980) 'The sexual status of Vestal Virgins', *JRS* 70: 12–27.
Bellen, H. (1987) 'Novus status – novae leges. Kaiser Augustus als Gesetzgeber', in G. Binder (ed.), *Saeculum Augustum I*, Darmstadt.
Biondi, B. (1954) *Il diritto romano cristiano*, vol. 3, Milan.
Birley, A. (1982) *Marcus Aurelius: A Biography*, New Haven, CT.
Bleicken, J. (1959) 'Ursprung und Bedeutung der Provocation', *SZ* 76: 324.
—— (1962) *Senatsgericht und Kaisergericht*, Göttingen.
—— (1968) *Das Volkstribunat der klassischen Republik*, 2nd edn, Munich.
Boyancé, P. (1970) *Etudes sur l'humanisme cicéronien*, Brussels.
Brasiello, U. (1937) *La repressione penale nel diritto romano*, Naples.
—— (1954) *Problemi di diritto romano esegeticamente valutati*, Bologna.
Brecht, C. H. (1938) *Perduellio*, Munich.
—— (1939) 'Zum römischen Komitialverfahren', *SZ* 59: 261–314.
Bretone, M. (1982) *Techniche e ideologie dei giuristi romani*, 2nd edn, Naples.
Broughton, T. R. S. (1951/2, 1986) *The Magistrates of the Roman Republic*, 3 vols, New York.
Brunt, P. A. (1975) 'Stoicism and the Principate', *PBSR* 43: 7–35.
—— (1980) Evidence given under torture in the Principate', *SZ* 97: 256–65.
Büchner, K. (1967) 'Humanitas', *Kl. P* 2: 1241–44.
Buckland, W. W. (1963) *A Textbook of Roman Law*, 3rd edn, Cambridge.
Burdese, A. (ed.) (1988) *Idee vecchie e nuove sul diritto criminale romano*, Padua.
Burton, G. P. (1975) 'Proconsuls, Assizes and the Administration of Justice under the Empire', *JRS* 65: 92.
Buti, I. (1982) 'La "cognitio extra ordinem": da Augusto a Diocleziano', *ANRW* II 14: 29–59.
Cantarella, E. (1972) 'Adulterio, omicidio leggitimo e causa d'onore in diritto romano', *Studi Scherillo*, Milan: 1.243–74.
—— (1991) *I supplizi capitali in Grecie e a Roma*, 2nd edn, Milan.
Cardascia, G. (1950) 'L'apparition dans le droit des classes d'*honestiores* et d'*humiliores*', *RHDFE* 28: 305–37, 461–85.

—— (1953) 'La distinction entre *honestiores* et *humiliores* et le droit matrimonial', *Mélanges Albertario*: 655–67.

Casavola, F. (1980) *Giuristi Adrianei*, Naples.

Cenderelli, A. (1965) *Ricerche sul 'Codex Hermogenianus'*, Milan.

Ciulei, G. (1972) *L'Équité chez Cicéron*, Amsterdam.

Cizek, E. (1982) *Néron*, Paris.

Classen, C. J. (1979) 'Bemerkungen zu Ciceros Ausserungen über die Gesetze', *RhM* 122: 278–302.

Cloud, J. D. (1969) 'The primary purpose of the *lex Cornelia de sicariis*', *SZ* 86: 258–86.

—— (1971) '*Parricidium* from the *lex Numae* to the *lex Pompeia de parricidiis*', *SZ* 88: 1–66.

—— (1994) 'The Constitution and Public Criminal Law', *Camb. Anc. Hist.*, 2nd edn: 9.491–530.

Colin, J. (1965) *Les villes libres de l'Orient gréco-romain et l'envoi au supplices par acclamations populaires*, Brussels.

Cornell, T. J. (1981) 'Some observations on the "crimen incesti", in *Le Délit religieux dans la cité antique*, Rome: 27–37.

Crifo, G. (1961) 'Ricerche sull'exilium', *Studi Betti*: 2.229–320.

—— (1984) 'Exilica causa, quae adversus exulem agitur. Problemi dell'aqua et igni interdictio', in Thomas 1984: 453–97.

Crook, J. A. (1955) *Consilium Principis*, Cambridge.

De Martino, F. (1972–4) *Storia della costituzione romana*, 2nd edn, Naples.

De Plinval, G. (1969) 'Autour du De Legibus', *REL* 47: 294–309.

De Robertis, F. M. (1939a) 'Arbitrium iudicantis e statuizioni imperiali: Pena discrezionale e pena fissa nella cognitio extra ordinem', *SZ* 59: 219–60.

—— (1939b) 'La variazione della pena *pro qualitate personarum* nel diritto penale romano', *RISG*: 59–110.

—— (1942a) 'Le sentenze *contra constitutiones* e le sanzioni penali a carico del giudicante', *SZ* 62: 255–66.

—— (1942b) *Sulla efficacia normativa delle costituzioni imperiali*, Bari.

Diliberto, O. (ed.) (1993) *Il problema della pena criminale tra filosofia greca e diritto romano*, Naples.

D'Orgeval, B. (1950) *L'Empereur Hadrien: Oeuvre législative et administrative*, Paris.

Drapkin, I. (1989) *Crime and Punishment in the Ancient World*, Lexington.

Ducos, M. (1984a) *Les Romains et La Loi*, Paris.

—— (1984b) 'Favorinus et la loi des XII Tables', *REL* 62: 288–300.

—— (1994) 'Philosophie, littérature et droit à Rome sous le Principat', *ANRW* II 36.7: 5134–5180.

Dupont, C. (1953–5) *Le Droit criminel dans les constitutions de Constantin*, Lille.

—— (1971) 'Les Constitutions *Ad Populum*', *RHDFE* 49: 586–600.

Durry, M. (1938) *Les Cohortes prétoriennes*, Paris (repr. 1968).

Eder, W. (1969) *Das vorsullanische Repetundenverfahren*, Munich.

Eisenhut, W (1972) 'Die römische Gefängnisstrafe', *ANRW* I 2: 268–82.

Ensslin, W. (1954) 'Praefectus Praetorio', *RE* 22: 2391–2502.

Fanizza, L. (1982) *Giuristi Crimini Leggi nell'età degli Antonini*, Naples.

Ferrary, J.-L. (1991) 'Lex Cornelia de sicariis et veneficis', *Ath.* 79: 417–34.

Ferrill, A. (1991) *Caligula: Emperor of Rome*, London.
Fillion-Lahille, J. (1989) 'La Production littéraire de Sénèque sous les règnes de Caligula et de Claude, sens philosophique et portée politique: les Consolations et le De ira', *ANRW* II 36.3: 1606–38.
Flach, D. (1973) 'Zur Strafgesetzgebung der graccischen Zeit, *SZ* 90: 91–104.
Fraschetti, A. (1984) 'La sepoltura delle Vestali e la Città', in Thomas 1984, 97–129.
Furneaux, H. (1896/1907) *The Annals of Tacitus*, 2 vols, Oxford.
Gallini, C. (1970) *Protesta e integrazione nella Roma antica*, Bari.
Garnsey, P. (1968) 'Why Penal Laws Become Harsher: The Roman Case', *Natural Law Forum*: 141–62.
—— (1970) *Social Status and Legal Privilege in the Roman Empire*, Oxford.
Garofalo, L. (1989) *Il Processo Edilizio*, Padua.
Gaudemet, J. (1951) 'Utilitas Publica', *RHDFE* 29: 465–99.
—— (1954) 'L'Empereur, interprète du droit', *Fschr. Rabel*, Tübingen: 169–203.
—— (1967) 'Indulgentia Principis', in *Conferenze Romanistiche* II, Milan: 3–45.
Genin, J.-C. (1968) *La Répression des actes de tentative en droit criminel romain*, Lyon.
Gioffredi, C. (1970) *I principi del diritto penale romano*, Turin.
Girard, P. F. (1913) 'Les Leges Iuliae Iudiciorum', *SZ* 34: 295.
Giuffre, V. (1980) '*Militum disciplina* e *ratio militaris*', *ANRW* II 13: 234–77.
Greenidge, A. (1894) *Infamia*, Oxford.
—— (1901) *The Legal Procedure of Cicero's Time*, Oxford.
Grelle, F. (1980) 'La "correctio morum" nella legislazione flavia', *ANRW* II 13: 340–65.
Griffin, M. (1976) *Seneca*, Oxford.
—— (1984) *Nero*, London.
Grilli, A. (1990) 'Data e senso del De Legibus di Cicerone', *PP* 250: 175–87.
Grimal, P. (1979) *Sénèque*, Paris.
Grodzynski, D. (1984) 'Tortures mortelles et catégories sociales. Les *Summa Supplicia* dans le droit romain aux IIIe et IVe siècles', in Thomas 1984: 361–403.
Grosso, F. (1964) *La lotta politica al tempo di Commodo*, Turin.
Gsell, S. (1893) *Essai sur le règne de l'Empereur Domitien*, Paris.
Gualandi, G. (1963) *Legislazione imperiale e giurisprudenza*, Milan.
Hasebroek, J. (1921) *Untersuchungen zur Geschichte des Kaisers Septimius Severus*, Heidelberg.
Heinemann, I. (1931) 'Humanitas', *RE* Supp. 5: 282.
Heuss, A. (1944) 'Zur Entwicklung des Imperiums der römischen Oberbeamten', *SZ* 64: 57.
Honig, R. M. (1960) *Humanitas und Rhetorik im spätrömischen Kaisergesetzen*, Göttingen.
Hurley, D. W. (1993) *An historical and historiographical commentary on Suetonius' Life of C. Caligula*, Atlanta.
Hüttl, W. (1936) *Antoninus Pius*, Prague.
Jolowicz, H. F. and Nicholas, B. (1972) *Historical Introduction to the Study of Roman Law*, 3rd edn, Cambridge. (Short citation: Jolowicz 1972)

Jones, A. H. M. (1972) *The Criminal Courts of the Roman Republic and Principate*, Oxford.

Jones, B. W. (1992) *The Emperor Domitian*, London.

Jones, H. (1992) 'L'Ordre pénal de la Rome antique: contexture et limites', *Lat.* 51: 753–61.

Jossa, G. (1964) 'L'*utilitas rei publicae* nel pensiero di Cicerone', *Studi Romani* 12 (3): 269–88.

Jung, J. H. (1982) 'Die Rechtsstellung der römischen Soldaten', ANRW II 14: 882–1013.

Kaser, M. (1949) *Das altrömische Ius*, Göttingen.

—— (1956) 'Infamia und ignominia in den römischen Rechtsquellen', *SZ* 63: 220–78.

Kelly, J. M. (1957) *Princeps Iudex*, Weimar.

Keyes, C. W. (1928) Cicero *De Re Publica, De Legibus*, Loeb edn, London.

Koch, C. (1958) 'Vesta', *RE* 8A: 1717–76.

Kornemann, E. (1960) *Tiberius*, Stuttgart.

Kunkel, W. (1962) *Untersuchungen zur Entwicklung des römischen Kriminalverfahrens in vorsullanischer Zeit*, Munich.

—— (1967) *Herkunft und soziale Stellung der römischen Juristen*, 2nd edn, Graz.

—— (1974) *Kleine Schriften*, Weimar.

Lapicki, B. (1969) 'L'Humanisme romain et son influence sur l'évolution du droit romain', in *Gesellschaft und Recht im griechisch-römischen Altertum*, Berlin: 121–38.

Lassen, E. M. (1992) 'The ultimate crime: Parricidium and the concept of family in the Late Roman Republic and Early Empire', *CM* 43: 147–61.

Levy, E. (1963) *Gesammelte Schriften*, 2 vols, Cologne/Graz.

Liebs, D. (1964) *Hermogenians Iuris Epitomae*, Göttingen.

—— (1980) 'Alexander Severus und das Strafrecht', *Bonner Historia Augusta Colloquium (1977/78)*, Bonn: 115–43.

—— (1990) 'Ist unter den römischen Juristen mit einem zweiten Cäcilius zu rechnen?', *SZ* 107: 371.

Longo, G. (1972), 'Utilitas Publica', *Atti di seminario romanistico internazionale*, Perugia: 155–227.

—— (1977) 'Delictum, e crimen', *Iura* 27: 216.

Luzzatto, G. I. (1971) 'In tema di origine nel processo *extra ordinem*', *Studi Volterra*, vol. 2: 665–757.

MacMullen, R. (1966) *Enemies of the Roman Order*, Cambridge, MA (repr. 1975).

—— (1976) *Roman Government's Response to Crisis*, New Haven, CT.

Manning, C. E. (1989) 'Stoicism and Slavery in the Roman Empire', *ANRW* II 36.3: 1518–43.

Marino, F. (1988) 'Il falso testamentario nel diritto romano', *SZ* 105: 634–63.

Marsh, F. B. (1931) *The Reign of Tiberius*, Oxford (repr. 1959).

Martin, J. (1970) 'Die Provokation in der klassischen und späten Republik', *Hermes* 98: 72.

Maschi, C. A. (1948) 'Humanitas come motivo giuridico', *Scr. Cosattini*, Trieste: 263.

Massei, M. (1946) 'Le citazioni della giurisprudenza classica nella legislazione imperiale', *Scr. Ferrini*, Milan: 403–75.

May, G. (1936) 'L'Activité juridique de l'empereur Claude', *RHDFE* 15: 55–97, 213–54.

Mayer-Maly, Th. (1964) 'Carcer', *Kl. P* 1: 1053–4.

Meise, E. (1969) *Untersuchungen zur Geschichte der Julisch-Claudischen Dynastie*, Munich.

Merrill, E. T. (1918) 'Some remarks on cases of treason in the Roman Commonwealth', *CP* 13: 34–52.

Michel, J.-H. (1991) 'Du neuf sur Gaius?', *RIDA* 38: 175–217.

Mignot, D.-A. (1988) 'Droit, équité et humanisme d'après la correspondance de Pline le Jeune', *RHDFE* 66: 587–603.

Millar, F. (1964) *A Study of Cassius Dio*, Oxford.

—— (1977) *The Emperor in the Roman World*, London.

Mommsen, Th. (1887–8) *Römisches Staatsrecht*, 3 vols in 5, Leipzig.

—— (1899) *Römisches Strafrecht*, Leipzig.

Monaco, L. (1984) 'Veneficia matronarum: Magia, Medecina e Repressione', in *Sodalitas: Scritti in onore di Antonio Guarino*, Naples: 2013–24.

Mortureux, B. (1989) 'Les Idéaux stoïciens et les premières responsabilités politiques: le De Clementia', *ANRW* II 36.3: 1639–85.

Mouchova, B. (1985) 'Crudelitas Principis Optimi', *Antiquitas* 17: 167–95.

Nicholas, B. (1962) *An Introduction to Roman Law*, 3rd edn, Oxford.

Nicolet, C. (1972) 'Les Lois judiciaires et les tribunaux de concussion', *ANRW* I 2: 197–214.

Nörr, D. (1974) *Rechtskritik in der römischen Antike*, Munich.

—— (1976) 'Der Jurist im Kreis der Intellektuellen: Mitspieler oder Aussenseiter?', *Festschr. Kaser*, Munich: 57.

—— (1983) 'C. Cassius Longinus: Der Jurist als Rhetor (Bemerkungen zu Tacitus 14.42–45)', *Hist. Einzelschr.* 40: 187–222.

Noyen, P. (1954) 'Divus Marcus', *RIDA* 3e serie, I: 349–71.

—— (1954/5) Marcus Aurelius: The Greatest Practician of Stoicism', *L'Antiquité Classique*, 24: 372–83.

Orestano, R. (1980) 'La "cognitio extra ordinem": una chimera', *SDHI* 46: 236.

Palazzolo, N. (1974) *Potere imperiale ed organi giurisdizionali nel II secolo D.C.*, Milan.

Parpaglia, P. P. (1987) *Per una interpretazione della lex Cornelia de edictis praetorum del 67 A.C.*, Moderna-Sassari.

Passerini, A. (1939) *Le coorti pretorie*, Rome.

Perelli, P. (1990) *Il pensiero politico di Cicerone*, Florence.

Pringsheim, F. (1934) 'The legal policy and reforms of Hadrian', *JRS* 24: 141–53.

Pugliese, G. (1982) 'Linee generali dell'evoluzione del diritto penale pubblico durante il principato', *ANRW* II 14: 722–89.

Raaflaub, K. A. (ed.) (1986) *Social Struggles in Archaic Rome*, Berkeley.

Rawson, E. (1973) 'The Interpretation of Cicero's De legibus', *ANRW* I 4: 334–56.

—— (1989) 'Roman Rulers and the Philosophic Adviser', in M. Griffin and J. Barnes (eds), *Philosophia Togata*, Oxford: 233–57.

Rein, W. (1844) *Das Criminalrecht der Römer*, Leipzig.

Riccobono, S. (1965) 'L'idea di "humanitas" come fonte di progresso del diritto', *St. Biondi* vol. 2, Milan: 585–614.

Richardson, J. S. (1987) 'The Purpose of the Lex Calpurnia de Repetundis', *JRS* 77: 1–12.

Rilinger, R. (1988) *Humiliores–Honestiores*, Munich.

Robinson, O. (1981) 'Slaves and the Criminal Law', *SZ* 98: 213–54.

Rogers, R. S. (1935) *Criminal Trials and Criminal Legislation under Tiberius*, Middletown.

Roncali, R. (1989) *L'Apoteosi Negata*, Venice.

Rotondi, G. (1912) *Leges Publicae Populi Romani*, Milan.

Rozelaar, M. (1976) *Seneca*, Amsterdam.

Sachers, E. (1954) 'Praefectus urbi', *RE* 22: 2502–34.

Schadewalt, W. (1973) '*Humanitas Romana*', *ANRW* I 4: 43–62.

Schiller, A. A. (1949) 'The jurists and the praefects of Rome', *RIDA* 2, 321–59.

—— (1978) *Roman Law: Mechanisms of Development*, The Hague.

Schulz, F. (1936) *Principles of Roman Law*, Oxford.

—— (1963) *History of Roman Legal Science*, Oxford.

Schumacher, L. (1982) *Servus Index*, Wiesbaden.

v.Schwnd, F. F. (1940) *Zur Frage der Publikation imrömischen Recht*, Munich.

Scott, K. (1936) *The Imperial Cult under the Flavians*, Stuttgart and Berlin.

Sherwin-White, A.N. (1966) *The Letters of Pliny*, Oxford.

—— (1972) 'The Roman Citizenship', *ANRW* I 2: 23–58.

—— (1973) *The Roman Citizenship*, 2nd edn, Oxford (repr. 1980).

Siber, H. (1936) *Analogie, Amtsrecht und Rückwirkung im Strafrechte des römischen Freistaates*, Leipzig.

Speyer, W. (1956) 'Zur Verschwörung des Cn. Cornelius Cinna', *RhM* 99: 277–84.

Spruit, J. E. (1969) *De Lex Iulia et Papia Poppaea*, Deventer.

—— (1975) 'The penal conceptions of the Emperor Marcus Aurelius in respect of lunatics', in *Maior Viginti Quinque Annis*, Assen.

—— (1992) *Enchiridium: Een geschiedenis van het Romeinse privaatrecht*, 3rd edn, Deventer.

Stalley, R. E. (1983) *An Introduction to Plato's Laws*, Oxford.

Starr, C. G. (1965) *Civilization and the Caesars*, New York.

Staveley, E. (1954) 'Provocatio during the fifth and fourth centuries BC', *Hist.* 3: 413.

—— (1972) *Greek and Roman Voting and Elections*, London.

Strachan-Davidson, J. L. (1912) *Problems of the Roman Criminal Law*, 2 vols, Oxford.

Stroux, J. (1929) *Eine Gerichtsreform des Kaisers Claudius*, Munich.

Thomas, Y. (ed) (1984) *Du Châtiment dans la Cité*, Rome.

Thome, G. (1992) 'Crime and Punishment, Guilt and Expiation: Roman Thought and Vocabulary', *Acta Classica* 35: 73–98.

Tomulescu, C. St. (1977) 'Les Douze Césars et le Droit Romain', *BIDR* 19: 129.

Treggiari, S. (1991) *Roman Marriage*, Oxford.

Tyrrell, W. B. (1974) 'The duumviri in the trials of Horatius, Manlius and Rabirius', *SZ* 91: 106–25.

Ungern-Sternberg, J. (1970) *Untersuchungen zum spätrepubilkanischen Notstandsrecht*, Munich.

Vander Waerdt, P. A. (1994) 'Philosophical Influence on Roman Jurisprudence? The Case of Stoicism and Natural Law', *ANRW* II 36.7: 4851–4900.

Van Sickle, C. E. (1928) 'The headings of rescripts of the Severi in the Justinian Code', *CP* 23: 270–7.

van Zyl, D. H. (1986) *Cicero's Legal Philosophy*, Roodepoort, South Africa.

Vittinghoff, F. (1936) *Der Staatsfeind in der römischen Kaiserzeit*, Berlin.

Vitucci, G. (1956) *Ricerche sulla praefectura urbi in età imperiale*, Rome.

Volkmann, H. (1969) *Zur Rechtsprechung im Principat des Augustus*, 2nd edn, Munich.

Volterra, E. (1949) 'Processi penali contro i defunti in diritto romano', *RIDA* 2: 485–500.

Waldstein, W. (1964) 'Untersuchungen zum römischen Begnadigungsrecht', *Commentationes Aenipontanae* 18: 1–209.

Warmington, B. H. (1981) *Nero*, London.

Wells, C. (1984) *The Roman Empire*, London.

Wenger, L. (1953) *Die Quellen des römischen Rechts*, Vienna.

Whittaker, C. R. (1970) *Herodian*, Loeb edn, London.

Wieacker, F. (1971) 'Le Droit romain de la mort d'Alexandre Sévère à l'avènement de Dioclétien', *RHDFE* 49: 201–23.

—— (1988) *Römische Rechtsgeschichte*, vol. 1 (a.p.), Munich.

Wilcken, U. (1920) 'Zu den Kaiserreskripten', *Hermes* 55: 1–42.

Wlassak, M. (1917) *Anklage und Streitbefestigung im Kriminalrecht der Römer*, Vienna.

Wolf, J. G. (1988) *Das Senatusconsultum Silanianum*, Heidelberg.

—— (1991) 'Claudius Iudex', in *Die Regierungszeit des Kaiser Claudius* (41–54 n.Chr.): *Umbruch oder Episode?*, Mainz: 145–58.

Wubbe, F. B. J. (1968) 'Benignus Redivivus', in *Symbolae M. David*, Leiden: 1.237–62.

Zumpt, A. W. (1865–69) *Das Criminalrecht der römischen Republik*, Berlin.

INDEX TO SOURCES

Entries in the text are designated by the page number; entries in the notes are designated by the page number followed by a decimal point and the number of the note.

213

GENERAL INDEX

Entries in the text are designated by the page number; entries in the notes are designated by the page number followed by a decimal point and the number of the note.

crimes against the state, *see maiestas,*
treason
crimina extraordinaria 106, 113,
119–21, 123, 127
criminal jurisprudence 116–23; *see
also De iudiciis publicis, De poenis,*
punishment, theories of
criminal, reform of, *see* punishment,
curative function of
criticism 8, 51, 144; *see also* black
comedy, *Rechtskritik*
crucifixion 7, 109–10, 126, 129,
141, 151–2, 159, 203.33
crudelitas 79

dardanarii 132
death by beating 9, 18, 43, 72–3,
76, 93–4, 96, 151
death penalty/sentence 6, 7, 12, 14,
18, 19, 26–7, 38, 44–5, 47–8, 54,
58–9, 62, 67, 71, 74, 76, 80–6,
103, 105, 114, 132, 135, 137,
141–6, 148–9, 151–4, 159,
162–3
decapitation 18, 19, 151
decemviri 70
decurial ornaments 132
decurions 128–32
delict 2, 34, 113, 128, 162
De iudiciis publicis 116–23, 148–9
De poenis 8, 124–40, 149, 156
deportatio in insulam/deportation 28,
53, 59–63, 67, 81–5, 89, 96, 101,
103, 105, 112, 114, 125–7,
129–30, 135, 137, 141, 143, 148,
151–2, 155, 179.62
deprecatio 40
deterrence, *see poenae metus*
differential punishments 124–36,
150
diminished responsibility 39, 116;
see also impuberes, insanity,
intention
Dio 106, 131
Diocletian (emperor) 135, 155
disciplina Augusti 131
discretionary punishment 5, 6, 11,
38–9, 50, 53, 58, 118, 121,
136–9, 146, 161, 175.2

dismemberment, *see* Mettius
Fufetius
Dolabella, C. 86, 101
Domitian (emperor) 8, 85–6, 92–9,
101–2, 107, 114, 125, 138,
144–5, 162
Domitilla 95
Domitius Ulpianus, *see* Ulpian
double jeopardy 12, 43, 93
duumviri 43, 47

Elagabalus (emperor) 106, 156
emperor, constitutions of 6, 65,
120, 126–7, 136–9, 152–6,
201.63; courts of 5, 50–1,
53–7, 65–75, 120; safety of
151
equites 75, 108–9, 114, 125, 128,
169.17
Erucius Clarus 103, 112
evocatio 42
execution, methods of, *see ad bestias,*
burial alive, crucifixion, death by
beating, decapitation,
dismemberment, *furca, liberum
mortis arbitrium,* molten lead,
poena cullei, precipitation,
strangulation, vivicombustion
exemplum 157–9, 201.63
exile 7, 14–18, 22, 26–30, 36, 44,
47–9, 54, 62, 79, 80, 93, 105,
110, 117, 135, 141–3, 146, 159,
163, 179.62, 204.58
existimatio 182.29
extortion, *see repetundae*
extraordinary jurisdiction, *see
cognitio extraordinaria*

Fabius Cilo 105, 113
Fadius 67
Faustus Sulla 89–91
Favorinus 145–7, 156, 159, 161,
163
fides 14
fine 11–13, 15, 20, 29, 30, 44, 135,
141; *see also multa*
fixed punishment, *see poena legis*
Flavius Sabinus 86, 101, 105, 144–5
foedus aequum 16

115, 122, 126, 133, 125–7,
139–40, 143, 146, 161–3,
182.32, 196.43; *parricidii* 117
poenae metus 8, 19, 29, 37, 49, 90,
94, 99, 141, 147, 156–9, 160,
163
Polluted Fields 93, 97
Polybius 14, 142, 163
Pompeia Macrina 63
Pompey 24, 28, 30–2, 56, 115, 143
Pontifex Maximus 18, 93, 96, 99,
102
Poppaea 89–9
popular assembly 5, 11, 12, 43
Postumius Pyrgensis 12, 15, 16, 19,
27
praefectus annonae 195.36; *praetorio*
5, 51, 71, 76, 86, 100, 106–14,
176.10, 185.33; *urbi* 5, 51, 86,
97, 100–6, 110, 112–14, 133,
144, 195.36; *vigilum* 103, 112
praetor 13, 17, 25–6, 29, 35, 40,
57, 79, 101, 104, 120–1, 146,
162, 189.5, 6, 196.41
praetorian prefect, *see praefectus*
praetorio
pragmatic conceptualization 4, 35
precipitation, *see* Tarpeian Rock
previous convictions 53, 103, 134,
158
Primus, M. 55
Priscus 129
provincial governors 5, 75, 80, 82,
97, 105, 118, 120–1, 134, 139,
150, 151, 154–5, 194.19, 195.36,
196.43
provocatio ad populum 10, 43, 165.5,
174.41
public accusation 23
publica clementia, see clementia
publica
public criminal laws, *see leges*
iudiciorum publicorum
public interest 27, 39–42, 44, 53,
81–2, 87, 144, 146, 157, 162; *see*
also utilitas publica, utilitas rei
publicae
Publicius Malleolus 30
punishment 1, 13, 14; attitudes to

141–60; by ancestral custom
72–3, 82, 84, 88, 95, 98; creative
role of 62; curative function of 3,
46, 56, 79, 80, 90, 143, 146,
157; entertainment value of 86–7,
159, 162; propaganda value of
92–7; purpose of 2–4, 7, 37, 147,
156–9; status symbol value of
129–32; theories of 2–3, 35–41,
77–81, 115–123, 124–140,
145–9; *see also clementia*,
confiscation, crime, gravity of,
criminal jurisprudence, decurial
ornaments, *deportatio in insulam*,
differential punishment,
discretionary punishment,
execution, methods of, exile, fine,
hard labour, imprisonment,
ignominia, infamia, interdiction,
ius gladii, ius occidendi, leniency,
mines, penalty, *poena, poenae*
metus, previous convictions,
relegatio, renuntiatio amicitiae,
reprimand, second grade, the,
senatus consultum Silanianum, servi
poenae, severitas, summum/ultimum
supplicium, torture

quaestio 17, 21–5, 29, 32, 55, 96,
106, 118–20
quick pursuit 55, 143
Quintilian 51–2

Rabirius, C. 35–6, 41–4, 47, 49,
143, 161–3
Rechtskritik 149; *see also* black
comedy, criticism
relegatio/relegation 29, 32, 52, 54,
62, 74, 84, 96, 101, 103, 127,
132, 135, 137, 141, 151, 155,
158, 163
remittal 102, 112–13, 189.6
renuntiatio amicitiae 54, 58, 60–1,
88
repetundae 15, 22–6, 30, 52, 59, 81,
115, 128, 141, 168.5
reprimand 56, 78, 103–5
rescripts 57–8, 138–9, 153; *see also*
emperor, constitutions of